Sociology th

Sociology through the Projector takes issue with the question of how contemporary film can help answer the general, abstract but still urgent question: what is the social today? This book explains the performative relation to contemporary social theory in which cinema functions as a tool for social diagnosis.

There is much to be learned about social theory through an encounter with films as films are part and parcel of the society they portray. Increasingly, more lay knowledge about social problems and facts stems from cinema as it offers to large audiences a popular and pedagogical introduction to social knowledge. Social theory cannot avoid a critical engagement with cinema as cinema interprets, invents, displaces and distorts the object of sociological inquiry.

This book will provide a deeper understanding of contemporary social theory as the chosen films will work as a pedagogical route into contemporary social theory. The films represent a mix of European and American blockbusters and more aesthetically oriented films.

The authors question several dominant topics and concerns within social theory and film studies. First, by cross-examining a series of concepts such as identity, representation, memory and surveillance (filming social behaviour) which are of concern to both film theory and social theory. Second, by trying to develop imaginative approaches to standard social concerns such as exclusion, gender roles and inequalities, power, infantilization and commodification of the social and psychological bonds.

This book will be a great resource for students and researchers of Sociology, Contemporary Social Theory, Film Studies and Cultural Studies.

Bülent Diken is Senior Lecturer in the Department of Sociology, Lancaster University. **Carsten Bagge Laustsen** is Associate Professor in the Department of Political Science, Aarhus University, Denmark.

International Library of Sociology
Editor: John Urry, Lancaster University
Founded by Karl Mannheim

Recent publications in this series include:

Risk and Technological Culture
Towards a sociology of virulence
Joost Van Loon

Reconnecting Culture, Technology and Nature
Mike Michael

Advertising Myths
The strange half lives of images and commodities
Anne M. Cronin

Adorno on Popular Culture
Robert R. Witkin

Consuming the Caribbean
From Arwaks to Zombies
Mimi Sheller

Crime and Punishment in Contemporary Culture
Claire Valier

Between Sex and Power
Family in the world, 1900–2000
Goran Therborn

States of Knowledge
The co-production of social science and social order
Shelia Jasanoff

After Method
Mess in social science research
John Law

Brands
Logos of the global economy
Celia Lury

Sociology through the Projector

Bülent Diken and Carsten Bagge Laustsen

Routledge
Taylor & Francis Group

LONDON AND NEW YORK

First published 2008
by Routledge
2 Park Square, Milton Park, Abingdon, Oxon, OX14 4RN

Simultaneously published in the USA and Canada
by Routledge
270 Madison Avenue, New York, NY 10016

Routledge is an imprint of the Taylor & Francis Group, an informa business

This book is a NSU book
http://www.nsuweb.net/wb/

Typeset in Garamond 3 by Keyword Group Ltd
Printed and bound in Great Britain by TJ International Ltd,
Padstow, Cornwall

British Library Cataloguing in Publication Data
A catalogue record for this book is available from the British Library

Library of Congress Cataloging in Publication Data
Diken, Bülent.
    Sociology through the projector / Bülent Diken and
        Carsten Bagge Laustsen.
    p. cm.
    "Simultaneously published in the USA and Canada by Routledge."
    1. Sociology. 2. Motion pictures–Social aspects. I. Laustsen,
        Carsten Bagge. II. Title.
    PN1995.9.S6D54 2007
    302.23'43–dc22
    2007012707

ISBN10: 0-415-44597-3 (hbk)
ISBN10: 0-415-44598-1 (pbk)
ISBN10: 0-203-93439-3 (ebk)

ISBN13: 978-0-415-44597-9 (hbk)
ISBN13: 978-0-415-44598-6 (pbk)
ISBN13: 978-0-203-93439-5 (ebk)

Contents

Foreword by Slavoj Žižek

Projector in the heart of the social

Perhaps the best way to render palpable the theoretical and political bearing of Bülent Diken and Carsten Bagge Laustsen's *Sociology through the Projector* is to focus on the two Hollywood productions that were released to mark the fifth anniversary of 9/11: Paul Greengrass's *United 93* and Oliver Stone's *World Trade Center*. The first thing that strikes the eye is that both try to be as anti-Hollywood as possible: both focus on the courage of ordinary people, with no glamorous stars, no special effects, no grandiloquent heroic gestures, just a terse realistic depiction of ordinary people in extraordinary circumstances. There is undoubtedly a touch of authenticity in the films – recall how the large majority of critics unanimously praised their avoidance of sensationalism, the sober and restrained style. It is this very touch of authenticity that should make us suspicious – we should immediately ask ourselves what ideological purposes it serves.

There are three things to note here. First, both films focus on an exception: *United 93* is about the only one of the four hijacked planes in which the terrorists failed, it did not hit its destination; *WTC* tells the story of two of the twenty people who were saved from the ruins. The disaster is thus turned into a kind of triumph, most notably in *United 93*, where the dilemma the passengers confront is: what can they do in a situation in which they know for sure they will die? Their heroic decision is: if we cannot save ourselves, let us at least try to save others' lives – so they storm the pilot's cabin to bring the plane down before it will hit the target intended by the hijackers (the passengers already knew about the two planes hitting the Twin Towers). How does this telling the story of an exception function?

A comparison with Spielberg's *Schindler's List* is instructive here: although the film is undoubtedly an artistic and political failure, the idea to choose Schindler as a hero was a correct one – it is precisely by presenting a German who DID something to help Jews that one demonstrates how it was possible to do something, and thus effectively condemns those who did nothing, claiming that it was not possible to do anything. In *United 93*, on the contrary, the focus on the rebellion serves the purpose of preventing us asking the truly pertinent questions. Let us indulge in a simple mental experiment and imagine both films with the same change: *American 11* (or another flight which did hit its target) instead of *United 93*, the story of *its* passengers; *WTC* remade as the story of two of the firefighters or policemen who *did* die in the rubble of the Twin Towers after prolonged suffering. Without in any way justifying or showing an 'understanding' for the terrible crime, such a version would confront us with the true horror of the situation and thus compel us to think, to start asking serious questions about how such a thing could have happened and what does it mean.

Second, both films also contain notable formal exceptions: moments which violate their basic terse realistic style. *United 93* starts with hijackers in a motel room, praying, getting ready; they look austere, like some kind of angels of death – and the first shot after the title-credits confirms this impression: it is a panoramic shot from high above Manhattan in the night, accompanied by the sound of the hijackers prayers, as if the hijackers stroll above the city, getting ready to descend on earth to reap their harvest. Similarly, there are no direct shots of the planes hitting the towers in *WTC*; all that we see, seconds before the catastrophe, when one of the policemen is on a busy street in a crowd of people, is an ominous shadow quickly passing over them – the shadow of the first plane. (Plus, significantly, after the policemen-heroes are caught in the rubble, the camera, in a Hitchcockian move, withdraws back into the air to a 'God's view' of entire New York City.) This direct passage from the down-to-earth daily life to the view from above confers on both films a strange theological reverberation – as if the attacks were a kind of divine intervention. What is its meaning? Recall the first reaction of Jerry Falwell and Pat Robertson to the 9/11 bombings, perceiving them as a sign that God lifted protection of the USA because of the sinful lives of the Americans, putting the blame on hedonist materialism, liberalism and rampant sexuality, and claiming that America got what it deserved. The fact that that very same condemnation of 'liberal' America as the one from the Muslim Other came from the very heart of *l'Amerique profonde* should give us thought.

In a hidden way, *United 93* and *WTC* tend to do the opposite: to read the 9/11 catastrophe as a blessing in disguise, as a divine intervention from above to awaken us from moral slumber and to bring out the best in us. *WTC* ends with the off-screen words which spell out this message: terrible events like the destruction of the Twin Towers bring out in people the worst AND the best – courage, solidarity, sacrifice for community. People are shown to be able to do things they would never imagine being able to do. And, effectively, this utopian perspective is one of the undercurrents that sustain our fascination with catastrophe films: it is as if our societies need a major catastrophe in order to resuscitate the spirit of communal solidarity.

This brings us to the last and crucial feature: both films restrain not only from taking a political stance about the events, but even from depicting their larger political context. Neither the passengers on United 93 flight nor the policemen in *WTC* have a grasp on the full picture – all of a sudden, they find themselves thrown into a terrifying situation and have to make the best out of it. This lack of 'cognitive mapping' is crucial: both films depict ordinary people affected by the sudden brutal intrusion of History as the absent Cause, the invisible Real that hurts. All we see are the disastrous effects, with their cause so abstract that, in the case of *WTC*, one can easily imagine exactly the same film in which the Twin Towers would have collapsed due to a strong earthquake. Or, even more problematically, we can imagine the same film taking place in a big German city in 1944, after the devastating Allied bombing. (In a TV documentary on that epoch, some surviving German pilots who had defended German cities with the few military planes Germany still had at its disposal in 1944, claimed they had nothing to do with the Nazi regime, they were totally out of politics, just bravely defending their country.)

Or what about the same film taking place in a bombed high-rise building in southern Beirut? That's the point: it CANNOT take place there. Such a film would have been dismissed as 'subtle pro-Hezbollah terrorist propaganda' (and the same would have been the case with the imagined German film). What this means is that the two films' ideological-political message resides in their very abstention from delivering a political message: this abstention is sustained by an implicit TRUST in one's government – 'when the enemy attacks, one just has to do one's duty'. It is because of this implicit trust that *United 93* and *WTC* differ radically from such pacifist films as Stanley Kubrick's *Paths of Glory*, which also depicts ordinary people (soldiers) exposed to suffering and death – here, their suffering is clearly presented as a meaningless sacrifice for an obscure and manipulated Cause. Remember Sherlock Holmes's famous repartee from Arthur Conan Doyle's 'Silver Blaze':

'Is there any point to which you would wish to draw my attention?'

'To the curious incident of the dog in the night-time.'

'The dog did nothing in the night-time.'

'That was the curious incident', remarked Sherlock Holmes.

One can say the same about *WTC*: 'Remember, in the film, the curious incident of the terrorist attack!' 'But we see no terrorist attack.' 'That was the curious incident'. This brings us back to our starting point, to the 'concrete' character of the two films, depicting ordinary people in a terse realistic mode. Any philosopher knows Hegel's counter-intuitive use of the opposition between 'abstract' and 'concrete': in ordinary language, 'abstract' are general notions, as opposed to 'concrete' really existing singular objects and events; for Hegel, on the contrary, it is such immediate reality which is 'abstract', and to render it 'concrete' means to deploy the complex universal context that gives meaning to it. Therein resides the problem of the two films: both are ABSTRACT in their very 'concreteness'. The function of their down-to-earth depiction of concrete individuals struggling for life is not just to avoid cheap commercial spectacle, but to obliterate the historical context. Here, then, is where we are five years later: still unable to locate 9/11 in a large narrative, to provide its 'cognitive mapping'.

The lesson of this short analysis is deployed in detail in Diken and Laustsen's admirable book: films are never 'just films', lightweight fiction destined to amuse us and thus to distract us from the core problems and struggles of our social reality. Even when films lie, they tell the lie which dwells in the very heart of our social edifice. This is why this book should be read not only by those who are interested in how films reflect or legitimize social reality, but also by those who want to get an idea of how our societies themselves can only reproduce themselves through films – in short, this is why pretty much *everyone* should read *Sociology through the Projector*.

Recall the memorable scene from *The Matrix* in which Neo has to choose between the red pill and the blue pill: either the traumatic awakening into the Real or persisting in the illusion regulated by the Matrix. He chooses Truth, in contrast to the most despicable character in the movie, the informer-agent of the Matrix among the rebels, who, during the dialogue with Smith, the agent of the Matrix, picks up with his fork a juicy red bit of a steak and says: 'I know it is just a virtual illusion, but I do not care about it, since it tastes real'. The choice between reading and not reading this book is the choice between the red and blue pill.

Acknowledgements

We are very grateful for the inspiring discussions with Niels Albertsen, Alison Armstrong, İhsan Erdoğan, Leon Gurevitch, Civan Gürel, Mark Lacy, Nayanika Mookherjee, Jackie Stacey, Majid Yar, Rodanthi Tzanelli and the participants of Nordic Summer University and Sociologisk Forum. We have greatly benefited from their comments on the different parts of the book. We would also like to thank Jens Blom Hansen for his support of the project.

We have received very valuable technical support from Helle Bundgaard, Marianne Hoffmeister, Else Løvdal Nielsen and Mette Ahlers Marino. Many thanks!

Some parts of the book were previously published in: 'From War to War: *Lord of the Flies* as Sociology of Spite', *Alternatives* 31(4): 431–52 (2006); 'City of God', *City* 9(3): 307–20 (2005); 'Enjoy Your Fight! – *Fight Club* as a Symptom of the Network Society', *Journal for Cultural Research* 4(4): 349–68 (2002); 'The Ghost of Auschwitz', *Journal for Cultural Research* 9(1): 69–86 (2005); 'Postal Economies of the Orient', *Millennium* 30(3): 761–84 (2001). Thanks for the permission to reprint parts of the articles.

Bülent Diken and Carsten Bagge Laustsen
December 2006

1 Introduction

Cinema and social theory

> Holding together this magical quality and this objective quality, bearer of all possible magico-affective developments, the cinema is like a kind of great archetypal womb that contains in embryogenetic potential all visions of the world.
>
> (Morin 2005: 169)

At the end of the nineteenth century two new machines almost simultaneously saw the light of the day: the Lumière brothers' cinematograph and the airplane (see Morin 2005). Both were technologies of mobility, allowing for movement between different spaces. While the airplane realized the most archaic dream of humans to have wings, the contribution of the cinematograph was constrained to merely reflecting images as realistically as possible. Soon, however, the roles were reversed. The airplane became a practical means of travel, of commerce and war, while cinema, allowing for escape from the mundane world, gradually became a provider of dreams (ibid.: 5–6).

Hence it is common today to compare cinema to dreaming; Hollywood to a 'dream factory'. Further, when dreaming we are physically immobilized while emotionally and visually creative, or, mobile. Also at the cinema we are equally physically immobile but emotionally mobile in a 'psychological coenesthesia' (ibid.: 97). Herein lies the most remarkable experience that pertains to cinema: it allows one to deviate from oneself, to become another. Cinema allows one to become a nomad on the spot. It deepens the social imagination and may even, in some cases, be ahead of social reality, allowing one to imagine the consequences of actions not yet taken. In other words, cinema can function as an indicator of the virtual, a coming society. Which is why social reality sometimes appears as a fallout effect of cinematic virtualities, producing the uncanny impression that reality mirrors cinema and not the other way around.

This impression visited us most visibly in September 2001, just after we finished an article on *Fight Club*, in which the violent reaction to the social 'unreality' of consumer society culminates in the final 'romantic' scene, where the protagonists walk hand in hand, while behind them is performed a catastrophic orgy of devastation as buildings explode and collapse. We finished the article, sent it to a journal, but later, just a couple of weeks later, on September 11, the film came, so to speak, to haunt us. It was as if, with real terror, the fantasy of violence in *Fight Club* – that is the image of violence without the real event – had come to coincide with its exact opposite: the unimaginable sublime event, the violence without an image. It was as if evil were coming directly out from the screen. We were left with the sensation that the film was not just an image of a reality, a shadow or appearance of a social fact, but the opposite was the case: that the reality itself had become an appearance of an appearance, a shadow of a shadow.

How can one make sense of such a play of shadows? The earliest attempt in this context is perhaps Plato's allegory of the cave, according to which humanity is chained in a cave, ensnared in its own ignorance, and is unaware of the possibilities of flight to a higher realm. The cave here stands for the world of images, of simulacrum or unreality, which is juxtaposed to the realm of reality, of Forms behind the simulacra. Without the knowledge of these Forms, according to Plato, the subjects are like the chained prisoners who cannot see anything other than the wall of the cave on which shadows from a fire are cast. Without being able to distinguish the real objects from the shadows, the prisoner/subject is condemned to seeing and hearing echoes only. Indeed, as Brians (1998) suggests following Baudry's classical essay (1974), 'if he were living today, Plato might replace his rather awkward cave metaphor with a movie theater, with the projector replacing the fire, the film replacing the objects which cast shadows, the shadows on the cave wall with the projected movie on the screen, and the echo with the loudspeakers behind the screen'.

Is cinema not, after all, merely a shadowy representation of reality rather than reality itself? The problem is that this question posits two kinds of beings – the actual (reality, society) and the virtual (copy, cinematographic image) – assuming the originary character of the first, the actual. First reality, and then its copy/representation. More often than not, social theory also buys into this hierarchy and thus perceives cinema as a mirror of the social. In contrast, ours is a 'pop sociological' take on a cinematic turn in social theory. In doing this, we get rid of the distinction between cinema/reality or between image/body. In a dialectical perspective, cinema is life and life is cinema; they tell the truth of each other.

Indeed, the truly Platonic problem is not representation as such but distorted or perverted representation. In other words, what we have here is not merely an opposition between essence and appearance, between an original and a copy; the question is not merely that of the difference between reality and representation or between 'social fact' and cinematic image. Rather, the significant Platonic distinction is that between two images: the copy and the simulacra. Whereas the copy is a true representation of pure Forms, Ideas, on the basis of resemblance, simulacra are no more than false or illegitimate pretensions which imply a perversion or deviation from pure Forms (Deleuze 1989: 256).

The copy is an image endowed with resemblance, the simulacrum is an image without resemblance. The catechism, so much inspired by Platonism, has familiarized us with this notion. God made man in his image and resemblance. Through sin, however, man lost the resemblance while maintaining the image. We have become simulacra.

(ibid.: 257)

In other words, the real opposition is between representation (good images founded on the idea of resemblance or identity) and simulacra (founded on the idea of difference). In contrast, we take a non-representationalist view on cinema in this book: cinema does not only represent the social but, provoking a machinic, spiritual response from the audiences, opens it up to the Virtual. Which is also the reason why the dialectic of the actual and the virtual is essential. Life in general, and social life in particular, is never fully actualized. Existing, actual sociality and virtual social 'events', that is incorporeal effects or 'entities' which are not actual but nevertheless real, exist side by side (ibid.: 4). What makes the social is not only its actualized structures, stratifications and segments but also its virtual potentialities which are significant without becoming necessarily actualized.

Hence what is significant is the interactive surface between social reality and cinema as an arena where virtual intensities gain resonance, cinematic surface effects cast out the social world anew. As Deleuze has shown, this surface, which both joins and separates the actual and the virtual, is the source of sense. However, sense must not be confused with meaning. In contrast to meaning, which is the derivation of the subject and structures, sense relates to impersonal and auto-poietic, machinic processes. Sense is an 'incorporeal event' that 'results from bodily states' (ibid.: 187). In other words, it is outside the law of the signifier, or 'outside the concept', that is sense is asignifying and hence irreducible to a state of affairs, particular images and beliefs, and to general concepts. Sense is 'neither word nor body, neither sensible representation nor rational representation' (ibid.: 19). What we have here is a paradoxical zone of indistinction, between the proposition and the state of affairs, between subjects and objects. In its 'extimacy', being both external and intimate to both the proposition and the thing it represents, sense 'subsists' in both and yet escapes them.

In relation to the social, cinema is an indicator of a virtual, a coming society, which does not exist but rather persists alongside the actual society. We cannot say persona or situations in films exist but rather, as incorporeal entities, they 'subsist or inhere' (ibid.: 5). Thus, rather than negotiating the relationship between cinema and social theory, we are interested in analysing films as not actualized but nevertheless real phenomena, as 'social facts'. The relationship between cinema and sociality must be seen as a two-way relationship based on virtualization (producing images of the social) and actualization ('socialization' of the image, inclusion of the symbolic element or image within 'reality'). In this sense, cinema offers us a transcendental analysis of the social, an analysis in which one is not only interested in actual 'social facts' but also virtual entities that transcend the domain of the empirical. It is in this sense that cinema makes, can make, a valuable contribution to social diagnosis. Social theory, in turn, has a means of relating to the virtual through cinema as a mode of registering the (social) world in a different, more effective, more intense way.

Sociology and the problem of correspondence

Sociology has always, both before and after its encounter with cinema, been haunted by the question of representation, of how to relate representation and reality. It has often dealt with this question in terms of correspondence: if representation can correspond to the represented reality more or less, then the task must be to construct as precise representations as possible. In this perspective, cinema represents the social world only in an indirect, artistic way. Indeed:

> We sociologists might consider it our duty, perhaps, to 'rewrite' the misguided vision of the filmmakers by imposing on the film a more socio-logical overlay. The films would be richer and more realistic if the character would behave in a manner that indicated their implication within social worlds that are wider, fuller, and older than their own individual lives. To do this requires that we stray outside the boundaries of the fictive world created by the filmmaker.
>
> (Dowd 1999: 329)

That is cinema is a secondary pursuit that awaits sociological illumination. In this approach, the filmmaker and the sociologist are necessarily in competition because they both offer representations of the social world – and luckily, or so it seems, this is a game the sociologist easily wins. After all, filmmakers are not professional observers of the social world! Consequently, such a con-ventional approach reduces the study of cinema to a subfield within sociology, to a 'sociology of cinema', or merely to a pedagogical device that stimulates teaching and learning (Demerath III 1981; Burton 1988).

To be sure, cinema is today one of the most important arenas for the dis-tribution of lay knowledge regarding social distinctions. Indeed, as Deleuze said, cinema is the 'contemporary art of the masses' (1989: 157–62); seen and intensely discussed by many, it is a great equalizer. Indeed, to the extent that films become popular introductions to social issues and they take poetic as well as visual liberties, social theory cannot avoid a critical engagement with cinema. Cinema has a distinct power to shape and fold the contempo-rary social (non)relations as well as the most intimate and the most public desires and fears of individuals. In a sense, cinema functions as a kind of social unconscious: it interprets, invents, displaces and distorts the object of soci-ological inquiry. What films offer is not just a reflection on society; they are a part and parcel of the society they portray. Cinema does not, however, only mirror/distort an external reality but also opens up the social world to a vast domain of possibilities. Cinema is often an experiment with changing social forms.

Ours is a society increasingly concerned with signs, images and sign systems, an increasingly 'cinematized' society. Thus, reality is increasingly staged and social production and everyday experiences are judged against their staged cinematic counterparts (see Denzin 1995: 32). As Morin claims, man has become a 'homo cinematographicus' (2005: 3). To a large extent, indeed, being social means today making and consuming images. Hence the first mystery of cinema: its obviousness. 'What is astonishing is that [cinema] does not astonish us. The obvious "stares us in the face", in the literal sense of the term: it blinds us' (ibid.). It blinds us towards the fact that the whole society has become cinematic.

> And it isn't just the reality of the real that's at issue in all this, but the reality of cinema. It's a little like Disneyland: the theme parks are now merely an alibi – masking the fact that the whole context of life has been disneyfied. It's the same with cinema: the films produced today are merely the visible allegory of the cinematic form that has taken over everything – social and political life, the landscape, war, etc. – the form of life totally scripted for the screen. This is no doubt why cinema is disappearing: because it has passed into reality. Reality is disappearing at the hands of the cinema and cinema is disappearing at the hands of reality. A lethal transfusion in which each loses its specificity.
>
> (Baudrillard 2005: 124–5)

In this book, we try to find a resonance between sociology and cinema, tracing the surface between them, oscillating between sociological concepts and cinematographic images. What allows for this union in separation or separation in union between the two activities is creativity, sense-making. And we want to make sense in a sociological style. That is we are not applying sociological knowledge *to* cinema; we are doing sociology by using cinema for sociological purposes (see Tomlinson and Galeta 1989: xv). We are not aiming at producing more film studies or theories of cinema; our project is a sociological project. Yet, we do not think that cinema can be reduced to sociology or one can study cinema through sociology only. We are also interested in studying cinema cinematically and tarry with the question of how sociology itself can become different through its confrontation with cinema.

On the basis of an external reading, one could say that, as a cultural artefact, a film can be inscribed into a 'network' of social determinants and can become an object for sociological research as such. However, an internal reading would hold the view that, as an artistic product, a film cannot be reduced to its network. As an artwork every film contains an excess, an intensity, which transcends its social network, its conditions of production and reception. Indeed, cinema is an art precisely because of this intensive surplus, its sense-making capacity, and analytic sociological concepts cannot capture this surplus unless they themselves (can) engage with artful commentary that can do justice to the artistic aspect of cinema. We want to navigate, then, in a zone of indeterminacy between cinema and social science, artwork and network, or, in a zone of indistinction between internal and external approaches to cinema.

On the one hand, we approach a film as a work positioned in a broader field, as something 'necessitated' (Bourdieu 1992) by the social structures and struggles within the artistic field which is itself positioned in relation to other fields such as economic, social, political and so on. Fiction is, of course, in itself a historical and socially conditioned product (Morin 2005: 168). 'Necessitation' means showing the necessity of a film as it is determined by the position of the work and its creator in the field. The singular work emerges from the singularity of the position as well as the singularity of the person that takes up the position in the broader social network. Film and the commentary on it, in this perspective, are part of a network. And the task of sociology in this context is to give an insight into the social conditions of the artwork, to liberate from misrecognitions and 'false transcendences' common in the field of art (Bourdieu 1982: 56).

Cinema is an art form that borrows from other forms of art, from the theatre, music, photography, etc. (Badiou 2005: 84). It is 'impure'. A similar impurity manifests itself in the relationship between cinema and 'social reality' – between the cinematic network and the social field. 'The cinema is a place of intrinsic indiscernibility between art and non-art. No film, strictly speaking, is controlled by artistic thinking from beginning to end. … Artistic activity can only be discerned in a film as a *process of purification of its own immanent non-artistic character*' (Badiou 2005: 84). Cinema is necessitated but at the same time it strives for autonomy and 'purification'.

Thus, on the other hand, we want to avoid sociologism, that is we are not saying that its network can ground cinema. Sociology tends to stratify and reify social life, focusing on regularities, repeated practices, systems and structures, and types. The 'cinematic gaze', however, can be liberating in the sense that it can relate the actual sociality to the virtual, to the Open. There is a possibility of artistic 'purification' or at least of a step in that direction. A work of art is, as Schlegel put it, a self-contained fragment, like a 'hedgehog' (1967). If it is not autonomous, it is not art. However, one could against Schlegel claim that no piece of art really is *it*, that is no artwork is truly autonomous; yet the defining characteristic of art is its striving for autonomy, its *attempt* at purification. Indeed, one could say the same about social theory as well; social theory, too, is conditioned by and tied to the empirical, the society it observes, but it also strives for independence and autonomy, which allows it to develop a critical stance towards its object. Social theory is a challenge to the social.

Socio-fiction

The relationship between art/cinema and the social is one of contamination and irreducibility. The cinematic and the social are like twins, separate in togetherness and together in their separateness. Which is why hierarchic approaches to the relationship between social theory (as being rigorous, serious and scientific) and cinema (as playful, artistic and fiction) must be challenged. Indeed, already Goffman (1959) understood social life as acting, as fiction, and the social as a scene with a front stage and a back stage. Small wonder, that sociology has borrowed some of its core concepts such as 'role' and 'actor' from theatre.

However, the dramaturgical approach 'communicates' with theatre, and later with cinema, at a metaphorical level: social reality is *like* theatre, *like* a film, etc. As such, it remains indifferent to the narrative content of particular films and to their artistic dimensions. To avoid this, we opt for a dialectical approach and consider film both as an allegory of the social and as an object that itself contains social theory. The relation between social theory and film is indistinct in so far as the distinction between fiction and non-fiction, representation and reality, has to be redoubled on both sides of the relation. The cinematic cannot be treated as just a metaphor. Thus, by interrogating films we want to do a cinematic social theory which, attempting to go beyond the dichotomy of social reality and fiction, (re)conceptualizes its object as a 'socio-fiction'.

'Reality' is always traversed by fiction, by fantasy. Fantasy is not a dreamlike illusion that serves to escape reality but the very basis for social life (Žižek 1989: 45). In other words, reality and fiction are not two opposed realms. Indeed, 'even in the state of wakefulness man walks surrounded by a cloud of images' (Morin 2005: 210). Fantasies are on our minds; but they are also manifested in social practices irreducible to individual behaviour. Thus fantasy belongs to the strange realm of the 'objective subjective':

> What, then, is fantasy at its most elementary? The Ontological paradox, scandal even, of fantasy resides in the fact that it subverts the standard opposition of 'subjective' and 'objective': of course, fantasy is by definition not objective (referring to something that exists independently of the subject's perceptions); however, it is also not subjective (something that belongs to the subject's consciously experienced intuitions, the product of his or her imaginations). Fantasy rather belongs to the 'bizarre category of the objectively subjective – the way things actually, objectively seem to you even if they don't seem that way to you'.
>
> (Žižek 2006)

The two realms, the subjective and the objective, are always blurred and always interact in subtle ways. We are always within the 'objectively subjective'. It is indeed therefore that cinema, a fantasy-producing machine, is a resource for diagnostic social analysis. Cinema displays the social unconscious, offering a mirror that allows for identification and social control. Hence there is a close relationship between ideology and cinema. Althusser (1984) once claimed that the school and the church were the most important ideological apparatuses. Today, we would say, cinema must be added to the list. There is, however, an additional reason why cinema is a privileged object of study: today social reality itself is cinematic, that is it is grounded in a fiction, in something that is contingent and reflexive in the sense that 'everything could have been otherwise' is a common sensibility. Society never exists 'as such' but is only 'seen' as distorted through a gaze. Consequently, one could reverse the distinction between reality and fiction:

> [T]he ultimate achievement of film art is not to recreate reality within the narrative fiction, to seduce us into (mis)taking a fiction for reality, but, on the contrary, to make us discern the fictional aspect of reality itself, to experience reality itself as a fiction.
>
> (Žižek 2001a: 77)

Cinema both represents and signifies. It remixes 'the real, the unreal, the present, real life, memory, and dream on the same shared mental level' (Morin 2005: 202). For Morin, cinema parallels the human psyche. We all have a little cinema in our head (ibid.: 203). The imaginary capacity of cinema, its production of images, is paralleled by the imaginary potential of the human mind. Cinema makes participation in others' lives and identification with them possible; thus through a film a conservative housewife might feel empathy for the prostitute (ibid.: 104–5). In other words, cinema increases the capacity for interaction between individuals and their world. 'Cinema is exactly this symbiosis: a system that tends to integrate the spectator into the flow of the film. A system that tends to integrate the flow of the film into the psychic flow of the spectator' (ibid.: 102).

However, the relationship works the other way around as well. Thus it is possible to say that it is not cinema which serves as a royal route to the understanding of the mind but inversely it is the mind, or rather the unconscious, that manifests itself in social reality. Indeed, the unconscious is outside. 'This exteriority of the symbolic in relation to man is the very notion of the unconscious' (Lacan 1966: 469). Whereas Morin considers the 'unconscious' as the imaginary capacity of the human mind to overflow social reality, for the young Lacan it is contained within the symbolic order. The unconscious, he claimed, is 'structured like language' (Lacan 1993: 167). The stuff of the unconscious is signifiers and it works through displacement (metonymy) and condensation (metaphor). Later Lacan claimed that a third concept, that of the real, had to be added to those of the imaginary and the symbolic. The symbolic (language, the law, or what sociology calls rules and norms) is not a self-contained unit. The big Other, the entity in which we mirror ourselves (the nation, the Lord,

God, etc.), can only exist as a mirror projection, it can only have an imaginary unity. 'In spite of all its grounding power, the big Other is fragile, insubstantial, properly *virtual*, in the sense that its status is that of a subjective presupposition' (Žižek 2006, italics added). It is this fictional character of the big Other (society?) that allows us to claim that the unconscious is structured like a film.

The cinematic apparatus

Lacan's work on the mirror stage proved to be highly influential within the study of cinema and it is of interest to us here because it initiated a way of analysing the relation between cinema and the surrounding society. Drawing on Lacan and Althusser, film theory began to analyse the analogies between the working of the mind/the psyche and the cinematic apparatus. In his 'The Mirror Stage as Formative of the I' (in Lacan 1966), Lacan claims that the child sees itself as a self-contained and autonomous being already between its first 6 and 18 months. Confronted with its mirror image, it reacts with the assumption: the image in the mirror looks exactly as me, an autonomous being. Later the child also reflects itself in the care of the mother and the father or in language, society and so on. Thus 'mirror' can also be used as a metaphor for the social. Lacan claims that the evolution of the mirror image is a precondition for the subject's maturation. The child is immature and depends on its mother/father/society/language.

Althusser linked this model of subjectivation to ideology. Ideologies might differ in content but as a form, as ideology in general, they are always an integral part of the social reality (Althusser 1984: 33ff.). This is because ideologies are 'representations of the imaginary relationship of individuals to their real conditions of existence' (ibid.: 36). This imaginary stance towards society blinds the subject to the constitutive role played by the social factors in the same way as the child misperceives its dependence on the mother's care. Following Lacan, Althusser claims that the idea of autonomy is a necessary illusion that allows the subject to feel an obligation towards ideological messages. Thus there is always a dialectic between the imaginary and the symbolic: '[T]he category of the subject is constitutive of all ideology, but at the same time and immediately I add that the category of the subject is only constitutive of all ideology insofar as all ideology has the function (which defines) of "constituting" concrete individuals as subjects' (ibid.: 45). Althusser's concept 'interpellation' describes this double constitution. The illusion of a pre-constituted 'I' is created in seeing oneself as an addressee of a call, e.g. an authority addressing a person. The subject thinks it responds to the call as an autonomous being while this very subjectivity is in fact produced through the call, which is also why ideological content always appears necessary and natural (ibid.: 48–9). The act of interpellation blinds the subject to the fact that the ideological message has an enunciator.

This idea initiated a series of studies on how cinema serves to reproduce the bourgeois ideology. Films do not, in this context, necessarily legitimize the dominant ideologies; rather, they serve as an outlet, making sure that the subjects do not challenge the system. As such, the actual content of the ideological images matter less. Thus, in Badiou's list (2005: 89–91), the basic elements of Hollywood ideology are erogenous nudity, extreme violence and cruelty, nostalgia, Millenarian motifs and the petit-bourgeois comedy. In other words, the ruling ideology is not necessarily the ideology of the ruling class.

The complication emanates from the fact that the ideological nature of cinema cannot be limited to its content; it is also manifested in the cinematic form. The subject identifies not so much with the actual ideological content as with the staging of the cinematic spectacle. According to Baudry (1974: 540), the spectator fails to notice that the cinematic gaze is situated through the symbolic. That is film is experienced as a product without a producer. Hence what is experienced is experienced as truth. Cinema is as such the 'ventriloquist of ideology' (Dayan 1976: 451). As ideology, for Althusser, cinema has no outside – it appears as a self-contained whole. 'The film is ideology presenting itself to itself, talking to itself, learning about itself' (Comolli and Narboni 1980: 34).

Cinema establishes the spectator as the active centre and producer of meaning. Thus, the filmic images, their fictional reality, are experienced from a fixed point in an imaginary space (Lapsley and Westlake 2006: 79, 83). The film is produced to allow the spectator to identify with the pure act of perception, which is precisely what Oudart's (1977) concept of 'ideological suture' refers to. Techniques such as shot/reverse shot allow the spectator to identify with the actor's gaze and make it his/her own. In this, all signs of the materiality regarding the medium are effaced. At the same time, however, the freedom of the spectator is completely conditioned by the cinematic setting.

> No doubt the darkened room and the screen bordered with black like a letter of condolences already present privileged conditions of effectiveness – no exchange, no circulation, no communication with any outside. Projection and reflection take place in a closed space and those who remain there, whether they know it or not (but they do not), find themselves chained, captured, or captivated. ... The paradoxical nature of the cinematic mirror-screen is without doubt that it reflects images but not 'reality'. ... In any case this 'reality' comes from behind the spectator's head and if he looked at it directly he would see nothing except the moving beams from an already veiled light source.
>
> (Baudry 1974: 44–5)

Interestingly, Baudry goes on, against this background, to compare cinema with Plato's cave and Lacan's mirror stage. Indeed, Lacan's two conditions that pertain to the formation of the imaginary, the 'immature powers of mobility and a precocious maturation of visual organization', apply to cinema as well (ibid.: 45). Yet, even though we know what we are watching is fiction, that we are entrapped in a 'cave', we still enjoy watching films. In other words, there is, in cinema, something more than imaginary delusion and its 'symbolic' staging at work. Film is, as Bertolucci said, an animal act that eludes reflective consciousness (Davis 2005: 73–4). It works directly on our emotions, on our desires. It is precisely as such, as a sense-making machine that can look beyond the reflective consciousness, that cinema is interesting to sociology.

In watching a film, we participate in a totality of beings, things and actions, which the film carries along in its flux (Morin 2005: 105–6). And herein lies the weakness of the 'apparatus approach' to cinema: cinema is not only a matter of receptivity to the images, of the spectator being 'chained, captured, or captivated'. Cinema also contains images that escape the panoptic enclosure of the 'cave'. The imaginary, as such, is also about creation and becoming. For interpellation to be able to work, the subject requires certain skills and capacities, such as the ability to understand, judge and interpret and so on. No doubt that these abilities allow the ideological images to be fastened onto the subject, but they also provide the resources for the subject to resist these images (Lapsley and Westlake 2006: 15). Interpellation, in short, can fail (see McGowan and Kunkle 2004: xvi). In other words, production and reception are both active and creative processes; hence there is always something that escapes the dialectic of the imaginary and the symbolic. The cinematic 'real', what cannot be contained in the dialectic of the symbolic and the imaginary, opens up the field of representation to a plurality of readings; it is this crack in the ontological edifice that makes creative film analyses possible.

Double readings

Filmic narratives and images can be transposed into a more or less ideological space through practices of reading and might as such be transfunctioned for a critical end (Lapsley and Westlake 2006: 51). To this effect, the situationist Asger Jorn overpainted kitsch paintings to release their utopian potential through what he called 'modifications' (Jay 1993: 424). In this way the protopolitical impulses that are managed and channelled through mass culture can be activated (Jameson 1981: 287). However, it seems to us that the situationist ontological assumptions are problematic. They saw bourgeois art (or mass culture) as regressive in character and understood their mission as adding to it something that can displace its meaning. Thus, there were two ontological layers: the ideological canvas and its avant-garde modifications. Like the sociologist caricatured in the beginning of this chapter, the situationists add something to an already devalued medium. Bourgeois art was kitsch in the same way as film for Dowd is a layperson's sociology.

The situationists expected that experimentation with new forms of art would break the power of the reified image. One way to fight the reified image was to create works of art manifestly marked by its producer's presence. For instance,

Lemaitre's *Syncinema* aimed at transgressing the spectator–spectacle divide by making the actors reappear as physical persons mingling with the spectators. Likewise, Brechtian techniques, epic cuts, etc., were applied to reinsert the artist within the filmic narrative. In a similar way, Debord made use of various *Hulements* such as introducing a disjunction between the voiceover and the images to force the spectator out of 'the cave'. In short, stories were no longer told from nowhere and this forced the spectator to reflect upon the 'real', the materiality of the cinematic media.

There are plenty of variations on the difference between ideological and avant-garde texts. In *Cahiers*, for instance, an influential journal on cinema, a sevenfold classification of film was developed: films falling in category A were those that reproduced the dominant ideology 'in pure and unadulterated form', while in category B were those films that attacked the dominant ideology in style/form as well as narrative. The remaining five categories designated various middle positions (Lapsley and Westlake 2006: 9). We want to attack this idea of regressive and progressive filmmaking on two fronts.

First, following Derrida's idea of non-masterable dissemination or Lacan's concept of the real, one could claim that all texts are incoherent. It is this incoherence that allows for the displacement of its meaning. Hence, we are not using filmic images and narratives as analogies or as symbols; this would have required a closer fit between the cinematic and the social, that is a realist ontology. Neither are we adding something to films to displace their meaning. Instead, we read films allegorically, with emphasis on ambiguity. Hence a stress on presence, identity and transcendence is replaced with the allegory's focus on qualities such as non-identity, rupture, disjunction, distance and fragmentation (Day 1999: 106).

Second, filmic narrative is always displaced by the context of reading. A film that appears to be avant-garde in one context may in another be judged as reactionary. Likewise, a reactionary film might later on rebel against the context in which it is framed; what once appeared avant-garde subsequently might become mainstream or vice versa. Indeed, the transfunctionalization of its messages, sharpening of its edges, is part of what makes an artwork work. In this book, therefore, we are interested in discussing such transformations in the context of cinema, a pursuit which also could vitalize social theory, sharpen or displace its concepts.

In our oscillation between external and internal approaches to cinema, cinematic figures convey for us sociological meanings apart from their literal, cinematic meanings. That is we read films allegorically. Instead of analysing 'social facts' through abstract theory, we analyse films as social facts through allegory. In this regard we have found Benjamin's notion of the dialectical image, a notion which he deduced from the baroque emblematic, the ideas represented by pictures and allegory, useful. In other words, we treat the themes, the people and the objects inhabiting the films as emblems whose interactions produce meanings relevant to social theory. Such fragments taken from the films and placed in the field of social theory can stimulate sociological imagination. Most significantly, however, dialectical images or allegories can suspend movement temporarily, a suspension which Benjamin himself referred to as 'dialectics at a standstill'. Cinema is a privileged site of encounter in so far as it can use such techniques:

> Lovers' looks, catastrophes, collisions, explosions, and other supreme moments tend to bring time to a standstill. By contrast, empty moments, secondary episodes, are compressed to the point of volatilization. Certain special effects related to acceleration even literally represent time's flight: calendar leaves flying away, clock hands spinning around.
>
> (Morin 2005: 57)

As well as structuring our perspective on cinema, allegory enables us to produce an interlinked series of double readings (actualization/virtualization, past/present, society/cinema). Hence when we talk about film, we talk about society and vice versa. Assuming that allegory is a structural reality within the cinematic narrative, we seek to understand the social through film by encoding its complex, often ambivalent, multiple and shifting meanings. But why allegory, and not analogy? Because, as we have already mentioned, we want to appeal to sense as well as meaning, to sociological imagination as well as sociological reasoning. In this context, putting sociology in motion, in action, is our prime concern. How can sociology activate its imagination, move beyond representational mediations? This is, of course, a Deleuzian question of 'dramatization'.

> [I]t is a question of producing within the work a movement capable of affecting the mind outside of all representations; it is a question of making movement itself a work, without interposition; of substituting direct signs for mediate representations; of inventing vibrations, rotations, whirlings, gravitations, dances or leaps which directly touch the mind. This is the idea of a man of the theatre.
>
> (Deleuze 1994: 8)

Dramatization through films is a useful tool for sociology to appeal to imagination and sense, to creativity, without confining itself to representations. Such an undertaking often enables the experience of intensities, of affects, which cannot be conceptualized in analytical terms or analysed empirically. Indeed, dramatization might become one of the most creative moments of social theorizing in which the sociologist himself is transformed through the encounter with cinema. Cinema is interesting for sociology precisely in this context, in its capacity of dramatization and, in a certain sense, 'actualization' of sociological ideas in particular sensations.

Finally, we are interested in a double reading of the aesthetic and the political/ethical. Thus, aiming for a social diagnosis, we deal with topics relevant to contemporary society. For this reason we cannot avoid, for instance, interrogating the present war against terror. Discourses of despotism (*Hamam*), partisan warfare and torture (*Brazil*), lynching and spite (*Lord of the Flies*), networks and strategies of resistance (*Fight Club*), crime and camps (*City of God*) and mourning the dead (*Life is Beautiful*) are all contemporary concerns highlighted in the context of the war against terror. This is the context for which the films are allegorized.

The contents of the book

This book can be read at least in three ways. First, as an attempt at analysing films while doing social theory; thus, all chapters explicitly deal with the relationship between reality and fiction, cinema and social theory, and they do it through discussing from different perspectives the possibility of critique today. Second, it can be read as an encounter with a series of significant fields and concepts within social theory: gender, identity and the other in Chapter 2; terror, fear and security in Chapter 3; capitalism and resistance in Chapter 4; various forms of crowds in Chapter 5; camps and poverty in Chapter 6; and finally ethics and testimony in Chapter 7. And third, finally, the book can be read as an attempt at social diagnosis where films function as tools of analysis.

Chapter 2 is built upon an analysis of Ferzan Özpetek's film *Hamam* (also known as *The Turkish Bath*) (1997). Having fully absorbed the structuralist and poststructuralist influences, it has become a commonplace within social theory to stress the 'relationality' of things. Thus, most scholars would agree that the vision of the East has played a significant role in the construction of European identity. However, using arguments from Lacanian psychoanalysis, we argue that the configuration of the self and the other is not primarily related to the construction of differences within a symbolic space. Rather, the Orient functions as a fantasy space of that which is prior to social or linguistic differences. In this context the Orient demonstrates a remarkable formlessness: the Orient is not only the other but also the hyperbolic. In this context we show how in *Hamam* the fantasies about perversion, bodily enjoyment, gender (especially homo- and heterosexuality) and despotism are sustained and stabilized through different economies of desire. The chapter unfolds further by relating *Hamam* to other representations of the Orient including Montesquieu's *Persian Letters* (1973 [1721]) and by elaborating on the ideological background of the fantasies of the East. In this context it develops two different readings: Foucauldian and deconstructivist methods constitute the first reading, Lacanian psychoanalysis the second. As well as discussing important questions of identity and gender/sex, the chapter thus aims to introduce the reader to the field of poststructuralist social theory.

Chapter 3 takes issue with Harry Hook's film *Lord of the Flies* (1990) based on Golding's novel, a dystopic comment on the Second World War. For Golding the reality of this war was more than just a brief disruption in the enlightened progress of civilization. Hence the state of exception, or the island life depicted in *Lord of the Flies* with ruthless precision, is not a regress into pre-social forms but rather an ever-present possibility of our own social system. Indeed, in stark contrast to the standard interpretations, the two 'clans'/crowds on the island, led by Ralph and Jack respectively, explicate the two sides of the same social bond. The 'upper' side consists in the image of society as rule governed and institutionalized, and citizens as law-abiding. On the 'downside', however, we encounter the fantasies of transgression, potlatch and perversion: Ralph's democratic utopianism versus Jack's fascistic warrior ethics. Ralph continuously appeals to reason and order (symbolized by his references to his parents) while Jack empowers his discursive position through references to the 'monster'. Ralph's mistake (and the shortcoming of democracy in general) is his denial of what Bataille called 'heterogeneity': the importance of expenditure, play, war and disorganization. What Jack can neither predict nor perceive, on the other hand, is that his disorganizing lines of flight can easily turn into an orgy of violence and spiteful murder. Interestingly, on their rescue, the boys answer their rescuers as to why they set the island on fire, they were 'just playing'; it was all a state of exception! The crucial question in today's society is whether this is still a valid answer. Is the contemporary state of exception merely an exception, a temporary phenomenon, or do we already live in a permanent state of exception?

Chapter 4 takes us to *City of God*, Fernando Meirelles's film about Rio de Janeiro's most notorious favela, which resembles a space of absolute exclusion or a dumping ground for human waste. The chapter addresses the situation of the favela dweller as an instantiation of *homo sacer*, the ultimate biopolitical subject whose life is stripped of cultural and political forms. The focus is on the socio-spatial mechanisms that immobilize the favela in which people lead a life in a permanent state of exception. To offer a systematic account of this immobilization we elaborate on the concepts of exception and camp. In this, favela life is periodized in three successive stages. The first is the 'age of innocence', in which the law is operational despite being in crisis. In the second period, crime and perversion increase, but communal ties continue to exist. As sovereign, the gang establishes an order, which it is itself excepted from. When exception becomes the rule, *City of God* enters its third period. Now, ceasing to have any referent any longer, violence takes the form of a pure, naked violence; everybody becomes *homo sacer*. We end with a discussion of how the movie *City of God* creates the illusion that the 'camp' is or can be contained in the favela, that outside the favela there is a 'city'. In this context we show how the logic of the camp is generalized, and how it can be detected in more positive forms such as gated communities and the like. How then are we to counter, to criticize this splintering society?

Chapter 5 takes its point of departure in the powerful blockbuster *Fight Club*. It deals with masochism as a form of (un)bonding. We focus on the question of how micro-fascism persists in the network society in spite of its public denial. We argue that every social order has an obscene supplement that serves as the positive condition of its possibility, and that increasing reflexivity today is accompanied by (re-)emerging non-symbolic forms of authority. In this context, the chapter deals with the question of violence and relates this to the problematics of critique, flight and act(ion) in contemporary societies. Considering micro-fascism as a line of flight with respect to the social bond, we ask what happens to the project of subversion when power itself goes nomadic and when the idea of transgression is solicited by the 'new spirit of capitalism'. Can the distinction between the mobile and the static serve as a critical tool in today's global consumer culture – the moral grammar of which is well adjusted to different forms of mobility and transgression? Dealing with the idea of transgression, we discuss that transgression has paradoxically become the law today. When the distinction between transgression and the law (between exception and the rule) disappears, capitalism starts to justify itself with reference to mobility/transgression/perversion. This chapter develops the analysis by addressing the two major aspects of contemporary society: its way of production (capitalism) and the dissolution of the disciplinary dispositif in the 'society of control'. Focusing on how resistance might be thought in such a society, the chapter opens the path for Chapter 6 which explicitly deals with terror, the strategies to counter it, and the danger of these counterstrategies becoming terroristic themselves.

Chapter 6 revisits the dystopic universe of Terry Gilliam's *Brazil*. It all starts when an insect enters the Ministry of Information causing an electronic typewriter to misspell the name of an enemy terrorist, Mr Tuttle. With the mistake Mr Tuttle becomes Mr Buttle, a family man living an ordinary life. Based on the piles of intelligence reports, the unfortunate Mr Buttle is now violently arrested and brought to the ministry for 'information retrieval', that is torture. He knows nothing and thus has nothing to tell, which however just makes him seem even more dangerous. The society we meet in *Brazil* is one in which surveillance and intelligence are everything and where the threat of terrorism is so omnipresent that people hardly notice the attacks anymore. In short, what we are facing in *Brazil* is a reactionary state of exception. The only person who challenges the state of affairs is Sam Lowry, the paper worker from the Ministry of Information who is made responsible for the mistake. However his attempts to convince the system that it all was a mistake remain unsuccessful, which is mainly because the idea of making a mistake is inconceivable to the authorities. Further, there is Mr Tuttle, whose terror is a 'good' one, that is it helps the people as against the Orwellian state. Against this background, *Brazil* forces us critically to analyse the concept of terror, linking this to the question of a society for which terrorism has become its sole *raison d'être*.

Chapter 7, the final chapter, concludes the book by elaborating on the question of ethics, especially ethics after the camp. It focuses on the 'riddle' of testimony in the context of Auschwitz. Trying to move beyond the reliance on 'experience' on the one hand and the danger of 'trivializing' the Holocaust on the other, we seek to develop an intermediary position in between the two approaches to the Holocaust, and discuss the possibility of an ethics that takes its point of departure in the *Muselmann*'s naked body. In this context we read *Remnants of Auschwitz* to render visible the (im)possibilities of representing the 'unspeakable'. The Holocaust, we argue, is that which resists a 'realist' archivation for it escapes both the appropriating memory and the willed forgetting. But then, how can we keep alive the aporia, the tension between speech and naked life, between the traumatized testimony and the appropriating forgetfulness, and thus 'mediate' between the past and the present? How can one represent the impossibility of depicting horror? We argue that the Holocaust cannot be represented in its horror for its essence precisely consists in making testimony impossible. The horror of the camp can only be depicted indirectly. 'The spirit of Auschwitz' is thus neither incarnated in those who died of gassing nor in those who survived, but in the bond that exists between them. We are all descendants of Auschwitz, and we are all obliged to bear testimony.

Finally, in the Afterword, we return to the question of critique. In this context we focus on the contemporary society as a postpolitical society and reformulate, from the perspective of this book, a possible role of cinema in terms of critique.

2   *Hamam*

Postal economies of the Orient

> Istanbul is what I was searching for. I have been here a week and it has taken
> my breath away, my slumber. How much time I wasted before reaching here!
> I have the feeling it was waiting for me, silently, while I chased for a life, as
> tiring as it was useless. Here things flow more slowly and softly, this light
> breeze dissolves your worries and vibrates your body. I finally feel that I can
> start again.

The above quotation is from a letter from the Orient, written by Madame
Anita, a fictive character in the film *Hamam*. Madame travels from Rome to
Istanbul just after the Second World War and never returns. In her letters back
to Rome, she describes her life in Istanbul as 'one long holiday': transgressing
the borderline between work and leisure, her life is light and joyful. In Istanbul,
she marries a local businessman, the owner of a series of coffee houses, but alas,
the marriage lasts only a few months. With the money she is entitled to after
the divorce, Madame Anita buys a decaying Turkish bath, a hamam. She
restores it and runs it for many years, until hamams begin to lose popularity
in Istanbul.

In *Hamam*, we do not meet Madame in person. The film opens with her
death and we are informed about her life only through the letters she wrote
to her sister in Rome. When Madame passes away, her only remaining Italian
relative, her nephew Francesco, inherits her possessions. Francesco is the owner
of a successful business (an interior design office) in Rome together with his
wife, Marta, and their associate, Paolo. The film depicts none of these people
as charming or warm: their habitus is characterized by a stressful, image-
conscious and career-oriented lifestyle. The Italian personae of the film embody
everything associated with the Orientalist image of the cold and rational Westerner. And then, of course, Istanbul, in stark contrast to Rome, stands for the
ancient, tantalizing erotic allure and idleness of the Orient. The film seeks to
reveal the secrets of the old, labyrinthine, narrow, intimate streets of Istanbul,
the feasts of circumcision, the sensuous atmosphere of the hamam and other
excessive joys of the flesh. The Turkish bath itself is depicted as a house of
pleasure and tranquillity, and it clearly symbolizes Europe's 'other'.

One could of course criticize *Hamam* for arranging everything in clean-cut, dichotomous terms: the West versus the East; Rome versus Istanbul; Francesco and Marta versus Madame Anita and the Turks in her neighbourhood. But such a critique, which focuses on the juxtaposition of the self and the other, misses something essential regarding Orientalism. Something has to mediate between the two poles, letters, persons and objects, allowing for substitutions and metamorphoses. *Hamam* is also about mediators who bridge West and East, a mediation inscribed in travel narratives on the strange and the exotic. In this respect *Hamam* is a post-1968 version of Montesquieu's *Persian Letters* (first published in 1721 [1973]). As in Montesquieu's work, *Hamam* allows the West and the East to be compared with a view to moralistic lessons. Both works are organized around letters. However, the letters in the film do not address the Orient to introduce it to the world of knowledge, rationality and reason as is the case with Montesquieu's letters; rather, they inversely address European travellers longing to escape from their stressful lives. In other words, the Orientalist dichotomy remains the same while the positively valorized pole is changed; relaxation and enjoyment now beat rationality and wealth.

Let us open up our question: how are we to read these postal economies? Are Montesquieu's *Persian Letters* and Madame Anita's letters to be interpreted as merely variations on the same theme (Orientalism)? Accordingly, how are we to read the distinction between West and East, Europe and the Orient? If we are dealing with the very same postal economy, then how do we explain this remarkable sameness between *Hamam*'s and Montesquieu's letters? And, finally, how can our reading inform the way the self and the other are juxtaposed? To answer such questions, we first deal with an interrogation of Montesquieu's *Persian Letters* and *Hamam*. Second, we discuss the texture of Orientalism in general terms. Then, by counterposing two different critical styles of reading Orientalism – a discourse analytical reading that focuses on the construction of binary distinctions and a psychoanalytic reading that focuses on the construction of the Orient as a fantasy space – we want to stress the advantages of the psychoanalytic reading. After discussing narratives (in *Hamam* and *Persian Letters*), the theme (Orientalism) and methodology (discourse analysis and deconstruction versus psychoanalysis), we end with our considerations on the question of critique: is there an ethical or a genuinely critical way of reading the Orient? In this context, we offer three different readings of the final scene of *Hamam*, which are organized according to the Lacanian distinction between the imaginary, symbolic and the real.

Hamam

Which images and narratives are deployed in *Hamam*? And is it justified to see them as representative of Orientalism? To begin with, let us interpret these images and narratives as elements of a distinction between West and East, masculine and feminine, or the normal and the perverted, a distinction that as a rule privileges the first term. By doing this, we interpret Orientalism in the way cultural theory usually does: by focusing on the construction of the self and the other and the accompanying strategies of stereotyping, devaluing and disqualifying the other (Neumann 1999: 1–38).

The first letter of *Hamam* informs Francesco about Madame Anita's death. Indeed, the longest sequence of the film, following the initial scene in which we are informed about her death, is based on the movements of this letter. We see the letter posted in Istanbul, stamped at several Turkish offices, sorted and finally delivered to Francesco in Rome. This might be seen as merely an introductory scene. However, as the film unfolds it becomes clear that *Hamam* is in fact structured around the very circulation of letters, which is why the initial scene is especially significant. Most often these letters are read by the characters while they cross the Bosphorus that (dis)connects the two continents. Hence the significance of postal economies in relation to *Hamam*: they effectively mediate between East and West.

The letter urges Francesco to go to Istanbul to sell what he later discovers to be a Turkish bath. Yet the sale is continually delayed: everything is in slow motion in the Orient. Finally, however, Francesco is ready to sign the contract for the sale with a greedy speculator. Yet he refuses to do so, because he happens to learn that the company wants to demolish the area to build parking lots, hotels, tennis courts and so on. Francesco warns the poor neighbourhood against the company's plans. Warned about the cold, calculating Western modernity, the people in the neighbourhood now follow his example and refuse to sell their homes. Once again the same old Orientalist image surfaces: in the West people barely know their neighbours; in the Orient you just open your window if you seek intense communication with others; everybody knows each other, news travels fast. *Hamam* focuses on a very specific area of Istanbul, presenting it as everything that urbanism has destroyed in the West: a big village untouched by modernity.

When modernity is brought to the Orient in an unreflected manner it gives rise to awkward effects; what is needed is therefore more Western involvement. It is hence Francesco, the European hero, who saves the primitive and backward Oriental subjects from themselves (in this case from the speculator). Istanbul is a beautifully decaying ruin waiting to be restored by entrepreneurial Europeans, first Madame, then Francesco and finally Marta. In a multiculturalist manner, the hamam remains a beautiful and exotic place thanks to the West (compare Žižek 1999: 215–21; 2001d: 69).

Enlightening the Orient and saving its cultural heritage is, however, only one aspect of the encounter. Francesco himself changes too. One of the reasons for his prolonged stay in Istanbul is his homosexual relationship with the Turk Mehmet, who lives in the same neighbourhood with his family, obviously Madame's closest neighbours. Homosexuality is an important element in that the Orient, particularly the Turkish bath, is depicted as a den of iniquity (Shohat 1997). Whereas the West is entrapped in rigid rules and ossified customs, desire flows smoothly in the Orient: '[l]ike a light breeze that vibrates your body'. The homosexuality of Mehmet and Francesco is perverted in the sense that it transgresses the Western heterosexual norm. This element of perversion is further underlined through Francesco, Mehmet and Madame's practice of peeping at naked bodies from the roof of the hamam. This peeping is perverted not because it sustains a forbidden eroticism, but especially in relation to enjoying the multitude, just as the Sultan previously enjoyed not just the female body but the multitude of harem women (Grosrichard 1998: 141–6).

Marta, suspicious of Francesco's excuses for being away, makes the next move by travelling to Istanbul to see him. During her first night, she discovers the relationship between the two men when she sees them make passionate love in the hamam. This glimpse of the Oriental hothouse of desire is an updated vision of the harem: a space of limitless and intense enjoyment. Water, steam and heat are all symbols of relaxation and smooth movement. Intense ethnic music with fast drumbeats underpins this atmosphere of corporeal passion.

The next day, Marta and Francesco agree to divorce, and Marta decides to leave Istanbul. On the same day, the mafia murders Francesco; the building company has taken out a contract on him. The Turkish mafia here serves as an updated version of despotic power (just as the hamam refers to the harem). What unites the despot and the mafia is the omnipotent power characterized by a complete disregard for human life. The Mafioso is now the absolute master: the neighbourhood is terrorized just as the Oriental subject was terrified of the Sultan's power (ibid.: 36–40). One does not go against the will of the despot. In this respect, Francesco seems to remain a European: stubborn as he is, he goes against the rules of the game, which an effeminate Oriental subject, motivated by fear rather than courage and individual will, would never do. The price he pays for his stubbornness is life itself.

After Francesco's death, Marta returns to Istanbul. As his wife, she receives Francesco's wedding ring (she had given her own to a poor woman after she discovered his betrayal). This reconciliation is significant since Marta in the final scene decides to run the hamam herself. However, her reconciliation is not only with Francesco but also with the repressed 'Orientalized' side of her own personality. Hence, Marta is in the final scene depicted smoking using Madame's cigarette holder while the narrator reads her letter, remarkably similar to Madame Anita's letters. She writes to Mehmet, who has left Istanbul after Francesco's death, to say that the hamam is now completely renovated.

> Sometimes at sunset, I get melancholy, but then suddenly this cold breeze rises and takes it far away. It is a strange breeze, like no other I have ever felt. A light breeze and it loves me.

One could say that Madame Anita's letters *did* reach their destination, that their true addressee was Marta, allowing her to take her position and realize her latent 'Orientalism'. Marta becomes the new Madame and Francesco is thus reduced to a vanishing mediator. In this context, too, letters play a significant role: they allow the metamorphosis of the characters to be completed and their 'fates' to be realized. 'Lost' letters finally reach their intended recipients even though they were initially returned to sender.

Writing *Persian Letters*

It is no coincidence that Montesquieu's *Persian Letters* (1973 [1721]), perhaps the most famous Orientalist piece, and Özpetek's *Hamam* have the form of postal economies. The letter obviously has a mediating function; it links home and abroad. Moreover, when Montesquieu wrote *Persian Letters*, his choice of form was well considered. Whereas his *The Spirit of the Laws* (1989 [1748]) is written as a *tractatus* proceeding according to the logic of reason, *Persian Letters* is deliberately excessive in style. *Persian Letters* are not just *about* the Orient, they are also written in an 'Oriental' style (McAlpin 2000: 55): their composition does not follow a logic and the story is not told as a linear narrative; rather, they give body to a polyphony of voices (ibid.: 45). There is not one narrative or one topic, but many. The letters shift from serious political business to reflections over ways of dressing. Sometimes a moralistic tone is applied, while other letters are intended to be funny. The most important aspect is the way the letters are selected: we are left with the impression that some are lost; others lack a sender or some parts of their content. Sometimes it is as if we have obscure letters within letters. In a similar way, we have in *Hamam* the returned letters of Madame Anita, which later are included in both Francesco's and Marta's narratives. Why this form? And why this consistent attempt to describe the Orient according to a characteristic *lack of form*?

To answer this question, a short detour around Derrida's *The Post Card: From Socrates to Freud and Beyond* (1987) is useful. Derrida's book is, among other things, an ironic critique of the teleological underpinning of many of Jacques Lacan's concepts. Derrida argues that no matter how enigmatic meaning is, for Lacan it is always open to interpretation: everything fits into the psychoanalytic scheme. Once, in a commentary on Edgar Allan Poe's 'Purloined Letter', Lacan even argued that the letter always reaches its destination (this point will be qualified later, see Lacan 1988). To illustrate the role of the performative misfire through the economy of lost letters is hence well done. Derrida further claims that this teleological structure, present in all of Lacan's concepts, is deeply flawed. Hence, he has written some unfinished and undelivered letters, some postcards, in order to subvert Lacan's teleology.

Thus, Lacan is for Derrida a representative of Western tradition's falling prey to 'logocentrism'. Logocentrism has many faces: the privileging of writing over speech, teleology over dissemination through time, the masculine over the feminine, the West over the East and so on. Everybody falls prey to such a logocentrism, except Derrida, of course, who is capable of uncovering through his impressive work the 'other' of this tradition (speech, woman, the hyperbolic, etc.). This is shown literally in Derrida's overwhelmingly difficult book *Glas* (1986a). In *Glas*, all pages are divided into two parts. The left part of the page is filled with quotes from Hegel, the Western logocentric philosopher par exellence, while the right part primarily contains references to the French author Jean Genet. Genet was a homosexual living on the margins of society, and Derrida takes his voice as a genuine other that subverts Hegel's text. While *The Post Card* can be read as written in an 'Oriental' style, the two columns in *Glas* can be read as referring to 'Western' and 'Eastern' ways of writing and being. The West is logocentric, rational, orderly, teleological, while the East is perversely hyperbolic. Genet is subversive and perverted just as the Orient is.

The question to be posed here is how genuinely critical Derrida's project is. Is this juxtaposition of logos and hyperbole not Orientalism at its purest? Has this 'other' of reason and rationality not always, at least since modernity, been present in Orientalist fantasies? Derrida has argued that Western logocentrism has been with us since Plato and the same goes for the 'other' of this tradition, 'Orientalism'. There is nothing subversive in stressing the existence of this other voice; in doing so one mainly consolidates a Western gaze. The Orient, the existence of this other voice, is nothing but an ideological supplement to Western logocentrism: it is a fantasy. This orientalized voice is not 'other', marginal or repressed. It takes no deconstructive labour to uncover it (for a deconstructive reading of Montesquieu focusing on postal politics, see Bennington 1994: 240–58). To clarify this point, let us return to Montesquieu's *Persian Letters*.

Montesquieu's popular book was published in 1721 and went through ten editions within a year (Betts 1973: 19). The place of publication was Holland, which was a normal practice when a work risked official disapproval (ibid.: 18). The book was not unexpectedly included in the Vatican's list of prohibited books (ibid.: 18). Montesquieu's English translator C. J. Betts characterized it as one of the main anti-Establishment works of the early eighteenth century. Yet it remains one of the classical examples of Orientalist discourse. *Persian Letters* is not, however, a singular achievement: around 30 per cent of all books published in Montesquieu's time had the Orient as their theme (Kaiser 2000: 16).

The most important voice in *Persian Letters* is Usbek, a rich man travelling to Europe to be enriched. He sets off, leaving his seraglio and harem in the custody of his chief eunuch. In the book, we also meet another traveller from Persia, Rica. The two men are usually interpreted as the two sides of Montesquieu's own personality: Usbek is the curious man seeking enlightenment, while Rica, constrained by traditional ways of seeing, is the Orientalized figure (McAlpin 2000: 50). Taken together, their narratives offer a varied commentary to contemporary affairs, allowing Montesquieu to contrast West and East.

Persian Letters are highly moralistic in preaching a golden rule that can apply to everything from government to sexuality. Both the complete denial of freedom that supposedly pertains to the East and the unlimited pursuit of freedom as premised in the philosophy of Thomas Hobbes are under ruthless attack.

The women in the harem and the eunuchs unfold their sexuality in an unnatural and too restrained way (Montesquieu 1973: letter 114). Marriage as practised in the West is a much better way of uniting man and woman. On the other hand, Montesquieu criticizes monastery life and the Catholic Church in general for being too strict, recommending that his readers strive for the right balance in all aspects of life (ibid.: letters 116 and 117: 209–13). This double-edged analysis is present in all of Montesquieu's concerns. His letters are both 'Persanes' and 'Parisiennes' (Trumpener 1987: 180). The main focus is a critique of the Orient: through the work of reason, Usbek learns to appreciate knowledge, rationality and freedom. At the same time, however, an implicit critique is offered of the abuse of privileges in France. The emperor's abuse of government in France is claimed to mirror Oriental despotism (Betts 1973: 26–7; Grosrichard 1998: 26–7). Orientalism is not just, as Said often argues, a tool used to repress the Orient (Said 1978), it is and has always been a double-edged sword (Kaiser 2000).

Three themes are central in this Orientalist discourse – religion, sex and politics – enabling a distinction between Islam and Christianity, between perversion and heterosexuality and between despotism and republicanism (Grosrichard 1998). Islam is a fake religion based on a lack of inner conviction. Mahomet is an impostor who gave birth to a religion of empty rituals (ibid.: 85–119; Joubin 2000). The image of sexuality relates to the eunuch, the harem and the fantasies of secret enjoyment: lesbian relationships (Montesquieu 1973: letters 4 and 20), the unfulfilled sexual desires of the eunuchs and so on (ibid.: letters 79 and 96). The Sultan himself is a pervert who turns his household into one of lust and pleasures: a brothel where all women (and men) are brought in to please the Sultan. Finally, the Orient is described as a place without separation of powers. Everything exists for and belongs to the Sultan; nothing has an independent existence (Grosrichard 1998).

More than 250 years later, we find these narratives reappearing in films like *Hamam*. We have already mentioned that the mafia stands for the Sultan (the complete disregard for human life, the politics of fear) and the hamam for the harem (the enjoyment of the manifold, the bodily pleasures, illicit pleasure obtained through a hidden gaze). *Hamam* is also an ambivalent narrative, as is Montesquieu's *Letters*. It contains not only a stereotypical image of a backward East but also a critique of contemporary Western culture. False gods are now Western (design, money or excessive materialism). Furthermore, as is the case with Montesquieu's narrative, *Hamam* is about the metamorphosis of the West and the East; hence the importance of letters in both narratives.

It is in this context tempting to argue that Orientalism has remained unchanged. Indeed, this seems to be Said's conclusion in *Orientalism* (1978). A whole range of analyses in cultural theory have taken up this idea and mapped the different ways in which the West constructs the non-Western world. Much is gained through these analyses, but one thing is always missing: scholars are not attentive to the ambivalence of the Orientalist discourse (Bhabha 1972). The Orient is neither near nor distant, but both, and simultaneously. It is not necessarily a positively or negatively valorized social topology, but a utopia and a dystopia at the same time.

This ambivalence is clearly present in the famous concluding letter 161 of Montesquieu's *Persian Letters*. Lacking the firm hand of Usbek, his seraglio and harem slowly but inevitably disintegrate. There are indications of lesbian relationships among women of the harem, and the hierarchy of power is turned upside down (power has moved from the powerful eunuchs to the manipulative harem women). Already in letter 156, Usbek's first wife reports: '[h]orror, darkness, and dread rule the seraglio: it is filled with terrible lamentation; it is subject at every moment to the unchecked rage of a tiger' (ibid.: letter 156: 276–7). Later, in letter 161, things become clearer when Roxana explains to Usbek the reasons for her suicide:

> Yes, I deceived you. I suborned your eunuchs, outwitted your jealousy, and managed to turn your terrible seraglio into a place of delightful pleasures. ... How could you have thought me credulous enough to imagine that I was in the world only in order to worship your caprices? That while you allowed yourself everything, you had the right to thwart all my desires? No: I may have lived in servitude, but I have always been free. I have amended your laws according to the laws of nature, and my mind has always remained independent.
>
> (ibid.: letter 161)

Like Montesquieu's whole book, this ambivalent letter can read in two different ways. The first reading places more emphasis on the geographical or the geophysical. In accordance with Montesquieu's climate theory, all power constructions in the Orient are permanently corrupted. At the same time, however, the Oriental system, that is despotism, is unnatural for it denies human freedom. How, then, is the persistence of the Oriental system explained? Obviously, it is a difficult question to answer and Montesquieu's way out is to argue that the climate makes people lazy and prone to accept domination: physical nature corrupts human nature. Accordingly, Western ideals of freedom and self-rule cannot be introduced in the Orient. If they are introduced, they will have negative effects. True freedom, as marked by the absence of Usbek, the master, is not possible in the Orient.

In a rather different feminist reading, female enjoyment or female voices exist beyond the reach of the despot. His power is never total. Hence, the image of despotic power is claimed to be Orientalism at its purest. The women (in Montesquieu's narrative: Roxana), are not completely controlled, there is always the possibility that they take control of their own lives and manipulate the sultanate. Whereas the first reading assumes the need and possibility of complete domination, hence the collapse of the harem with Usbek's absence, this second reading stresses a dialectics of master and bondsman. Perhaps it is the women who rule while the sultan remains tied to his role. Perhaps the women have secret enjoyments and a secret language.

Focusing on the content of the Orientalist narrative as we did in this section, one can conclude that Orientalist themes are both persistent and ambivalent. We started the above line of argumentation by ordering our discourse according to the distinctions between East and West and then went on to draw a more complex picture. However, something important is missing in this textual universe, which is organized according to the reifying logic of binaries. Hence, the next section aims at reconstructing our analysis according to a theoretical scheme of Lacanian origin.

The Orient as a zero-institution

Europe's identity is defined in relation to its 'other', predominantly the Orient, and this is what is commonly argued within cultural studies. Identity is not given through references to intrinsic qualities of objects, places or people, but rather through a relational web of differences. Accordingly, the Orient condenses what Europe is *not*: a kind of negative photographic image, which operates through the logic of oppositional differences between normality and perversion, law and despotism, mind and body, reason and desire (Neumann and Welsh 1991: 329, 331, 334). Thus, such images of the Orient – as the hothouse of desire and the cradle of despotic power – tell us more about the identity of Europe itself. They are images that unfold before a Western gaze. Through a power-knowledge nexus, the Orient is fixated in Western stereotypes.

Are Montesquieu's and *Hamam*'s letters then to be read along the same lines as yet other versions of a well-known story? We want to resist this temptation. Since it was published in 1978, Said's *Orientalism* has become a standard approach to the topic. Yet the following year, an equally interesting but much less known book on the Orient appeared in France: Alain Grosrichard's *Structure du sérial: La fiction du despotisme Asiatique dans l'Occident classique* (Grosrichard, *The Sultan's Court*, 1998). Grosrichard's major source of inspiration was not Foucault but Lacan, and that makes a significant difference.

Our first argument is that the relationship between the West and the Orient is not merely one of a difference between two elements within the same space. Rather, the Orient signifies that which is prior to difference. In other words, difference is not that of the masculine and the feminine, but between (sexual) difference and the lack of difference. Hence, the eunuch, not the woman, is the emblem of the Orient (ibid.; Trumpener 1987). Similarly, despotism is not merely a political form as are monarchy, tyranny and democracy, but rather an a-political 'formlessness'; the Orient is defined by the lack of form as such (Grosrichard 1998; Boer 1996: 46). It is constituted as a space in which the distinction between the social and the political does not hold. The discourses on sex and power are thus intertwined. The Orient does not belong to the symbolic order; it is a narration of what is prior to or beyond the symbolic.

In Lacanian terms, the Orient is constituted as a fantasy space that both conditions and escapes the 'social'. Fantasies create objects of desire, but these objects are perceived to be out of reach. The law, that is the prohibition of various activities, creates a desire to surmount constraints. The Orient is a product of such a desire to transgress. It is, in this sense, not a hallucination of fulfilled desire, but an answer to the question: why this desire? Through the law, the fantasy of a beyond (and before the law) is made possible. Fantasy is not primarily sustained through semantic interventions but through investments of psychic energies, desires and drives. Fantasy stages desire, freezes it in fixed patterns and hence protects the subject by keeping enjoyment at bay. The object of desire is transposed to another space, 'Orientalized', enabling it to remain sublimated, that is unreachable. Indeed, as we will argue later, to realize one's fantasy is often to dissolve it.

Concomitantly, the social bond has two sides (Žižek 2001b: 93). Life within the domain of the law, that is life organized by the separation of powers (the separation of the political and the domestic, male and female) is sustained through fantasies of transgression. Such fantasies form the 'downside' of the social bond that guarantees the strength of its up side. In this sense, Western rationality, reason and morality (the up side) and its dark, 'Orientalized' downside are parts of the same economy (Grosrichard 1998: 137–8). The downside, however, must remain disavowed, 'Orientalized', in order to remain functional.

Against this background, Said *à la Foucault* and Grosrichard *à la Lacan* produce two different forms of critique. The first is discursive and focuses on a 'symptomal reading' of the ideological text to 'deconstruct' its meaning by showing how the text constructs a field organizing a heterogeneous set of 'floating signifiers' around certain 'nodal points' while pushing other signifiers to the margin by devaluating them. Hence, it focuses on the upper side of the social bond, on the construction of dichotomies between West and East, and on how traces of these constructions can be uncovered when reading in the margins of classical texts. This is also how we have analysed Orientalism so far. The second mode of analysis, in contrast, 'aims at extracting the kernel of enjoyment, at articulating the way in which – beyond the field of meaning but at the same time internal to it – an ideology implies, manipulates, produces a pre-ideological enjoyment structured in fantasy' (Žižek 1989: 125). This is how we want to proceed.

What status is accorded to the Orient in this second reading? To answer this question, let us initially focus on Claude Lévi-Strauss's *Structural Anthropology* as discussed by Slavoj Žižek (1994: 25–6; 2000a). Here, Lévi-Strauss describes the behaviour of the members of the Winnebago tribe. This tribe is divided into two subgroups, 'moieties'. Asked by an anthropologist to draw a spatial representation of their town in the sand, the two groups draw different pictures. Whereas one group perceives the city as a circle with a central house in the middle, the other group divides it into two halves. Žižek labels these two groups conservative-corporatists and revolutionary-antagonists. These two camps could likewise be labelled left and right, or men and women. The temptation to be resisted here is the straightforward claim that the West and the Orient, Rome and Istanbul, are like moieties, like positions within the same symbolic space. On the contrary, these two positions express two ways of dealing with a fundamental deadlock. They are two attempts at symbolizing a traumatic core or, in other words, two ways of covering a primordially given and traumatic lack.

> Lévi-Strauss' central point is that this example should in no way entice us into cultural relativism, according to which the perception of social space depends on the observer's group membership: the very splitting into the two 'relative' perceptions implies a hidden reference to a constant – not the objective, 'actual' disposition of buildings but a traumatic kernel, a fundamental antagonism the inhabitants of the village were unable to symbolize, to account for, to 'internalize', to come to terms with – an imbalance in social relations that prevented the community from stabilizing itself into a harmonious whole. The two perceptions of the ground plan are simply two mutually exclusive endeavors to cope with this traumatic antagonism, to heal its wound via the imposition of a balanced symbolic structure.
>
> (Žižek 2000a: 112–13)

How are the two tribes brought together? Through what Lévi-Strauss calls a 'zero-institution'. The zero-institution is 'a kind of institutional counterpart to the famous *mana*, the empty signifier with no determinate meaning, since it signifies only the presence of meaning as such' (ibid.: 113). It is an institution that allows the symbolic to be installed and differences to be represented. The Orient works as a zero-institution characterized by a lack of difference; it is a fantasy of the pre-social, of what precedes difference.

It is worth taking Lévi-Strauss's concept of the zero-institution literally here. The Orient functions as the number zero, as that which does not have an objective counterpart. It can only be represented as a lack, as a black hole, a desert (ibid.). As such, however, it lays the foundation for all series of numbers (all series of differences: man versus woman, ruler versus ruled, and so on). Zero is involved in all rows of numbers even though it is literally not there. The Orient is the zero degree of political order. 'Despotism functions as the degree zero in Montesquieu's system of ordering' (Boer 1996: 47).

Yet, this 'beyond the law', the traumatic 'Real' prior to difference, can only be represented through the symbolic. Hence, it becomes a zero-*institution*. The concept of the letter is again useful here. The letters bridge and represent the beyond, the other space where no constraints are felt. They are as fictions or imaginary simulacra: the fantasy space of *Hamam* is thus not an empirical Istanbul; rather, it is a space constructed through Madame Anita's letters. Yet, the stuff of the letter is literally letters, signifiers; it creates difference by way of signifiers and, as such, the letter belongs to the symbolic register (Lacan 1977: 146–78). Thus, fantasy has a double, spectral, structure (Žižek 1994).

The difference between the Lacanian concept of fantasy and the common understanding of ideology should be noted here. Fantasy is, as we mentioned, fundamental in staging desire. There is nothing, no truth, to be discovered behind it (ibid.). It only covers a traumatic abyss. There is no real Orient behind the Orient caught by the Western gaze. Said's *Orientalism* implies that there is a true Orient distorted by the European gaze. From a Lacanian perspective, the Orient could be located anywhere; everything can be 'Orientalized'. When one merely asks whether Orientalist fantasies are true or not, what one forgets is that desire, not truth, sustains ideological fantasies. Hence, the only function of the zero-institution:

> is the purely negative one of signalling the presence and actuality of social institution as such, in opposition to its absence, to pre-social chaos. It is the reference to such a zero-institution that enables all members of the tribe to experience themselves as such, as members of the same tribe. Is not this zero-institution, then, ideology at its purest, that is the direct embodiment of the ideological function of providing a neutral all-encompassing space in which social antagonism is obliterated, in which all members of society can recognize themselves?
>
> (Žižek 2000a: 113)

Fantasies and ideologies should be analysed as given in discursive practices in which signifiers are fixed. This would be the first, the Foucauldian, mode of analysis mentioned above. Such operations are, however, only possible with reference to a more fundamental level. Fantasies and ideologies are sustained through desire. Thus, we now want to describe this interplay of desire and social taxonomies. To begin with, we take the final scene of the film as our point of departure and read the film as a meta-narrative about desire, enjoyment, drive and their social settings. Then we show a way of 'going through fantasy' that culminates in the ethical attitude of four female heroes: Marta, Antigone, Roxana and Lady Montagu.

Returned to sender

The interpretation of Marta's position in the final scene of *Hamam* is essential in that it allows for a reading that is not linear and chronological. Reading the film backwards it becomes clear that a Hegelian cunning of reason has led each personal story to its true conclusion. If the film is read as a contemporary version of an ancient Greek tragedy, the core concept in this context is fate. Due to the mediating activities of Francesco, Marta realizes her fate: through him, her transformation into Madame becomes possible. Francesco enables Marta's arrival in Istanbul twice and makes it possible for Marta to read Madame's letters. Finally, she is transfigured from an addressee to a sender (the last letter of the film is, as we mentioned, sent by Marta).

In *Hamam,* we primarily follow Francesco's actions and hence he appears to be the central character. The final scene, however, makes it perfectly clear that Francesco is a secondary character whose only purpose is to enable

Marta to assume Madame's mantle both socially and physically. Francesco is what Frederick Jameson has called a vanishing mediator (Jameson 1988). It is he who allows the letters to reach their destination: he is a 'post-man'. In the beginning of the film, we are informed that Madame's letters to Rome were returned. Yet, focusing on the characters in the film, one could say that the letters finally reach their destination and Francesco and Marta finally realize their common fate. But what is this fate? Let us begin by qualifying Lacan's claim that 'the letter always reaches its destination' and by explaining the way in which letters allow for Francesco's and Marta's metamorphoses.

The reason the letter always makes it to its addressee is, first, with a reference to the imaginary, that everybody experiences herself or himself as an addressee (Žižek 1992). A message in a bottle is the paradigmatic example. Louis Althusser's concept of interpellation describes this imaginary lure (1984). The person interpellated by a policeman shouting 'hey you' is interpellated because by turning towards the policeman, he identifies himself with the addressee of the call. This 'I' which turns around is created through the call; it is a product of the process of interpellation. The addressee is thus everyone who turns around, recognizing the policeman as an authority. Madame's letters reach their destination because persons who happen to read them are interpellated. Furthermore, Madame's letters also have the audience of the film as their addressee. Like the person interpellated by the policeman, the audience readily turns around, confirming the banal fantasies of the Orient. The film offers a fantasy structure, which is accepted in so far as it helps us to overcome our 'symbolic' castration.

'A letter always arrives at its destination since its destination is wherever it arrives' (Johnson 1988). In this sense, the success of the letter has to be explained by the fact that it offers a screen for the projection of our fantasies. In Edgar Alan Poe's story 'The Purloined Letter' (1988), the policeman never finds the letter of the criminal due to the fact that he has an already established image of what the letter of a criminal may look like. Actually, the letter is in front of him but carries the seal of the chief police officer. That the letter always reaches its destination implies, with reference to 'the symbolic', that the letter is simply a signifier, which is then interpreted according to the fantasies of its receiver. In Poe, it is the police officer's image of a criminal mind that keeps him from finding the letter. Likewise, the film is a chain of signifiers ready to be interpreted. Homosexuals read the film in the context of gay liberation (the message of the film being in this case that no sexual practices can be claimed as sick or perverted: everyone has that sexuality which is just right for him or her). Communitarians read it as a narrative of cultural and social decline in the West. Some Turks take it as a celebration of Turkey's unacknowledged silent acceptance of sexual and cultural diversity, in opposition to the Western images of Eastern intolerance, while others dislike the film because of its homosexual scenes, Orientalism and so on. Which reading to prefer, then? This question is a false one in so far as one accepts that the

Orient is a fantasy space, and the film plays to (can confirm) all spectators' fantasies.

Now, we can investigate how the letters in *Hamam* reach their destination allowing the main characters to change. We offer three different readings of the film. The first two readings confirm the Western construction of the Orient as a fantasy space, while the third attempts to go through fantasy, breaking its spell and its power to fascinate.

From the symbolic to the imaginary

Smoking is a central signifier of enjoyment in the film. In the final scene, for instance, Marta smokes on the rooftop of the hamam she now owns. This is the culmination of the process in which she finds herself: she moves from a socially mediated desire (Rome) to enjoyment (Istanbul), from Marta to Madame. This would be a commonsensical reading of the scene. Marta has found what she was searching for, just as Francesco and Madame had done before her. The Oriental way of life is worth desiring, or better, enjoying, in contrast to the false and empty desires staged in Rome. Moving to Istanbul, both Marta and Francesco realize that this Western way of life is false and conformist: the European self is a surface self, a mask, in contrast to the Oriental self, which is based on inner truth and conviction. In this reading, the film is about finding oneself behind the mask.

However, Rome is here associated with the symbolic in a second sense. Lacan wrote that the sexual relationship is impossible and that the partners are forced to play the role of partial objects for each other's desires (Lacan 1975: 58). The image of love as unity is a mystification (ibid.). Life in Rome is a precise manifestation of this impossibility. In their pursuit of great love both Marta and Francesco are caught in a game of betrayal. The desire for the sublime love only creates unhappiness, for the ideal partner is always somebody else; desire is always the other's desire. However, in Istanbul they approach the object of desire directly and accept the socially mediated fantasy of the great love as hollow. Francesco finds true happiness by living out his denigrated love; he lives out his fantasies, accepting the position of a pervert, falling short of the heterosexual norm, for him Istanbul is a way of escaping social taxonomies.

This reading, however, must be rejected, or better, its ideological under-pinnings must be uncovered. What makes it ideological is its attempt to conceal the void on which all identities are based. In 'The Mirror Stage as Formative of the Function of the I', Lacan claimed that the child misinterprets its unity (Lacan 1977: 1–7). When it sees its reflection in a mirror, it sees an autonomous self existing independently of its parents. This perception is a misperception for the child is crucially dependent on its parents and their care. Later, Althusser gave Lacan's idea a sociological twist by claiming that the bourgeois subject, defined through the concepts of autonomy and freedom, misperceived its lack of unity and independence (Althusser 1984). Along the same lines, Lacan stated that 'the woman does not exist' (Lacan 1973: 60). The basic idea is the same as in Althusser's essay on ideology: people of the female sex do of course exist, but the woman as such does not exist as an independent being outside the play of sexual difference. In short, this reading falls prey to the lure of ego psychology, whose contemporary form is according to Žižek 'Western Buddhism':

> The recourse to Taoism or Buddhism offers a way out of this predicament which definitely works better than the desperate escape into old traditions: instead of trying to cope with the accelerating rhythm of technological progress and social changes, one should rather renounce the very endeavour to retain control over what goes on, rejecting it as the expression of the modern logic of domination – one should, instead, 'let oneself go'. Drift along, while retaining an inner distance and indifference towards the mad dance of this accelerated process, a distance based on the insight that all this social and technological upheaval is ultimately just a non-substantial proliferation of semblances which do not really concern the innermost kernel of our being.
>
> (Žižek 2001d: 12–13)

Seen from this perspective, *Hamam* parallels Western Buddhism. Find your true self, give up the desire to express yourself through commodities, career and prestige; let yourself liquefy in the light oriental breeze. Such Western Buddhism is a fantasy used to conceal one's fundamental castration or lack.

From the imaginary to the symbolic

In contrast to the illusory life in Rome, tranquillity, relaxation and social and physical proximity characterize Istanbul. Everybody seems to know one another in what is portrayed as a gigantic village untouched by modernity and capitalism. Enjoyment is not tied to individualistic aspirations as in Rome, but is rather a matter of occupying a place within community. No conflict between the individual and the social is experienced, no class divisions. We are within the symbolic order, not in the sense of a castrating and limiting law that constrains the subject, but in the sense of a spirituality shared by all members of the community. Whereas in the first reading the focus was on finding one's self, here the focus is on finding one's place within the community. Hence, the scene of circumcision in *Hamam* is significant: in the East, people are properly 'castrated', their entry into a given community is properly marked and secured. As such, the film is a critique of Western individualism and materialism, and a tribute to community life.

Again, the structure is redoubled in the relationship between Francesco and Marta. After Francesco's death, Marta and Francesco are reconciled, and their love culminates in the acceptance of each other's fantasies. The reconciliation is marked by Marta's acceptance of Francesco's wedding ring, which she is offered after his death. Francesco and Marta, so to say, 'marry' a second time, re-establishing the symbolic bond between them, thus signalling the transcendence of difference. What we have here is the image of pure love, of two becoming one, just as community members become one by transcending their antagonisms.

However, we must be critical towards this reading too. Ernesto Laclau has stated that 'society does not exist' (Žižek 1990). Not that Thatcher was right when she claimed 'there is no such thing as society' (quoted from *Woman's Own*, 31 October 1987). But 'society' as an image of an entity without antagonism, that is society as one big individual continuously repeating some previously shown aporia, is an illusory idea; the 'social' is always antagonistic to begin with. It is no easier to find one's place in the community than it is to find one's self (Dolar 1993). The communitarian paradise is a melancholic construction, something lost and mourned (Shohat 1997: 25–6). *Hamam* mourns the loss of *Gemeinschaft* in the West. Žižek's discussion on the way Tibet (as Istanbul in *Hamam*) functions in the Western narrative is useful in highlighting this melancholia (for a discussion of melancholia and fantasy, see Žižek 2001c).

> What characterizes the European civilization is, on the contrary, precisely its ex-centered character – the notion that the ultimate pillar of Wisdom, the secret agalma, the spiritual treasure, the lost object-cause of desire, which we in the West long ago betrayed, could be recuperated out there, in the forbidden exotic place. Colonization was never simply the imposition of Western values, the assimilation of the Oriental and other Others to the European Sameness; it was always also the search for the lost spiritual innocence of OUR OWN civilization.
>
> (ibid.: 67–8)

We are again within the domain of ideology. The Orient, be it Istanbul or Tibet, works as a fantasy space that conceals the antagonistic character of 'society'. Fantasy enables a melancholic attitude in which a lost paradise is mourned. In a similar way, the relationship between Marta and Francesco is a failure until Francesco's death. The film repeats the grand old Hollywood cliché in which the partners are reconciled just before the death of the beloved (Žižek 2000b: 223; 2001e). Marta has to lose Francesco in order to realize their love as pure, as given without conflicts, cheating and perverse fantasies.

Now, having demonstrated two different readings organized around the categories of the imaginary and the symbolic, let us develop a third one by focusing on the concept of the real. Here a central question is this: are the Orientalist fantasies of *Persian Letters* and *Hamam* really the same? Yes and no. They are the same, but they work in different ways. Montesquieu's fantasy was hidden and censored; as such it reflected Montesquieu's split personality. The contemporary Orientalist fantasy, in contrast, is neither hidden, nor censored.

There is nothing to transgress; everything is already seen and approved. We are today not facing a strict superego bombarding us with demands and prescriptions, but rather an imperative to enjoy, as illustrated in the critique of Western Buddhism.

Yet, paradoxically, the lack of censoring weakens the hold of fantasy rather than the other way around. The worst thing that can happen to fantasy is that it is realized. When realizing a fantasy, what previously seemed sublime becomes just one more trash object. *Hamam* displays a nostalgic attitude that also reflects the anxiety related to loosing the Orient as a fantasmatic frame. A scene in the film is telling. Both Francesco and Marta, on different occasions, visit a ravaged house in the old part of Istanbul. What is interesting is that its missing parts make a 'void' visible. Focusing on this scene, one could argue that the critical twist of the film lies in showing that behind the fantasy of the Orient there is merely a void. Let us now focus on this void by using the Lacanian concept of 'the real'.

Four heroines

As we have seen, Francesco's death is a prerequisite for the symbolic marital bond. Ultimately, Marta comes to love what she has lost. However, *Hamam* is not as melancholic as it is tragic. Indeed, Marta could be compared to the classical Greek heroine Antigone in that she seems to have moved beyond any desire. While Francesco becomes 'like a son' in the Turkish family, she remains a stranger. She comes to occupy Madame's position, which is why she, in the final scene, stands alone on the roof of the hamam. The difference between Francesco and Marta can be illustrated if we compare the two smoking scenes. Francesco and Mehmet are smoking together; Marta is alone. Francesco and Mehmet are making love in the hamam while Marta is standing on the rooftop, gazing at the Oriental panorama. After being transformed into the new Madame, Marta becomes a kind of asexual being, living alone, as a stranger, embodying an a-social drive beyond the socially mediated desire.

Marta has sacrificed herself to fulfil Francesco's project. We should here distinguish between two kinds of sacrifice. The first aims at securing one's position within the symbolic: one sacrifices oneself for the good of a community and in return gets a place in it. In contrast, the second sacrifice aims at sacrificing this very place within the symbolic. It is as such a matter of sacrificing the sacrifice itself, accepting condemnation by and exclusion from the community. Antigone is a good example. She undertakes a mad, suicidal act by burying her brother Polyneikes, who has been condemned as an enemy of the city and hence denied burial. Antigone buries him, forcing Creon to punish her by imprisoning her in a cave with just enough food to survive. In this, Antigone comes to occupy the position of neither being dead nor alive. Is Marta a modern Antigone? She sacrifices her life in Rome in order to bury her husband and she stays in Istanbul to make sense of his heroic act, which is her sacrifice. Neither Antigone's nor Marta's space is, as in Hegel, given within the symbolic; it is not that of a 'family-ethics' but rather they occupy a non-place, that of the real:

> In Hegel, the conflict is conceived as *internal* to the socio-symbolic order, as the tragic split of the ethical substance. … Lacan, on the contrary, emphasises how Antigone, far from standing for kinship assumes the limit-position of the very instituting gesture of the symbolic order, of the impossible *zero-level* of symbolisation, which is why she stands for death drive. While still alive, she is already dead with regard to the symbolic order, excluded form the socio-symbolic co-ordinates.
>
> (Žižek 2001b: 101. Italics added)

The concept of drive is crucial in this context for it enables desire to break out of the framework of fantasy, which freezes the metonymy of desire in fixed coordinates. Thus, drive is disruptive. Death drive is Freud's and Lacan's prime example; Lacan states that suicide is the only successful act as it is the only act through which the subject undergoes a radical change. Suicide here does not have to be taken literally. Death drive is the force enabling the subject to redefine itself, to be reborn as somebody else; or, in Marta's words: 'I finally feel I can start again'. 'Suicide' is not mere *action* (conditioned by a symbolic space) but an *act* (destroying this space and the fantasy that sustains it). Accordingly, the final scene of *Hamam* is not about desire or enjoyment, but about drive. Here, to use Lacan's phrase, Marta 'goes through fantasy'. This transition is not from the symbolic to the imaginary or from the imaginary to the symbolic, as indicated in the first two readings, but towards the real. Marta does as Antigone did: she has a debt to pay and she pays it with her 'life'. She decouples herself from the symbolic and accepts a process of subjective destitution. The space beyond fantasy is a non-space, the place of death. Marta comes to occupy such an impossible position. She invites us, the audience, to repeat her gesture, going through our fantasies. Thus, in the final scene, and for the first time, the camera identifies with Marta's gaze and invites the spectator to identify with it too. This reading transforms the narrative of *Hamam* into a Greek tragedy: could one think of a better way to dissolve the fantasy space of the Orient than to situate it in ancient Greece?

However, we have to be precise when describing 'going through fantasy'. Crucially, the fundamental move in this respect is not to rearrange signifiers but to uncover the economy of desire and enjoyment underlying the Orientalized images. There is no way out of fantasy, no other space, for what is beyond fantasy is a void. Identity is basically about covering, hiding, this void through fantasy; hence dissolving fantasy brings with it the dissolution of the symbolic structure (and thus the identity) sustained by fantasy. This is also to say that Europe will always have its 'Orient'. It can be situated anywhere. The critique of fantasy and ideology is therefore an endless process; we are urged to tarry with the negative although it is an infinite task. Still, we have to insist on it.

Although ideology is already at work in everything we experience as 'reality', we must none the less maintain the tension that keeps the *critique* of ideology alive. Perhaps, following Kant, we could designate this impasse the 'antinomy of critico-ideological reason': ideology is not all: it is possible to assume a place that enables us to maintain a distance from it, *but this place from which one can denounce ideology must remain empty, it cannot be occupied by any positively determined reality* – the moment we yield to this temptation, we are back in ideology.

(Žižek 1994: 17)

Is this impossible space also the space occupied by Marta in the final scene? Does Marta transcend the symbolic frame or does the final scene merely confirm her inscription into it? Is it Marta or the narrator who comes to occupy the impossible space of the real? To be able to read the Orientalist discourse critically, one must insist on the existence of a 'female' drive beyond the socially mediated desire, be it Marta's or the narrator's drive. It is from this place that a new, critical story can unfold, dissolving the stereotypes about Europe's others. Not to replace them with more 'true' identities, but to highlight their fantasmatic status. Only in this sense is it possible to articulate a critical project through an economy of letters, that is from within the symbolic order.

Reading *Hamam* as a Greek tragedy, one could similarly read Roxana in Montesquieu's letters as a female heroine who breaks the spell of fantasy. Such a reading is characterized by the intention of giving women a voice and insists on subverting the male-dominated power relations. Men install and control the symbolic space and the economy of letters; the female heroine is the one who challenges this monopoly (Grosrichard 1998: 63–7). Katie Trumpener writes, '[t]he women in the seraglio are punished and controlled by the interception of *leurs paroles les plus secrètes*, by enforced silence, by not being allowed to speak to one another or to write letters' (Trumpener 1987: 184). Following this, Usbek's 'letters of instruction and command are intercepted or lost or reach the seraglio only to sit unopened and unheeded for months of time', while his wives 'have begun to carry on their own correspondence with the outside world: a mysterious letter, of which the chief eunuch can guess neither the author nor the intended recipient, circulates clandestinely in the seraglio' (ibid.: 185).

Criticizing the dominant economy of letters that circulate between West and East, one must search for a new economy. It will be a new one because there is no way to escape the symbolic order, only a moment of death, sacrifice and revolution. Inge E. Boer criticizes Grosrichard for merely repeating the Orientalist fantasy of the almighty Sultan, the effeminate subjects, and she searches for another voice from within the harem (1996: 51–5). Grosrichard's work is, concomitantly, written from the despot's point of view (ibid.: 53). The point is well taken, although Boer seems to be unaware of the crucial twist at the end of Grosrichard's book, where he describes the power of the subjects, their secret language and the Sultan's mother, the de facto ruler.

Boer mentions Lady Mary Wortley Montagu's *Turkish Embassy Letters* (1717–18) as an example of a female narrative from within the harem. The lady stresses that the veiling of the women protects them from being looked upon and allows for masquerade and free movement (ibid.: 56). Let us close with a consideration from one of her letters:

> It is very easy to see that they have more liberty than we have, no woman of what rank so ever being permitted to go in the streets without two muslins, one that covers her face all but her eyes and another that hides the whole dress. … You may guess how effectively this disguises them, that there is no distinguishing the great lady from her slave, and 'it is impossible for the most jealous husband to know his wife when he meets her, and no man dare either touch or follow a woman in the streets … the perpetual masquerade gives them entire liberty of following their inclinations without danger of discovery'.
>
> (Montagu, quoted in Halsband 1965: 96–7)

There are specific female spaces that cannot be invaded by men and in which women enjoy more privileges than in the West (Boer 1996: 57). The harem 'is not merely an Orientalist voyeur's fantasy of imagined female sexuality: it is also a possibility of an erotic universe in which there are no men, a site of social and sexual practices that are not organized around the phallus or a central male authority' (Lowe 1991: 48). Boer mentions the braiding of hair as a countering of the despot's gaze. The braiding of hair is a secret female way of communicating and a specific female enjoyment (ibid.: 61; Miles 2000). It is a counter-institution to the coffeehouse, which serves as a male forum for discussion, information exchange and male bonding (Boer 1996: 64). But at the same time, these practices do, as in the story of Roxana, bear the seal of death. It is a focus of critique, which can, however, only be articulated in a negative way.

What is crucial in our context is that the fantasy of the Orient is not dissolved merely through critique that shows the contingency of articulation. Everybody knows that the image of the Orient is a semblance, but they still enjoy it. In other words, in Orientalist practices a cynicism is at work. How can one explain the moderate success of Said's intervention otherwise? The image of the Orient works as a zero-institution enabling desire to proliferate in a smooth space. Thus the discourse on the self and the other is caught up in a fascination with the Orient, the avoidance of which can only be accomplished by going through fantasies. Which is why it is necessary to deterritorialize the distinction between the self and the other, between West and East, but without forgetting that it is not a difference between two poles within the same symbolic space, but between the two sides of the social bond. The symbolic is always supported by a downside, by fantasies of transgression and of unlimited enjoyment. There is no escape from the circulation of letters, the flowering of desires and the staging of enjoyment in fantasies. But there is a responsibility to attempt to install a new economy of letters less violent than the old ones.

3   *Lord of the Flies*
Sociology of spite

Lord of the Flies, which depicts the life of a group of boys on a desert island, is a dystopian comment on war. Yet, for Golding, as well as for his contemporaries such as Adorno and Horkheimer, war was more than just a dark spot, an anomaly, in the history of civilization. Indeed, the life portrayed in the film is an ever-present possibility of our system: a state of exception. Following this, social life on the island oscillates between two poles: on the one hand, we have an image of a rule-governed society with its law-abiding citizens; on the 'downside', however, we encounter fantasies of transgression, potlatch and perversion. Democratic utopianism versus fascist violence, society versus mob. The two topologies coexist, which is also why the social bond is always based on a fragile balance between the two tendencies.

It is this fragility, the split character of authority, which is dramatized in *Lord of the Flies*. Ralph continuously appeals to reason and order, while Jack empowers his discursive position through references to an enemy, the 'monster' on the hill. Ralph's mistake and the shortcoming of democracy in general, is his denial of what Bataille called 'heterogeneity': the importance of expenditure, play, war and disorganization in social life. What Jack can neither predict nor perceive, on the other hand, is that his disorganizing lines of flight have the potential to turn into an orgy of violence and, ultimately, a gruesome death.

Play

The film opens with an accident; a plane evacuating military students from England during the Second World War crashes in the Pacific Ocean. The only survivors are a group of boys aged from 5 to 13. They end up on a tropical desert island on which they are determined quickly to re-establish civilization. Indeed, in this respect the story brings to mind *Robinson Crusoe*, where the world is recreated on a deserted island. Thus, as soon as two of the central figures in the film Ralph and Piggy meet, they try to find the other boys and begin to re-establish the social order.

An important object in this context is a conch shell they find on the beach. Functioning as a symbol of civilization (its sound being used as a call for gathering), the conch holds the boys together; the one who holds the conch has the right to speak, etc. In a sense, therefore, the conch is an instrument of democratic governance and legitimacy, a token necessary for preserving the agora and keeping violence at bay. At this stage, even Jack, the figure who represents the anti-democratic tendency in the film, is content with remaining the leader of his own pack, the 'hunters', when he loses the leadership election to Ralph. He is on the whole uneasy with the idea of violence; thus, when he finds a pig caught in a tangle of vines in the jungle, he hesitates, along with the other boys, unable to kill the pig. The boys watch the pig free itself and run away. However, the similarity to Robinson's island ends here. Because in *Robinson Crusoe:*

> Everything is taken from the ship. Nothing is invented. It is all painstakingly applied on the island. Time is nothing but the time necessary for capital to produce a benefit as the outcome of work. And the providential function of God is to guarantee a return. God knows his people, the hardworking honest type, by their beautiful properties, and the evil doers, by their poorly maintained, shabby property. Robinson's companion is not Eve, but Friday, docile towards work, happy to be a slave, and too easily disgusted by cannibalism. Any healthy reader would dream of seeing him eat Robinson.
>
> (Deleuze 2004: 12)

In a sense, this anti-Puritan dream is realized in *Lord of the Flies*, in which invention and creativity abound, the 'work ethic' does not work, God too easily abandons His subjects, and evil thrives in the boys' increasing fear. Thus, things change quite early in the film; the boys start to drift away from order/civilization, and towards the end of the film, as the group moves further and further away from civilization, even the conch loses its attraction and is crushed by one of the boys, Roger, the sadist who also kills Piggy, the 'inventor' of the conch.

It all starts when the boys discover that they are alone. They think their life on the island will be like in a comic book, a life without adults: 'until the grown-ups come to fetch us we'll have fun' (Golding 1954: 33). The disappearance of authority figures and the prospect of fun, however, also embody fear; the boys are scared of the possibility of long-term abandonment on the island, a fear that is to be reinforced later by the 'monster'. Frightened, the boys expect to be rescued and, helped by Piggy's intelligence, they decide to build a signal fire to attract the attention of passing ships.

This fire, one of the most significant metaphors in the film, signifies a bond with, a desire for (returning to) civilization; as long as the fire is alive, so is their hope of escape. However, from the very start, the fire turns out to be a double-edged sword. Thus, the first fire the boys make burns out of control and a tree is set on fire. What promises escape can bring destruction. As the boys become more and more violent in the following scenes, they completely lose interest in the signal fire. Their process of dissociation from civilization is completed when the fire finally burns down. At this stage, the boys return to the state of nature.

Initially, the fire accidentally burns down because of the search for 'fun'. To ensure their collective survival, everybody in the group must work. There is much to be done: building huts, finding fruit to eat, securing the well-being of the smaller boys so that they stop having nightmares, and so on. Ralph is keen on the division of labour. But Jack and his group use hunting as an excuse to escape from real work. As Ralph and Jack grow increasingly hostile, the thematic conflict of the film (civilization versus violence, building huts versus hunting, territorialization versus deterritorialization) is articulated in the form of verbal arguments. Ralph defends the common good; Jack is obsessed with power. Concomitantly, Ralph's group is held together with reference to reason; Jack's in identification with a charismatic leader. At this stage, however, Jack still in part has to justify hunting with reference to the common good: 'the boys want meat'.

As a whole, life has a normalcy to it: the boys live according to a daily rhythm; mornings are play time, in the tropical afternoons they sleep, in the evenings they tell each other horror stories about the 'beast', they eat fruit, suffer diarrhoea, and so on. There are, however, signs of violence and perversion of this normalcy. Thus, we see that the bigger boys bully the others. But such violence primarily works against the background of a normality, as an exception that proves the rule.

One day, unexpectedly, Ralph and Piggy see a ship on the horizon. Precisely at the same moment, they realize that the signal fire has burned down! And it turns out that on that particular day, the signal fire should have been the hunters' responsibility. Ralph and Piggy are enraged with Jack. Jack and his boys, however, are increasingly obsessed with hunting and are totally unaware of the ship. Ralph and Piggy find them on their way back from the jungle, covered with blood and carrying a pig they have killed. Significantly in this context, killing the first pig is Jack's first taste of sovereignty, the power to decide on life and death: a 'knowledge that they had outwitted a living thing, imposed their will upon it, taken away its life like a long satisfying drink' (ibid.: 74).

It is at this point that we get the first real confrontation between Ralph and Jack and the first signs of serious violence breaking out: 'Ralph made a step forward and Jack smacked Piggy's head. Piggy's glasses flew off and tinkled on the rocks. Piggy cried in terror: "My specs!"' (ibid.: 75). Excited with bloodlust, Jack and his boys ignore Ralph's and Piggy's criticism. In this scene, Jack for the first time explicitly denies Piggy the right to speak and refuses to apologize to him for breaking his glasses. In the following scene, Jack's hunters make a fire to roast the pig and start to dance in a frenzied ritual, re-enacting the savagery of the hunt: 'Kill the pig. Cut her throat. Spill her blood' (ibid.: 79).

It is significant that in the beginning of the film, that is under more 'normal' circumstances, none of the boys represents order more than Jack. He is the leader of a small boys' choir, whose members readily sing and march on his command. Now, however, in the exceptional state emerging, he becomes the primary source of disorder. Step by step, the de-civilizing process takes over. The boys' choir turns into a hunting pack. Thus, we witness increasing nakedness, escalating bullying and rudeness among the boys and a visible lack of hygiene and other signs of deterioration in their daily conduct. And in this context 'fun' plays a decisive role. Now, in contrast to Ralph's and Piggy's adult-like tone, most boys do not (want to) 'act properly' any longer. 'Fun' becomes a game without rules, increasingly including sadistic bullying and violence, especially of the most helpless victims, that is the smallest boys.

After having missed the chance of rescue, Ralph calls a meeting and attempts seriousness: 'This meeting must not be fun, but business' (ibid.: 81). But it is too late, and we quickly realize that 'fun' already has become the rule and perversion a law unto itself. Precisely at this point, the boys begin to behave like a mob, ruled and manipulated by Jack, without any perspective of their own. 'Like kids! They are acting like a crowd of kids!' (Piggy in ibid.: 37). 'Fun' transforms the desert island into a biopolitical space where the boys can exercise unlimited violence upon one another without the fear of punishment. The significance of post-Oedipal violence and the unlimited, carnivalesque enjoyment depicted in the film lies in this transformation. The resulting social condition closely resembles Bataille's 'festival', a state of exception in which sacrifice, lawful crime and sovereignty emerge in a pure form (Bataille 1993: 124). More than anything else, festival is a kind of potlatch, an opportunity to become naked, that is to get rid of one's markers of identity or 'civilized' manners. When naked, bodies 'open out to a state of continuity through secret channels that give us a feeling of obscenity' (Bataille 2001: 17–18). In the festival-crowd, that is, one can escape the 'feeling of obscenity' and embrace others without fear of touching (see Canetti 1962: 15).

One of Bataille's examples is from the Hawaiian islands where the death of the king meant a period in which all prohibitions were lifted: 'No sooner is the event announced than men rush in from all quarters, killing everything in front of them, raping and pillaging to beat the devil' (Bataille 1993: 89). As such, the festival does not threaten the established power; rather, it is a reactionary state of exception. In other words, the festival is an attempt to strengthen and legitimize the grip of the game rather than changing its rules. Hence the 'festival of the king's death' is authorized by the law itself through a regular self-suspension (ibid.: 129).

Likewise, in *Lord of the Flies*, this state of exception is imagined, by Ralph, like a festival limited in time and space; only 'until the grown-ups come to fetch us we'll have fun'. As such, as an exceptional, temporary condition, the festival signifies a transgression that does not suppress but suspends the rule (Bataille 2001: 36). Transgression completes the rule by transcending it (ibid.: 63). However, with Jack, who is keen to point out that their rescue is not probable – 'there are 8 million islands, they will never find us' – the festival becomes permanent, marking the birth of a paradoxical order based on transgression. And, not surprisingly, at a later stage in the film the desert island (the space of exception) becomes a (permanent) home: 'We like it here. We love it here. We finally found a home. A home away from home'. This paradoxical 'home', a permanent space of exception, is what Agamben has called 'camp', the space in which order and disorder, inside and outside, politics and biopolitics, or, in short, between exception and the rule, becomes indiscernible (Agamben 1998). Thus, the biopolitical element is explicit in the film; through accelerating violence, the boys transform into stripped-down naked bodies, 'animals'. However:

> we should not be misled by the appearance of a return by man to nature. It is such a return, no doubt, but only in one sense. ... [W]hen men, in the course of the festival, give free play to the impulses they refuse in profane times, these impulses have a meaning in the context of the human world: they are meaningful only in that context. In any case, these impulses cannot be mistaken for those of animals.
>
> (Bataille 1993: 90)

So how can we interpret this strange desire acted out by the boys in *Lord of the Flies*? How can 'becoming animal' be understood if it is always mediated by human 'law'? The boys are under the influence of two simultaneous emotions: they are both fascinated and terrified by nature. 'Taboo and transgression reflect these two contradictory urges. The taboo would forbid the transgression but the fascination compels it' (Bataille 2001: 68). Indeed, this strange dual economy of desire and disgust, of object and abject, or of transgression and confirmation, is the underlying matrix of *Lord of the Flies*. It is by oscillating between the two poles that the boys become 'animals'. Their formation of a crowd is crucial in this context.

The crowd

An 'organized crowd', writes Le Bon (2002: 2), presents 'new characteristics very different from those of the individuals composing it'. In the crowd, all sentiments and thoughts 'take one and the same direction'; conscious personalities disappear. Each subject in a crowd is always in a state of 'expectant attention', which makes it open to 'suggestibility': once in a crowd, the individual starts to obey all the suggestions of the 'operator', e.g. the leader, and can act in contradiction with his individual character (ibid.: 14, 7). In this sense, *Lord of the Flies* depicts a perfect example of a crowd formation as the fear of the beast first emerges as a suggestion and then gradually becomes the main preoccupation of the boys. Indeed, *Lord of the Flies* is the allegory of a society in fear, a society that perceives security as its *raison d'être*.

Relatively early in the film, when Jack tells the group frightening stories for entertainment, some of the boys, especially the little ones, get scared. Jack takes pleasure in their naivety, whereas Ralph tries to calm them down.

The group in general tries to ward off fear and seems to be aware of its destructive potential. 'What we need here is positive people. Not people trying to scare people!' However, the very suggestion of a beast turns out to be contagious and the fear it causes develops like a virus, terrifying the already fearful crowd and, ultimately, sending it spiralling into chaos.

Interestingly in this context, even though he knows that the 'beast' does not exist, Jack at one point claims that *if* there is a beast, his hunters will kill it. Based on mere suggestion, he starts to use the group's insecurity to consolidate his own position. Conscious of this, Ralph desperately tries to convince the group that the beast does not exist: 'We've got to talk about this fear and decide there's nothing in it' (Golding 1954: 88). However, Ralph's call for reason is ignored. Later on, as the fear of the beast proves to be more and more useful, Jack openly claims that the beast exists. And the more fearful the 'crowd' becomes, the more they listen to Jack; the more they listen to Jack, the more fearful they become. A perfect alliance emerges between the suggestion and Jack's commands. The rest of the film is a story of how fear, cynically amplified by leaders, drives a crowd into a state of terror.

In *Lord of the Flies*, the search for security fuelled by increasing fear only brings with it more violence, and thus more fear. Manipulating their fear, Jack can easily make the boys act as a mob. The belief in the beast quickly becomes antithetical to democracy. The more the beast gains reality, the more the conch loses its meaning. Growing certainty about the beast translates into growing uncertainty for Ralph and Piggy. Jack problematizes Ralph's leadership. Ralph is not *voted* out of power, though; instead, Jack angrily leaves the group, saying that anyone who would like to join him is welcome. Ralph is left frustrated and, together with Piggy, he tries to convince the 'crowd' to remake the signal fire. But the other boys start to leave his group to join Jack's, also tempted by pig meat.

In short, the struggle over 'deciding on the fear' ends with Jack's sovereignty, with his definition of what the enemy is: for Ralph it is disorder, for Jack the monster. When the balance of power between Ralph and Jack radically shifts, Jack pushes Ralph and Piggy to the margins. A growing number of boys, virtually everybody except Ralph, Piggy and Simon, no longer want to be bothered with rules. As the beast increasingly enables the breakdown of morality, order and civilization, the lack of rule becomes the only rule. Even Ralph is exposed to manipulation and forced to act irrationally in order to maintain his symbolic position, which is why he starts to join hunting sessions.

On one such beast-hunting jaunt, the boys find pig droppings and decide to hunt the pig instead of looking for the beast. The pig escapes, yet the boys remain in a frenzy. That same afternoon the 'hunting pack' transforms itself into an 'increase pack' characterized by the 'desire to be more' (Canetti 1962: 107), a desire that can be transferred to everything around a crowd, including animals. Thus, in a thoroughly ritualistic manner, the boys re-enact the hunt among themselves with one of the boys (Robert) playing the pig.

A communion emerges in this very transformation of the hunting pack into the increase pack (see ibid.: 114). The boys jab the pig/boy with their spears while they dance and chant. At one point, however, the game turns real, and they start to beat Robert, almost killing him. Frightened to death, Robert suggests they use a real pig next time: "'You want a real pig", said Robert, still caressing his rump, "because you've got to kill him."' Exactly at this point, and it is a significant detail in the book omitted in the film, Jack suggests using one of the small boys instead. 'And everybody laughed' (Golding 1954: 126). The crowd cheers this idea of abandoning the communion.

Later, after Jack gathers his own tribe and declares himself chief, his hunters manage to kill a sow, and in a scene, which is visibly sexualized, one of the boys (Roger) drives his spear into the anus of the sow. The boys leave the sow's head on the spear as a sacrifice to the beast. In this way, the pig becomes the boys' totem animal, that is a substitute for the father (Freud 1960: 141). The flies are soon attracted to the rotting head, their Lord, which is an allegory for the dissolution of civilization. Jack being the Lord of the Flies, the crowd (the boys) represents the flies. Flies are indeed, as suggested by Canetti, one of the best symbols of the crowd (1962: 23, 42, 46).

Having killed and yet mourning their totem animal, the boys are filled with contradictory, neurotic feelings: on the one hand, they hate the beast (their primordial father) because it is an obstacle to their freedom, power and sexual desires; yet, on the other hand, they admire and love the Lord of the Flies (Freud 1960: 141–6). As such, the totem becomes the source of the socio-symbolic order. And significantly, the beast/Lord orders enjoyment: 'We are going to have fun on this island. Understand? We are going to have fun on this island!' (Golding 1954: 158). Indeed, the film illuminates how the demise of authority, or the law, can lead to even more repressive authority structures based on superego figures supported by imaginary ideals/fears. What is characteristic of the superego, represented in the film by the Lord of the Flies, is that it does not require obedience but commands fun. It wants, in other words, to turn transgression into a law, the exception into a norm.

Significantly in this context, the social order in *Lord of the Flies* is founded on envy. The 'election scene' in the beginning of the film, for instance, where Ralph wins although Jack is the oldest in the group, is illustrative. Even though Ralph says 'it doesn't matter who is in charge', it matters to Jack, who envies Ralph's power, Piggy's intelligence and, above all, their relationship, which explains the homoerotic triangle thus formed between the three boys. Piggy's role is central: he is both an abject, hence has no name and, at the same time, a femininized figure, an object of desire. The two categories, the object and abject, completely overlap in him, and this coincidence is what explains Jack's envy/hate. Thus, Jack envies, that is 'demands justice':

> the demand for justice is thus ultimately the demand that the excessive enjoyment of the Other should be curtailed, so that everyone's access to *jouissance* should be equal. The necessary outcome of this demand, of course,

is asceticism: since it is not possible to impose equal *jouissance*, what one *can* impose is only the equally shared *prohibition*. However, one should not forget that today, in our allegedly permissive society, this asceticism assumes precisely the form of its opposite, of the *generalized* superego injunction 'Enjoy!'

(Žižek 2005)

It is no wonder that it is precisely when the promise of enjoyment – the lack of adults – turns into enjoyment as an imperative that the initial state of exception is normalized and democracy degenerates into the delirium of a lynch mob. Thus, in the frenzy of a wild hunting dance (during which Ralph and Piggy also get excited), while the boys dance and chant – 'Kill the pig. Cut her throat. Spill her blood'. – they notice the shadowy figure of Simon creeping up from the forest and mistake him for the beast. They attack him and violently tear him apart. Ironically, the reason why Simon came was to say that the beast does not exist; it was a dead parachutist – a 'sign ... from the world of grown-ups' (Golding 1954: 103). With the death of the scapegoat, Simon, Jack attains full sovereignty and starts to use it arbitrarily.

Indeed, in *Lord of the Flies* the scapegoat and the sovereign emerge as symmetrical figures. As a target of irrational violence the scapegoat is excluded from norms and rules and is killed with impunity. Lynching is an exercise of sovereignty by the many over a single individual. And herein lies the significance of the scapegoat. The scapegoat can do something that no object of desire can do: hatred towards him is not possessed individually but shared. In a mob, people can mimic one another's hatred, which is also what culminates in violence. Through the mimesis of hatred, the problem of conflict and difference is pushed aside, the group is united, and order is established. Indeed, the scapegoat is lynched 'to protect the entire community from *its own* violence', from disintegration (Girard 1977: 8). In this sense, scapegoating is the foundation of society. As with Hobbes's state of nature, Girard's origin of culture is characterized by envy and enmity. Whereas the conflict is overcome in Hobbes by the creation of a well-ordered state, Leviathan, in Girard a lynch mob does the job. Further, there seems to be an intimate link between scapegoating (that is the lynch law, mob rule) and Schmitt's state of exception:

There remains to this day one unashamedly primitive pack – the pack which operates under the name of *lynch law*. The word is as shameless as the thing, for what actually happens is the negation of the law. The victim is not thought worthy of it; he perishes like an animal, with none of the forms usual amongst men.

(Canetti 1962: 117)

Both the lynch law and the state of exception emerge as a lawless void within the domain of law itself. In both, the 'form of life' is reduced to the biopolitics of bare life (see Agamben 2000). In both, the relation between exception and rule is at the forefront, and the decision (to identify the scapegoat/enemy) is the basis of society. Just as the sovereign exception is the core of law, the scapegoat is what holds culture together (Palaver 1992). At this stage, torture is normalized. Thus, in a violent scene we see one of the boys tied up and beaten. It is also in tune with the emergence of this context that Jack wages war against the evil and demonizes Ralph's group, which is reminiscent not only of Cold War paranoia but also of the contemporary 'war against terror'.

Social theory has traditionally assumed that society is the norm and has conceptualized the crowd as an exception or deviation from society. But contemporary sociality now seems to be formed in the image of the mob. In a sense, the exception has become the rule. What we are witnessing is the loss of distinctive modern categories such as society and individual and the emergence of a crowd, a 'much less distinct mass' (Maffesoli 1996: 64). The individual and society were the two versions of the modern subject; what replaces them now is the crowd. However, becoming a crowd is an open-ended process. It can potentially remain a rhizomatous phenomenon, an intermezzo or inter-being. It can also, however, metamorphose into a re-stratified, paranoiac organization, as happens to our destructive mob around Jack's leadership in *Lord of the Flies*. Or, going even further, the mass can turn into an instrument of self-destruction, of spite (see Deleuze and Guattari 1987: 229–30).

Spite

After breaking away from the group, Jack and his hunters quickly realize that they need fire to be able to cook their kills. They therefore attack Ralph's group to steal Piggy's glasses to be able to make fire. When they lose their major technological support, Ralph's small group is left with no means of survival. Especially Piggy, completely dependent on his spectacles, is devastated. It is cold, they cannot make a fire and, even worse, there is no signal fire, hence no hope anymore. At this point, we get an ideologically rich comment from a crying Piggy: 'We did everything just the way grown-ups would have. But why did it not work? Why?'

In desperation, Ralph and Piggy feel that their only option left is to go to Jack's group and 'talk' them back to reason. But Jack's group, now totally indifferent to the signal fire, violently attacks them. Piggy starts crying again, and, clinging to the conch, makes an effort to make others listen by shouting as loudly as he can: 'Which is better – to have rules and agree, or to hunt and kill? … Which is better, law and rescue, or hunting and breaking things up?' (Golding 1954: 200). Exactly at this point, Roger, the most sadistic character in the film, rolls a boulder down the hill, killing Piggy, the most rational person of the story. It also shatters the conch. The last signs of democracy thus disappear, and Ralph takes refuge in the jungle. Jack's boys hunt him in the same way they hunt pigs. Hiding/dwelling now in the 'jungle', the proper place of *homo sacer*, Ralph loses all hope. To smoke him out Jack's group sets the whole forest on fire. And fire, initially the symbol of hope and contact with the outer world, turns into a symbol of lack of hope and a paranoid closure. Fire and the crowd coincide:

> Of all means of destruction the most impressive is fire. It can be seen from far off and it attracts ever more people. It destroys irrevocably; nothing after a fire is as it was before. A crowd setting fire to something feels irresistible; so long as the fire spreads, everyone will join it and everything hostile will be destroyed. After the destruction, crowd and fire die away.
>
> (Canetti 1962: 20)

> It is strange to observe how strongly, for the person struggling with it, the crowd assumes the character of fire. ... The manner in which fire spreads and gradually works its way round a person until he is entirely surrounded by it is very similar to the crowd threatening him on all sides.
>
> (ibid.: 27)

But to see the significance of this scene, we must look at it from the point of view of Jack's group as well. Is the forest they set alight not the forest that feeds them? Are they not, in their attack on Ralph, also harming themselves? Spite, willingness to destroy others at one's own expense, is key to understanding crowd behaviour here. As Le Bon formulates it most clearly, self-interest is 'very rarely a powerful motive force with crowds' (2002: 28). Regardless of how heroic or how cowardly the crowd behaves, 'even the interest of self-preservation, will not dominate them' (ibid.: 11). The crowd will readily sacrifice itself, desire its own death, for the death of its other. *Lord of the Flies* is above all an allegory of spite. An allegory of a society ready to destroy itself, not only through environmental catastrophes and other manufactured risks, but also through a 'war against the evil'. Let us at this point dwell on the precise character of the evil depicted in the film.

When the two boys (Sam and Eric) mistake the twisted body of the dead parachutist for the beast, they rush back to the group to tell what they have seen. Everybody is horrified and terrified, and an emergency meeting is called. The boys organize an armed expedition to search for the beast. In their search, they discover a narrow pathway that leads to a hill with small caves. At the summit, Jack 'sees' the monster and calls Ralph and Roger, who also climb up to have a look: a big, dark form which makes a flipping sound in the wind. Terrified, the three boys run down the mountain to join the group. Jack's 'discovery' of the beast is what lends legitimacy to his war against the evil; hence the significance of the non-existent beast.

Lord of the Flies depicts a war on an evil (that does not exist). The evil in the film is a virtual player, reminiscent of the devil in the Middle Ages which, even though it did not exist, was a significant dispositif of governance. In this regard, Jack uses the 'beast' in the same way as Stalin demonized Trotsky to legitimize his despotism, or as Bush uses Bin Laden, to justify the emerging control society. Significantly, in this context the first victim in the film is Simon, who symbolizes ethics in the film. Why?

In the film, two contrasting views on ethics emerge. First, in their war against the 'beast', the boys reduce ethics to a conformist rule-set, to a supra-individual social codex. As such, ethics only means following the rules of the 'game', obedience to the law (Bauman 1993: 8). Hence when the 'society' or 'civilization' loses its grip on the boys, their 'ethics' also immediately disappears. Simon, on the other hand, represents another take on ethics: instead of reducing ethics to the passive observance of a rule-set based on heteronomous definitions of what is good or evil, he looks evil in the eye and makes choices as an active, autonomous moral actor. Simon's ethics retains an impulse, and he is ethical not because of but rather in spite of the society surrounding him. For him, 'morality comes not as a secondary layer on an abstract reflection on the totality and its dangers; morality has an independent and preliminary range. First philosophy is ethics' (Levinas 1985: 77).

No wonder that Simon is the one who climbs to the cave on top of the mountain (pilgrimage?) to find the truth. And most importantly, throughout the film he is the only figure who manages to remain outside the power struggle between Ralph and Jack. He is a borderline figure directly placed between the actual and the virtual, between society and ethics: thus, he is especially in the book the only figure who can communicate with the beast.

In a sense, with the figure of Simon, the island comes to look like Deleuze's two-storey 'baroque house', where the folds of the soul (the virtual) occupy the dark upstairs space (the unconscious), and the sensible matter (the actual) dwells on the ground floor with its doors and windows to the outside world. The most interesting place in this house is of course the stairs, the link between the virtual and the actual, which is also the space of the 'event' (virtualization and actualization) without the virtual ever becoming fully actualized (Deleuze 1993; Frichot 2005). On this account, Simon's climb to the mountain cave is a truly 'insignificant' event with significant consequences. Thus, as the crowd is increasingly manipulated with the fear of the beast, Simon can see that the beast is their own creation: 'What I mean is ... maybe it's only us' (Golding 1954: 95–6).

Evil

The evil is us. The war against the evil is not a matter of opposing others but of confronting ourselves, our own desire. In this sense, *Lord of the Flies* is a story of latent fascism in us all. Thus, in the famous preface he wrote for a 'book of ethics', Foucault claims that the 'major enemy, the strategic adversary is fascism. ... And not only historical fascism, the fascism of Hitler and Mussolini ... but also the fascism in us that causes us to love power, to desire the very thing that dominates and exploits us' (Foucault 1983: xi–xiv, the quote is from p. xiii). Which is also the reason why Simon hears the following from the 'Lord of the Flies': 'Fancy thinking the Beast was something you could hunt and kill! ... You knew, didn't you? I am part of you? Close, close, close! I'm the reason why it's no go? Why things are what they are?' (Golding 1954: 158). This is ironic because the boys in *Lord of the Flies* are actually people who escaped Hitler's fascism (they are evacuated in the Second World War) but are then caught up in their own fascism. The 'beast' in the film is nothing other than the unconscious desire for power that seduces the boys to do evil things, to have 'fun'. With Simon as the only exception, this desire affects all the boys, including Ralph. 'Ralph too was fighting to get near, to get a handful of that brown, vulnerable flesh. The desire to squeeze and hurt was over-mastering' (Golding 1954: 125). He, too, is exhilarated with the taste of the chase and is caught up in his own desire for power. However, he is troubled about this. Thus, 'just a game', he says 'uneasily' (ibid.: 126). In a sense, then, the evil exists as a virtual entity, as the social unconscious. So the more the boys 'see' the beast, the more evil their actions become: the paradox of evil. How then does the evil materialize in the film?

First, evil appears as banal in Arendt's sense. In the beginning of the film the boys are startlingly normal. It is through routine rule adherence that they become evil. As long as they can hide behind the crowd, they can escape their own consciences. Thus, when Ralph and Piggy try to speak to the twins about the lynching of Simon, they look embarrassed but can only say: 'We were tired. We left early'. The truth, however, is that they participated in the event as though it were something commonplace. In the anonymity of the crowd 'the sentiment of responsibility which always controls individuals disappears entirely' (Le Bon 2002: 6). What is interesting here is that the twins are in no way pathological. Their 'banality' pertains to their following the group, the law of fun, and doing so 'blindly', that is without ethical reflection (Arendt 1978). Banality in this sense relates to the indifference of the crowd. And herein lies the crucial function of the mask in the film as a symbol of moral indifference and the suspension of sociality.

Indeed, every time there is a visible reaction ('politics') against Roger's and Jack's sadistic acts ('suspension' of politics or the state of exception), those who react are successfully pacified; it is only when the majority begins to show signs of indifference, only when Jack's and Roger's acts cease to be seen as being morally relevant, that evil takes root on the island with increasing heat. Under Jack's leadership, the boys are now 'protected' from the terror of the 'beast', but the emerging question is who is going to save the silent collaborators from themselves. After all, for evil to occur you don't need evil people.

Second, evil is rational in the sense that the role of technology (spectacles, spears, fire) and the organization of the hunters (army) are decisive for the scale of destruction in the film. Two kinds of objects are at play in the film, technological objects and fetish objects (the knife and the eyeglasses on the one hand, and the conch on the other) and it is hard to imagine events unfolding in the same way without these objects. The most technologically minded person (and thus the most indispensable person to Ralph) is Piggy. In one scene, he refers to Simon being lynched as an accident: 'No, they are not as bad as that. It was an accident' (Golding 1954: 204). Piggy's evil is banal in Arendt's sense, but for Jack and Roger, who are primarily engaged with spear production in the film, the evil is also rational. It is, after all, the spears that threaten democratic politics on the island, which presupposes a collective interest in the 'good society' and a collective responsibility for their 'rescue'.

Third, evil is radical. It targets the very humanity of a human being, reducing it to an animal, or a *homo sacer*, which is why it is radical (Arendt 1973). Such evil is hard to grasp. The philosophical tradition and Christianity have always understood evil as being determined by a lack, as a secondary phenomenon that can be eliminated (ibid.: 459). In contrast, *Lord of the Flies* expresses an explicitly evil will that cannot be understood as anything else. In this sense, *Lord of the Flies* breaks with every utilitarian doctrine and with the idea that every human being has an inherent value. The fire, or the paradise island turned hell, is the symbol of this radical evil.

Apropos of the metaphor of fire in the film, it is striking to remember that the Nazis increased the speed of the extermination of Jews when they began to lose the war, thereby wasting decisive resources that could have been employed in the war. It was, in other words, as if spite mattered more than anything else did. We see the radical evil in *Lord of the Flies* in the gesture of de-subjectifying or abandoning. It is important in this context to reconsider Simon's death, which is precisely not a sacrificial death, as such a death would have made him a Christ-like religious figure. Instead, he is a *homo sacer* who is not killed for his beliefs (sacrificed) but abandoned, reduced to an animal. It is telling in this respect that Jack's group 'mistakes' Simon for the 'beast' just before the lynching.

Is Roger or Jack an egotist? Hardly. 'An evil person is not an egotist' because a true egotist would take care of himself (Žižek 2005). What we have in the final scene, the scene of spiteful fire, is not a lynch mob whose mimetic desire, whose envy and egotism, establishes the society. On the contrary, in this case, the mimetic desire does not, as envisaged by Girard, establish but destroy the society. Here everybody, and not only the scapegoat, is threatened with destruction, with the war of all against all. Spite works regardless of the desire for self-preservation.

Exception

Paradoxically, the spiteful fire at the end of *Lord of the Flies* successfully summons a ship to the island. It does what the signal fire could not and saves the boys from themselves. As a whole, this ambivalence, which is also the ambivalence of the crowd, is at the heart of the film. Thus, fire, on the one hand, has civilizing functions, as is the case with cooking. After all, the signal fire is the boys' most important link with civilization. But, on the other hand, fire works to opposite ends, animalizing the boys and awakening their primitive instincts and spiteful desires. The dual nature of fire and the crowd move it 'beyond good and evil'. In this sense, the fire/mob resembles the Greek *pharmakon*, poison and remedy at the same time.

What is crucial here, however, is that in the face of such ambivalence, mere tolerance for the other does not suffice to establish a political ground. What Ralph and Piggy lack is not respect for the other but the capacity for antagonism, to be able to have conflicts with the other. In other words, what they lack is not just respect, but what Connolly (2005) calls 'agonistic respect', a concept that enables him to combine tolerance with the possibility of conflict and dispute. Agonistic respect is in a sense tolerance in conflict or conflict in tolerance, which is something one has to fight for. Agonistic respect must be created for it is not rooted in a habitus, in language, or in any other fundament. It is a question of grounding the political itself. But then again, ambivalence thrives in agonistic respect as a political gesture as well. That is it can easily turn into pure conflictuality, fundamentalism.

While hiding in the jungle, Ralph stumbles across the Lord of the Flies, the dead pig's head, and smashes it, a revengeful act that resembles the destruction of the conch. Significantly, this event is omitted in the film, which is also why we are left with only a nostalgic longing for an ethics of dialogue as the way out. Democracy is great, so the film tells us, but it is also impotent. It lacks mobilizing power and the capacity for radical acts. Both Piggy the intellectual and Ralph the democrat lack this ability. Except in this incident, where Ralph dares to look evil in the eye. The moment for a radical act is however surpassed. After Ralph has become the new enemy, no one needs the totem animal any more. Thus, Ralph's act does not amount to more than an empty gesture. But still, we should not exclude the possibility of such acts; they have a time and a moment. And radical they are in aiming for the destruction of our most cherished object. If evil is 'in us' then an ethical act must be an act of 'self-destruction', an act that undermines what make us a 'we'.

Significantly, in this respect Benjamin was the first to divide Schmitt's concept of exception, producing a remainder of it. For Schmitt, exception is a limit concept that presupposes a 'normal' situation as its background. The state of exception aims at the preservation of this normality with extraordinary means. In other words, Schmitt's project is to legitimize the state of exception, or to normalize what is exceptional. Along similar lines, we could argue that the state of exception on the island is reactionary or, to phrase it differently, that violence is rational. The generalized exception, the festival, is Jack's way of consolidating his power. In this, everything is made fluid, all hierarchies are reversed, but one thing remains constant: Jack, the leader.

Speechless

The whole jungle is on fire. Ralph is being hunted. He has lost all hope and is unable to find a shelter from violence. Running frenetically, he makes his way to the beach, but collapses there. Worn out, out of breath, he is about to surrender to his predators just behind him. But miraculously, at this point he notices the naval officer looking at him. A ship has obviously seen the fire. He is saved by that fire which was intended to destroy him. Shortly after, the other boys arrive with their painted bodies and with sharpened spears. They are startled when they see the officer. The officer, in turn, looks puzzled. With this scene, the film ends. But, unforgivably in our view, it omits an essential dialogue from the book. In the book, when the naval officer sees the naked boys with masks and weapons, he thinks that they are playing, having 'fun and games', and crucially (mis)interprets the situation as a 'Jolly good show. Like the Coral Island' (Golding 1954: 223–4).

Coral Island is R.M. Ballantyne's novel for children written in the nineteenth century, in which three British boys successfully 'defend' civilization against pirates, cannibals and wild animals on a tropical island. In other words, it is a naive version of *Lord of the Flies*. Which makes the dialogue essential, not least because it is here that the first living 'adult' figure appears. Crucially, this figure turns out to be an infantilized adult for whom war is a game, 'like the Coral Island'. Further, the boys in the film are 'rescued' by soldiers only to move to another war, to a more general state of exception. In a sense, therefore, the world the film depicts is one with no outside. The 'outside' is as violent, and as infantilized, as the boys' island.

Indeed, by omitting this crucial point, the film creates the illusion that outside the island, things are 'normal', that outside there is civilization. The irony, however, is that the boys are on the island because of a war in the first place. They are, so to speak, waging a war within a greater war. This 'official' war of the 'adults' is not less but – with more technology, bigger crowds and more powerful sadists – more violent than anything that happens on the island. The two worlds are continuous (Deleuze 2004: 13).

Herein lies the significance of the fact that the film is about boys. Why boys? Perhaps because Golding thought that boys, as half-formed beings, would make perfect symbols of the central conflict between civilization and barbarism. Thus, the boys in the film occupy a grey zone of indistinction between society and nature. But why does the only man in the film appear like a boy? That is because *Lord of the Flies* is an allegory of infantilization.

After all, the 'childhood' of society is the state of nature. And the 'nature' that comes *after* 'society' is the state of exception, a condition in which the 'citizen' is reduced to a member of a mob. As a first approximation, therefore, infantilization is about regressive evolution: a movement not from the child to the adult, but from the adult to the child, from the human to the orang-utan, from society, *bios*, to nature, *zoē*. The state of exception is a world in which orang-utans originate from human beings. And, in a sense, man becoming orang-utan is what explains the increasing infantilization of contemporary culture, especially in the context of consumption and the war against terror.

It is well known that in pre-modern times the 'child' did not exist, that is did not constitute a different being. Hence, in paintings, for example, the children were depicted as small grown-ups, as child-men (Aries 1962). Not until modernity did childhood take the form of an exceptional period in individual chronology and the child emerged as a subject to be normalized and disciplined: the child-man is, per definition, de-socialized. Therefore, some of the most significant panoptic institutions of modernity, the nursery and the school, for instance, mark the difference between the child and the man. To be a proper 'man' one should first be a proper 'child', that is disciplined and normalized in a site of confinement. And then one could move forward to other institutions, to factories, universities, marriage and, finally, to the elderly care, living a life on the move 'from one closed site to another, each with its own laws', each marked by an inside–outside divide (Deleuze 1995: 177). However, this is changing in today's 'control societies', whose main symptom is the breakdown of panoptic boundaries:

> In disciplinary societies you were always starting all over again (as you went from school to barracks, from barracks to factory), while in control societies you never finish anything – business, training, and military service being coexisting metastable states of a single modulation, a sort of universal transmutation.
>
> (ibid.: 179)

Perhaps today the discipline specific to the nursery is also moving beyond the panoptic walls, with the result that the man-child is once again everywhere, in every domain. That one's childhood 'never finishes' means that the nursery extends to the whole society, that the exception in a sense becomes the rule. In this sense, infantilization is the 'end of the outside', of the divide between child and adult. In the 'smooth' biographic space that emerges, the distinction between the child and the adult can only be created at fantasy level, obscuring the fact that the outside of the nursery is also a nursery: the infantilized world of the man-child.

Otherwise, outside this fantasy frame the child (the exception) and the adult (the rule) are indistinguishable, and thus the imperatives that govern adult life are the same as those that govern the nursery: play, learning, protection. In the 'new spirit of capitalism', it is imperative to play, that is to be nomadic, experimenting, and inspired (Boltanski and Chiapello 1999). Ours is a society in which play is consumption, consumption is play. Ideally, the consumer is a child who shops impulsively, whose desire is to be aroused, channelled and manipulated. Second, we live in a knowledge-based society where we 'never finish' learning. 'Continuous assessment' is thus indispensable (Deleuze 1995: 179). And finally, ours is a society of fear, of scare mongering, in which we are continuously told that we need to be protected. We are advised to sacrifice even democracy on the alter of security. After all, *in-fant* means speechless. The children need no agora; if they had one, they would destroy it anyway, like the conch in *Lord of the Flies*.

If the young human feels intense grief, anger, or other emotion, he is not able to contain it, and he is forced into 'acting out'. A frustrated child is unable to internalise the discomfort or to release it by verbal expression. He rids himself of this unbearable tension by an act, like kicking against the floor. ... Crying, head-banging, screaming, or other forms of temper tantrums are a child's way of obtaining a denied wish.

(Jonas and Klein 1970: 162)

It is no wonder that political infantilization today comes with a rigid polarization between good and bad ('you are either with us or against us'), which reduces reality to fairy stories, or rather, to a 'comedy of (t)errors': no weapons of mass destruction are found; Bin Laden is not caught; Afghanistan seems to be more deserted than ever; democracy has failed to arrive in Iraq, and so on, but everything goes on and on. In this, the 'audience' is treated like an infantilized mob. It is striking in this respect to observe the parallel between the infantilized subject of security and the frightened subject of terror, the hostage. The hostage is an anonymous figure, a naked, formless body, which is absolutely convertible: anybody and everybody can be a hostage (Baudrillard 1990: 34–5). Likewise, the politics of security redefines the citizen as a fearful subject, like a child to be protected. Anybody and everybody must be protected. Consequently, both the enemy and the friend are de-subjectified; while the 'enemy' is reduced to an illegal combatant or a fundamentalist, the 'friend', the subject of security, is infantilized.

It is against this background that *Lord of the Flies* is an allegory of a biopolitical or, even better, a postpolitical society that elevates 'security' to its most sacred principle of organization in the form of a permanent state of exception and tries to combine it with consumerism (so that we need security to be able to consume and need to consume to be able to feel secure). After all, violence in *Lord of the Flies* was just an exceptional circumstance; the boys were 'just playing'! The crucial question is whether this is a valid answer in today's society: is the exception just an exception or is it generalized? Who then counts as evil, as the contemporary Lord of the Flies? And how is evil to be fought?

A control society is one in which fear/terror and businesses, like non-identical twins, work together through a disjunctive synthesis to form a single dispositif. It is therefore no coincidence that spite as a postpolitical strategy re-emerges in today's society. Hence, with reference to the protests/fires in the French suburbs, Žižek asks:

Where is the celebrated freedom of choice, when the only choice is the one between playing by the rules and (self)destructive violence, a violence which is almost exclusively directed against one's own – the cars burned and the schools torched were not from rich neighborhoods, but were part of the hard-won acquisitions of the very strata from which the protestors originate.

(Žižek 2005)

In the contemporary postpolitical society, the 'agora' is not functioning as it is supposed to: violence cannot be translated into a political language and thus it can only assume the form of an obscene, irrational outburst. Such impotent violence is self-sacrificial and loudly so. It is spite. *Lord of the Flies* as *saviour*.

4 *City of God*

Camping as (non)relation

The film *City of God* (2002) opens amid a carnivalesque atmosphere, samba music is playing, the camera cuts from image to image, knives are being sharpened, chickens slaughtered and grilled, huge amounts of hash and cocaine consumed ... but then, all of a sudden, one chicken manages to escape the 'party'. The whole gang now frantically chases after the desperate runaway chicken, turning the chase itself into an instance of perverse enjoyment. Will the chicken manage to escape being slaughtered?

This bereft chicken living on borrowed time is an allegory for the f(l)ight for survival depicted in *City of God*, Fernando Meirelles's film about Rio de Janeiro's most notorious favela, which resembles a space of absolute exclusion. *City of God* 'has nothing to do with the Rio you see in the postcards'. It is a 1960s style housing project that, in tandem with increasing drug trafficking, by the 1980s had become one of the most dangerous places in Rio. It is a place abandoned by God and justice, where the police hardly ever come and where residents' life expectancy barely exceeds the twenties. Physically it is close to Rio de Janeiro, only 15 miles away. Socially, however, it is infinitely distant, almost 'an independent country' (Karten 2003), or a 'wild zone' characterized by a collapsing civil society and weak 'civilizing process' (see Lash and Urry 1994: 324). Hence, the narrator of the film, an escapee, introduces *City of God* as a garbage dump: 'this is where the politicians dump their garbage'. As such, *City of God* is a necessary outcome of order-building processes and economic progress, through which modern society also produces huge amounts of human waste, *homo sacer* (see Bauman 2003: 123–6). So human life is cheap; not only gangsters but also the police can kill with impunity in *City of God*. Consequently, the boundaries between the law and unlaw are unstable and the justice system is delegitimated (see Caldeira 2000: 157). The allusion to St Augustine's treatise *The City of God* is therefore interesting, not because *City of God* is ironically 'a city without God' but because it is a truly 'sacred' place provided that one recalls the originary meaning of the 'sacred': a situation of being *abandoned*, a state of being exempted from the domain of the law and ethical responsibility (Agamben 1998). *City of God* is, in other words, a 'city without citizens' as well.

City of God is a labyrinth, a no-go area. As is the case with the runaway chicken, 'you die if you escape and you die if you don't'. Those who attempt to escape fail (and are killed, as is the case with Hairy). Likewise, those who traverse the inside–outside divide through strategies of hybridization are denied existence (and are killed, as is the case with Bene, the most charismatic character in the film). There is one exception to this paranoid closure, though: Rocket, who signifies the search for the outside, the only upwardly mobile character ('rocket'), whose life miraculously changes because of his artistic practice as a photojournalist. Being both inside and outside (both resident and an escapee, both the narrator and protagonist), Rocket is the exception that proves the rule: there is no outside if one is not a Michael Jordan or an Eddie Murphy.

Three worlds of misery

'The story of *City of God* begins with the story of Trio Mortes', a three-man gang (one of whom is Rocket's elder brother) that robs gas trucks and distributes gas to residents in the 1960s, a time when *City of God* was 'without electricity, without roads and without buses'. Their violence is not violence for the sake of violence, which becomes characteristic of *City of God* at a later stage. As Rocket says, Trio Mortes consists of mere 'amateurs'; even their relationship with the police is playful (when the police arrive in the favela, they can easily and cheerfully vanish in the crowd of kids playing football). This is the age of innocence of *City of God*, and hence the use of golden colours and much light to depict a relaxed tempo, cosy houses, streets full of happy kids, and so on. The law and other father figures cannot fully assert their authority, but despite being in crisis they are nevertheless respected. The same applies to the police, for instance an older police officer rejects an indecent proposal from another (and significantly younger) police officer.

In the second period, colours are darker. The turning point is when Trio Mortes arranges a big-scale burglary in a motel/brothel. Everything goes wrong and 'Kid', a would-be gangster whom we meet later as 'Ze', gives the event a bloody turn. In order to be taken more seriously by the older boys in the hood and for his own enjoyment he shoots everybody left tied-up by the trio in the motel. Nobody suspects Kid. Instead, the trio becomes the target in the subsequent police raid in *City of God*. As they are held responsible for the massacre, the trio is chased and quickly ends up in violent disintegration. Their end is the beginning of Ze's gangster rule based on drug dealing and robbery.

During this second period, crime and perversion increase, but communal ties continue to exist. Ze has a significant function in this context. His rule is perverse and despotic but he unites the *City of God* by protecting it against kids' gangs who 'do not respect the rules of the ghetto' and rob the local shops. With Ze, *City of God* gets a master. However, unlike Rocket, Ze is blind to the outside of the favela; he is both the master and slave of the labyrinth.

In a sense, therefore, he marks the demarcation line between the inside and outside of *City of God*. As sovereign, he establishes an order from which he himself is excepted, and creates an internal cohesion, re-invoking the scandal of power: the 'Law itself relies on its inherent transgression' (Žižek 1997: 77). Hence this second period, the 1970s, refers to a kind of state of exception depicted in grey colours. What follows is an increasing 'blurring of good and evil' (Schwarz 2001: 105). The favela becomes a zone of indistinction between law and anarchy, city and nature, peace and war: 'In Rio de Janeiro we are and we aren't at war … [M]ore people died in Rio during the four-year siege of Sarajevo than in the city of Sarajevo itself' (João Moreira Salles in Jaguaribe 2003: 23, f19).

As Carl Schmitt showed, the law can be understood only through an investigation of the exception. In the state of exception, the distinction between a transgression of the law and its execution is blurred (Agamben 1998: 57). Consequently, a zone of indistinction emerges between law and nature, outside and inside, violence and law. However, the exception does not subtract itself from the rule; rather, the rule by suspending itself gives rise to the exception. The particular 'force' of law consists in this capacity of law to maintain itself in relation to an exteriority (ibid.: 18). Schmitt had argued that it is the link between localization and order that constitutes the 'nomos of the earth'. Through this link, the biological (*zoē*) and the social/political (*bios*), nature and the polis, are separated, and bare life (life reduced to biological existence) is excluded from the polis. In this context, the concept of exception points to an ambiguity: in the state of exception this link breaks down. Further, when the unlocalizable, the exception, achieves a permanent localization, the 'camp' emerges. The camp is a zone of indistinction in which law and chaos, inside and outside become indistinguishable: 'To an order without localization (the state of exception, in which the law is suspended) there now corresponds a localization without order (the camp as a permanent state of exception)' (ibid.: 175). It is precisely this dislocating location of unlaw within the law that transforms *City of God* into a camp, creating the confusion whether it is in fact an 'independent country'.

When the exception becomes the rule, *City of God* enters its third period. Now colours turn all grey and, ceasing to have any referent, violence becomes pure, naked violence; everybody becomes *homo sacer*, a concept that takes its point of departure in the classical understanding of sovereignty as the practice of abandoning subjects from the polis. Sovereignty works through an act of *abandoning* subjects, reducing them to bare life. *Homo sacer* and the sovereign are two symmetrical figures: 'the sovereign is the one with respect to whom all men are potentially *hominess sacri*, and *homo sacer* is the one with respect to whom all men act as sovereigns' (ibid.: 84). *Homo sacer* is inscribed in a zone of indistinction situated between the *zoē*, the natural life common to humans, Gods and animals, and the *bios* which is life proper to humans (ibid.: 1).

What triggers the emergence of the third period in *City of God* is the ferocious drug war between two local gangs. In this war, Ze arms street kids against the other gang. These two gangs by and large eliminate each other and the police catch their leaders. However, the police are corrupt; Ze is released again. What escapes the police does not escape the kids, though. In the end, Ze is violently murdered by the kids he himself had armed (in a way reminiscent of Kabila, the dictator of Zaire, who, after a coup against Mabitu, was killed by one of his own child soldiers). After killing the last 'father' in *City of God* the kids shout: 'we are the masters!' Their violent transgression brings with it naked violence. In a post-Oedipal ecstasy, perversion becomes the rule and *City of God* regresses to the state of nature. Favela life becomes a life outside the city, civilization and normality, a life characterized by the lack of law, irrational violence, perversion and despotism.

To this effect, *City of God* is Orientalized. Hence, the favela is reminiscent of the labyrinth-like Arabic casbah (inner city) and Ze resembles the Oriental despot with absolute disrespect for his obedient, massified subjects. In one scene, a police officer says 'let them kill each other'; in another, Ze visits an occultist to ask for help in his quest to gain absolute power; in yet another scene, women discuss anal sex and bananas, producing the Kama Sutra of the ghetto, and so on: what is relevant in these scenes, where the characters are predominantly black, is a reference to the African dimension of the Brazilian favela. Via the Orientalist twist, the favela becomes a space of limitless enjoyment, transgression and perversion, or, in short, the Orientalized 'other' of the city. No wonder that in the Brazilian popular imagination, the favela is a 'liminal space', housing not ordinary residents/citizens but 'marginal ... people who are not really from the city' (Caldeira 2000: 78–9).

The image of the darkening is particularly significant in this respect. Indeed, the founding metaphor of Western metaphysics, as Derrida writes, was a photological one, that of light and dark: 'The sensory sun, which rises in the East, becomes interiorized, in the evening of its journey, in the eye and the heart of the Westerner. He summarizes, assumes and achieves the essence of man, "illuminated by the true light"' (Derrida 1986b: 213). The 'East'/the favela, on the other hand, gets darker and darker.

Following this, one could criticize *City of God* for its use of dichotomous terms: the 'city' versus the 'liminal' favela, civilization versus gang violence, Rocket versus Ze and last, but not least, shooting pictures versus shooting people. But such an anti-Orientalist critique, which attempts at the deconstruction of dichotomies, oversees, as we have already seen in a Chapter 2, something significant, namely that something mediates between the two poles of the dichotomy, allowing for metamorphoses. *City of God* is also about mediators that bridge the city and the favela, civilization and nature. Hence, the mobile mediators such as Rocket's photographs play decisive roles in introducing the favela/Orient to the outer world of rationality and reason.

It is in this respect significant that *City of God* deliberately moves back and forth in time and decentres the narration by split-screening events. Although there is a single narrator, who himself is split, it has several stories to tell; its focus shifts from infrastructure to reflections on sexual enjoyment, combining moral tones with irony, and so on. It criticizes violence in the favela, while at the same time offering a critique of Brazilian institutions (democracy, the police). Religious motives (talismans), sexual symbols (bananas) and political characterizations (Ze as the pervert/despot) portray the favela as a space of transgression. Further, *City of God* is about the metamorphosis of the city and the jungle. The Orient/favela is neither outside nor inside but both, occupying a zone of indistinction, a utopia and a dystopia simultaneously. In a nutshell, the favela is characterized by decisive moments of mobility and mediation.

Indeed, in this respect *City of God* has a significantly fluid aspect: despite numerous attempts at planning, codifying or disciplining, it behaves as a flow, a flow of people and things. It remains heterogeneous and ambivalent, which is why it is both fascinating and anxiety provoking, more than anything else symbolizing a nomadic movement that transgresses limits and 'contaminates' that which is imagined to be pure.

Seen from the perspective of ambivalence, 'planning the favela' is thus often an attempt to segregate the desired and undesired flows from one another, a war waged against undesired flows. Planning is about clean-cut borders to help 'tame' and channel the flows in desired directions. But despite the ambition of neutralizing the ambivalent, the spatial order remains fragile. What is left out in rigid representations returns as anomaly. While order itself produces ambivalence as its own excess – by codifying the (un)desired flows – there is always a remainder that escapes the legislator's gaze. As Deleuze and Guattari (1987: 207) are keen on emphasizing, no power relation can be totally stabilized; something always escapes. Hence, power centres (and cities) should be defined primarily by what escapes them.

Whereas power seeks to territorialize a space as a conglomerate of more or less stable regions, there are always deterritorialized flows that transgress and destabilize them. Interestingly in this respect, classical social theory has predominantly focused on the life forms of the settled. Indeed, *Gesellschaft* and *Gemeinschaft*, the two central concepts of social theory, both express sedentary life forms. It is thus not surprising that the nomadic – that which is in movement – has been systematically excluded from the narrations of 'society' and 'community'. The basic antagonism that characterizes the constitution of 'the social' is therefore nomadic movement versus fixed territories, transgression versus the law, or flow versus borders. The 'other' of society is in other words not 'community', but the nomad. 'What is lacking is a Nomadology' (Deleuze and Guattari 1987: 23).

It is precisely in this context that Bauman's definition of globalization as the 'revenge of the nomads' is interesting in relation to *City of God* (Bauman 2000: 12). We are experiencing today a new phase of modernity, 'liquid modernity', which functions according to the logic of dis-embedding without re-imbedding, deterritorialization without territorialization:

> Throughout the solid stage of the modern era, nomadic habits remained out of favour. Citizenship went hand in hand with settlement, and the

absence of 'fixed address' and 'statelessness' meant exclusion. ... While this still applies to the homeless and shifty 'underclass', which is subject to the old techniques of panoptical control (techniques largely abandoned as the prime vehicle of integrating and disciplining the bulk of the population), the era of unconditional superiority of sedentarism over nomadism and the domination of the settled over the mobile is on the whole grinding fast to a halt. We are witnessing the revenge of nomadism over the principle of territoriality and settlement. In the fluid stage of modernity, the settled majority is ruled by the nomadic and exterritorial elite.

(ibid.: 13)

In a society dominated by nomads, the threat is to remain tied to the ground. If in 'solid' modernity the panopticon had become a symbol of engagement, in today's society nomadic power does away with engagement, that is with the necessity of discipline. Instruments such as volatility, liquidity and speed make power free to move on short notice, while the walls of the institutions of civil society wither away. Disengagement is no longer the outer limit of power relations, and uncertainty does not lead to conflict. They have both become effective strategies of power. Conflict requires relation; yet, one side of the mutual (panoptic) relation opted out. Even worse, you cannot strike against an exterritorial power that plays on absence rather than presence. The new game of domination is therefore between the quicker and the slower, not between the bigger and the slower (ibid.: 188).

In liquid modernity, 'hit and run' is the logic that makes people obey, a logic that increases the security for the mobile elite, while insecurity increases for those who remain immobile or become immobilized. As a template for imagination, take the police raids in and out of the favela. The ghetto dwellers are immobilized, unable as they are to move out of the favela, while the police can intervene in an undemanding hit-and-run manner. In short, power is the power to disappear: a power that can sail away from the agora, from parliaments and, beyond citizens' democratic control, disappear into the electronic network space (ibid.: 40). In a globalized world characterized by increasing mobility of both people and objects, mobility is 'a major, perhaps the paramount, factor of social stratification and the hierarchy of domination' (ibid.: 150–1).

What makes the favela interesting in this context is above all its ambivalence in relation to globalization. While the situation of the favela's inhabitants can be perceived to be rigid and fixed from the point of view of globalization, they are often perceived to be nomadic in terms of national or urban politics. In this context, they stand for the mobile evil whose 'flows' destabilize the supposedly stable society. They, the 'nomads', enjoy in excessive 'uncontrolled' ways, and the source of their enjoyment is of course *our* enjoyment, our wealth, which they seek to steal from us:

Why does the Other remain Other? What is the cause of our hatred of him? ... It is hatred of the enjoyment in the Other. This would be the most general formula of the modern racism we are witnessing today: a hatred of the particular way the Other enjoys … the Other as he who essentially steals my own enjoyment.

(Jacques-Alain Miller in Žižek 1993: 203)

Hence, the favela fights on two fronts, so to say: against the nomadic elite and flows on the one hand, and against the settled locals and the 'solid' borders on the other. They want to escape the favela – but nothing could indeed be more difficult.

City of God as a fantasy space

What can be said about the relationship between the 'favela' and the 'city' in this context? As mentioned before, the city has historically been imagined as an enclosed space surrounded by 'walls' demarcating the limits of inclusion and exclusion (see Virilio 1997). Enclosure establishes a distinction between the polis and (the state of) nature. Yet the transition from nature (the real) to polis (the symbolic) is not clear-cut and it is here we must look for the pre-ideological core of fantasies that sustain urban reality: 'in the fact that there is no reality without the spectre, that the circle of reality can be closed only by means of an uncanny spectral supplement' (Žižek 1994: 21). Urban reality is not a thing in itself but is always structured through symbolic mechanisms, and because this symbolization always ultimately fails, leaving part of reality non-symbolized, what is unsymbolized 'returns in the guise of spectral apparitions' (ibid.: 21). Urban reality presents itself via its failed symbolization and it can never be a whole. It is precisely this (w)hole in the 'urban' that is foreclosed through urban fantasies, and it is precisely through these fantasies that the unsymbolized remainder returns in the form of an abject or object of desire, constructing a scheme in which the lack in the urban 'reality' (the symbolic order) can be filled and the city can be experienced as an imaginary whole with fixed coordinates.

In this, the logic of fantasy is necessarily nostalgic, and the wholeness of the city is typically depicted as lost or destroyed, stolen. The best examples are those discourses that focus on the 'original' city. Neoclassicism and 'New Urbanism', for instance, look for the stability and order of a 'lost' city: the contemporary city lacks something that was destroyed by modernism, and that sublime 'something' is what would have given the city its identity, had it not been lost. The question is, of course, whether the pre-modern city really had that presumed order. Ironically, the same retroactive mechanism was also persistent in the pre-modern city, albeit in different forms. According to Sennett, for instance, when Venice entered its crisis in the eleventh century, its politicians created a scapegoat, the Jew, the phantasmatic identity that supposedly contaminated the morals of the city and gave rise to the social and economic crises. The fantasy created thus was: if the hole (in the symbolic incarnated by the Jew) did not exist, Venice would have been a whole city.

> The making of the Ghetto occurred at a crucial moment for Venice. The city leaders had lost a great advantage in trade, and suffered a crushing military defeat, a few years before. They blamed these losses largely on the state of the city's morals ... from this moral campaign to reform the city came the plan for the Ghetto. By segregating those who were different, by no longer having to touch and see them, the city fathers hoped peace and dignity would return to their city.
>
> (Sennett 1994: 216)

In other words, the symptom, the scapegoat, held Venice together; thanks to the Jew and the Jewish ghetto, Venetians could imagine their city as a non-antagonistic unity. Likewise, the favela as a fantasy space symbolizes what is beyond the ambitions of planning, or what the other of urban normality is. The favela thus serves as an image of a chaotic space, an archaic state of nature beyond 'our' space and time, and therefore beyond our responsibility: the space of secret enjoyment (idolized networks, sexual perversions, etc.) or of unlaw (crime, repression, etc.). As such, the status of the favela is similar to that of the 'zero-institution', which we discussed in Chapter 2.

Concomitantly, the favela is an antithesis; it is what we fantasize the city is not, and that is precisely why the favela not only interrupts but also participates actively in the construction of the urban reality. Thanks to the favela we can imagine a non-antagonistic, non-chaotic city in harmony: as a fantasy space the favela gives the city an identity. In this, the favela is a paradoxical construction: hence, if the favela dwellers work, they 'steal our jobs', if they are jobless, they are 'lazy'; if they enter interracial marriages, they 'steal our women', if they do not, they 'do not want to integrate' and so on. Indeed, it is perhaps this aspect of spatial exclusion related to fantasy that may account for the almost perverse criminalization and scapegoating of the favela. In a time of globalization, in which 'everything solid melts into air', the favela is one of the last frontiers where one can fight for the illusion of an ordered and purified city/ identity.

Thus, a radical position in the favela debate is to say that the favela does not exist: the city is always antagonistic to begin with, the city is an antagonism that can only be united through fantasy. The favela is the symptom of the postulated identity of the city. And if the symptom dissolves, the imaginary unity of the city cannot be sustained. The city is always already antagonistic. The city *is* an antagonism, which can be overlooked only through the fantasy.

Inclusionary exclusion

'The main problem of this society', says Luhmann (1994: 4), 'is indifference or neglect. ... We will have, apparently, in the next century a large mass of, say, bodies which have to survive somehow on their own, and not so much as kind of parts, or kind of persons used for whatever purpose in function systems'. Evidence of one of the most dramatic consequences of this process is found in the favela, where 'citizens' are excluded from autonomous function systems and reduced to *homo sacer*, to 'bodies'. To be sure, the favela emerges in a differentiated society in which the difference between 'inclusion' and 'exclusion' can never be decided once and for all: persons can simultaneously belong to different systems and, as social hybrids, be included in some systems while being excluded from others. However, despite the fact that 'even in favelas children are vaccinated to avoid illnesses' (Luhmann 2002: 136), what makes the favela an 'extreme' case is its exclusion from most function systems at once. Hence Luhmann's metaphor 'indifference' to characterize the way the function systems (fail to) observe the favela.

Other contemporary social theories also share this view of total exclusion. Castells (1996), for instance, perceives in contemporary society two distinct and contradictory topologies, the 'space of flows' and the 'space of places', which 'live by each other, but do not relate to each other' (Castells 1996: 476). That is the favela belongs to the space of places and 'does not relate' to the space of flows. However, some mediators exist and 'contact zones' link the favela to the rest of society through unequal exchanges or flows (see Jaguaribe 2003: 4, 5, 11). The favela is not unambiguously contained in a striated geographical space (in the 'space of places') but also participates in the 'space of flows', which is made possible by objects and subjects that act as mediators: drugs, guns and other commodities such as information (photos), and subjects such as Rocket. Such mediators or, to use Latour's concept, 'immutable mobiles', that can move and yet maintain their identity in movement, constitute the favela as a networked space (see Latour 1990: 27, 32). In this, they enter into different network relations in different periods.

There is another serious problem with the idea of total exclusion, which relates to sovereignty. Importantly in this context, the reduction to 'bodies' mentioned above is a process that takes place not outside, but inside the function systems. Indeed, it is the most fundamental gesture of sovereignty. Power emerges not as an expression of the social bond, but as an untying; the social bond itself has the form of exception (Agamben 1998: 90). The sovereign tie is more primary than inclusion in or exclusion from social systems. Hence, whenever the favela is depicted as an excluded space, as a 'wild zone', one should look for the inclusive gesture that follows, which is part and parcel of the social bond between 'us' and 'them'. For untying simultaneously excludes bare life as outside and captures it within the realm of the law, the sovereign tie does not distinguish between inside and outside (ibid.: 19). Favela is another name for the zone of indistinction where inclusion and exclusion become indistinct categories, where one can only speak of inclusionary exclusions and exclusionary inclusions. The problem with the 'horizontal' approaches to exclusion, then, is the disappearance of the dimension of verticality (power), which results in a postpolitical depiction of the favela.

Regarding this missing link, the role of dominance relations in the production of exclusion, 'vertical' theories of social space, can be of help. Also in Bourdieu's approach, for instance, 'society' consists of differentiated fields, or 'spheres of play', in which each prescribes its particular values and possesses its own regulative principles. In this sense *City of God* constitutes a field where its residents compete with one another, at least to some degree playing the same 'game' where the rules are, at least until the third phase, clear ('ghetto rules'). However, despite the relative autonomy of the fields, one can observe a range of functional and structural homologies across different fields. Because of these homologies (defined as 'resemblance within a difference'), the struggles that go on in a single field are always 'overdetermined' by the field of power (Bourdieu and Wacquant 1992: 106). Thus, the field of power can be thought of as a kind of 'meta-field' characterizing the general structure of the social space (Wacquant 1992: 18).

City of God too is hierarchically placed qua the field of power. Thus Ze, the local despot, is spectacularly powerless in relation to the arms dealers who symbolize the outside of *City of God* and introduce a verticality to 'exclusion', which, by the same token, 'includes' *City of God* in a broader context, that of the capitalist economy. And exactly the same point can be made regarding the media (e.g. the gangsters' competition for the limelight). The question is: what is a favela without drugs, weapons, media images and so on? One is tempted to say that, contrary to its intention of making a case for total exclusion, *City of God* portrays a world totally penetrated by the commodity form, a world in which human blood and money become one and the same thing. A world in which, with the 'real subsumption' of society under capital, the dialectic between inside and outside has come to an end (Hardt and Negri 2000: 188–9). Indeed, the spectral presence of capital is the figure of authority that remains operative in *City of God* when all other father figures disintegrate; it is indeed what directly causes this disintegration (see Žižek 1999: 354).

> But this is not all: players can play to increase or to conserve their capital, their number of tokens, in conformity with the tacit rules of the game and the prerequisites of the production of the game and its stakes; but they can also get in it to transform, partially or completely, the immanent rules of the game. They can, for instance, work to change the relative value of the tokens of different colours, the exchange rate between various species of capital, through strategies aimed at discrediting the form of capital upon which the force of their opponents rests ... and to valorize the species of capital they preferentially possess. ... A good number of struggles within the field of power are of this type.
>
> (Bourdieu and Wacquant 1992: 99)

Although a field is not a product of deliberate action, and although players agree not through a contract but by the mere fact of playing and concurring in their belief (doxa) in the stakes of the game, players can escape and/or change the rules of the game. In *City of God*, only Rocket can change his social position and does so on the basis of his cultural and symbolic capital, his photographs, which become his most important asset *vis-à-vis* others within the field of power. It is telling in this context that the film portrays Rocket as a creative person who can avoid the habitual inertia of the favela. Shooting pictures instead of people, he finds redemption in art and, in a society without fathers, he becomes his own father/creator (see Theweleit 1989 on this 'male fantasy'). Indeed, all the successful men in *City of God* seem to be those who create themselves (e.g. by killing the father). Women never come to occupy central positions and merely function as tokens of exchange for men. It is equally telling that Snatcher, the only exception in this respect and the only Trio Mortes member who stays alive, ends up as a monk-like religious figure. He is the one saved by God just as Rocket is saved by art. God = Art.

In Rocket's *City of God*, the only way out is through art, art in the classical sense of a transcendent inspiration that can transgress pre-established boundaries. There is in fact a direct relation between *City of God* and Augustine's *The City of God* in this respect. The latter delivers the grammar for an aesthetic mode of justification in which the grandeur is an immediate relation to an exterior source, God's (gift of) grace, expressed in the inspired manifestations of the body such as sacredness, artistic sense, creativity and authenticity (Boltanski and Thévenot 1999). One invokes this 'regime of inspiration' every time justification is included as an essential moment that it is valid regardless of others' opinions (ibid.: 370).

Against this background, the most important metaphor of the film is perhaps the juxtaposition of the talisman and the camera. Thanks to his photographs, Rocket is able to escape from *City of God* and get access to women. Thanks to the magic talisman, Ze gets access to *City of God*, but should abstain from women. The magic of camera is artistic creativity and inclusion in society. The magic of the talisman is the mastery of the ghetto and a Faustian exclusion. The camera brings to life (Rocket), the talisman sends to death (Ze). In short, the camera and the talisman are the positive and negative of the same photograph.

The return of the real

'All photographs are *memento mori*. To take a photograph is to participate in another person's (or thing's) mortality, vulnerability, mutability' (Sontag 1977: 15). In *City of God*, the camera functions as an inventory of death. Rocket wants to become a photographer the day he sees a camera in the crowd when Harry, a member of the Trio Mortes, was killed by the police. From then on, the camera signifies death. For instance, he only comes to own a camera when Bene dies (Ze gives Bene's camera to Rocket). Rocket becomes a photojournalist when he shoots Ze being shot. The camera functions as a transitional fetish object that demands sacrifices (Harry, Bene, Ze). In a sense, therefore, Rocket is parasitic on the death of others. Indeed, in a remarkable scene, the camera coincides with the gun: just as Rocket is about to shoot a picture of Ze's gang they are shot by the other gang. In this moment when the camera fixates/mortifies the gang, shooting pictures and shooting people completely overlap. 'Just as the camera is a sublimation of the gun, to photograph someone is a sublimated murder' (ibid.: 14–15).

For sublimation to be effective (that is for the elevation of an ordinary object to the status of the Thing to be able to take place), the gap between *small object a* and the *Thing* must be sustained. If the gap cannot be sustained, the socio-symbolic order disintegrates and the other coincides with the monstrous Thing (Žižek 2000c: 165). When, for example, violence is no longer sublimated qua the despotic leader (Ze), it turns into the monstrous evil, the Thing itself, which is symbolized by the kids' gang and their meaningless violence. In other words, the demise of symbolic authorities (the fall of the father) and the process of de-sublimation are parallel processes (see Žižek 1999: 322–34). Thus, already in its second phase, in *City of God* there is no father, only a simulacrum: a smooth space without symbolic hierarchies. Herein lies the source of naked violence: the demise of the symbolic law is 'supplemented by the re-emergence of ferocious superego figures' (Žižek 1999: 368, 373).

Thus we are dealing with two authority figures: authority qua the symbolic order (the Law) and authority qua transgression, qua the real (Thing). Whereas the first authority demands obedience, the latter demands transgression of the Law and thus enjoyment. Violence in *City of God* emerges as a result of transgression. So we potentially no longer have the Thing (das Ding) as the beyond of the Law: 'the ultimate horror is that of the real Thing itself which directly "makes the law"' (Žižek 2000c: 132). The Real of violence emerges at the point at which transgression (exception) becomes the rule. And at this point João Moreira Salles's parallel between Sarajevo and Rio acquires its true meaning. Aleksandar Tijanić, one of Milošević's ministers, says:

> In the time of [Milošević's] rule, Serbs abolished the time for working. No one does anything. He allowed the flourishing of the black market and smuggling. You can appear on state TV and insult Blair, Clinton, or anyone else of the 'world dignitaries'. … Furthermore, Milošević gave us the right to carry weapons. He gave us the right to solve all our problems with weapons. He gave us also the right to drive stolen cars … Milošević changed the daily life of Serbs into one great holiday.
>
> (Žižek 2000c: 133)

In another sense, too, the relationship between sublimation and seeing/being seen (e.g. through the camera) is decisive in *City of God*. The stakes of struggle for symbolic power are images that 'construct' social reality (Bourdieu 1990: 134). However, symbolic capital 'only exists in the eyes of the others' (Joppke in Çaglar 1995: 311). In this context, the photographic image is a *percipi*, a being-seen-ness, and functions as positive or negative symbolic capital (Bourdieu 1994: 191). For the favela occupies a dominated position in the field of power, it is categorized (the etymological root of the word, *kategorein*, means 'to accuse publicly'; Bourdieu 1990: 34). The people in *City of God* have an uncompromising deficit in symbolic power, which is accentuated by the fact that the struggle for symbolic capital goes through distinctively local paths within the favela. No wonder, then, that we learn about *City of God* only through Rocket, the escapee.

Pauolo Lins, the writer of the novel *Cidade de Deus* (1997), was a former favela resident and a research assistant to Alba Zaluar, a leading anthropologist who specialized in favelas, violence and drug trade. This role as researcher/insider produced a powerful reality effect, which was further intensified by the film in 2002. Thus, many commentators welcomed *City of God*, finding it 'realistic' because it is 'played by real slum kids' (Mourao 2003). After all, 'a true story can be as brutal as Pulp Fiction' (Karten 2003). As Jaguaribe (2003: 1) points out in a broader context, in Brazil the 1990s saw the 'return of the real' through a series of realist representations of the favela that effectively sought to produce a 'shock of the real', signalling the impossibility of representing Brazil as one nation. Or in Baudrillard's words, 'the characteristic hysteria of our times: that of the production and reproduction of the real' (Baudrillard 1994: 23).

It is naive, however, to suggest that the film merely re-presents a profound reality. To confer upon *City of God* a realism is merely to confirm one perspective – in this case the Orientalizing middle-class perspective of the successful black escapee – in the tautological conviction that an image of the favela 'which is true to its representation of objectivity is really objective' (Bourdieu 1990: 77). Fictionalizing the favela necessarily pushes away or masks some realities (e.g. contact zones, flows, etc.). However, what if the representations of the favela not only mask a reality but also an absence?

Indeed, the secret of *City of God* can only be understood when focus is shifted from the dissimulation of something (e.g. through 'fictionalizing the favela') to the dissimulation of an absence. As Baudrillard has shown, there are four discourses on the relationship between image and reality: an image can reflect a reality, it can mask a reality or it can disguise its absence and, finally, by itself becoming a simulacrum, an image can cease to bear any relation to a reality (Baudrillard 1994: 6). Presenting the favela as a state of nature, *City of God* projects the 'problem of despotism' to this fantasy space, creating the illusion that outside the favela this problem ceases to remain a problem, that outside the favela (the 'camp') there exists the 'city'.

Against this background, it is tempting to argue that the favela exists in order to hide the fact that it is contemporary society, all of 'real' Brazil, that is the favela (compare ibid.: 12). In a sense, there is no more favela: all contemporary urban space is organized according to the logic of favela. Which perhaps explains why *City of God* 'is a great movie to see, even if only to appreciate the relatively safe surroundings we live in in the western world' (Sheila 2003). Even if only to sustain the fantasy that we still live in the city.

This is indeed the most important characteristic, which *City of God* as a 'realist' film shares with reality-TV shows such as *Big Brother*. When 'society' and 'social facts' lose the weight once attributed to them in today's 'liquid modernity', that is say, when 'society' can no longer repress or promise salvation for individuals, it can only be staged as a spectacle, as a simulacrum of a 'society' that exists, masking the anxieties that follow the disappearance of 'society' and the privatization of politics (see Bauman 2002). The outrageous popularity of the TV show *Big Brother* is illustrative because this new version of *Big Brother* is 'the tragicomic reversal of the Benthamite–Orwellian notion of the panopticon society in which we are (potentially) "observed all the time" ... today, anxiety seems to arise from the prospect of *not* being exposed to the Other's gaze all the time' (Žižek 2001c: 249–51). *Big Brother* stages the big Other (the 'society' or the 'city') in a world where the camp is generalized.

Thus, regarding the 'return of the real', one should focus not only on how fiction is mistaken for reality (e.g. *City of God* distorts reality by 'fictionalizing' it) but also on how reality itself is mistaken for fiction (e.g. the camp as 'just a movie'). That brings us to the nature of the real that 'returns'. 'The real which returns has the status of an(other) semblance: precisely because it is real, that is on account of its traumatic/excessive character, we are unable to integrate it into (what we experience as) our reality, and are therefore compelled to experience it as a nightmarish apparition' (Žižek 2002: 19). In a sense, *City of God* is not so much about producing an 'effect of the real' through which fiction is perceived as real, but about producing an 'effect of irreality' through which the real itself (the camp, the favela) is perceived as a violent spectre, as a fantasy space. In *City of God*, images turn the favela into a virtual entity, into a simulacrum. The paradox is that the spectral presence of this 'fantasy-favela' starts to function as the sublime irrepresentable Thing. The lesson here is:

> We should not mistake reality for fiction – we should be able to discern, in what we experience as fiction, the hard kernel of the Real which we are only able to sustain if we fictionalize it. In short, one should discern which part of reality is 'transfunctionalized' through fantasy, so that, although it is part of reality, it is perceived in a fictional mode. Much more difficult than to denounce-unmask (what appears as) reality as fiction is to recognize in 'real' reality the part of fiction.
>
> (ibid.: 19)

City of God deceives, then, not by presenting what is fiction as true but by presenting what is true (the camp) as fiction. Hence, the camp/favela comes to be perceived as a spectre projected into a fantasy space. Herein lies perhaps the most significant deception of *City of God*: that it is merely its own simulacrum. It not only shows or masks a reality or hides an absence, it produces and reproduces a zone of indistinction in which the reality (the camp) is dissolved into a fiction (see Baudrillard 1994: 31).

5 *Fight Club*

Violence in network society

Fight Club (1999), David Fincher's blockbuster, poses significant questions about 'microfascism': the heterogeneous, subterranean 'other' of political and social theory that, in spite of public denial, persists as sexism, racism, hooliganism, terrorism, fundamentalism and other 'passionate attachments'. In the opening scene, we meet Jack, *Fight Club*'s protagonist, sitting in a chair with a gun in his mouth. He recalls the events that led him here, which are also the reason for the destruction of the skyscrapers he is watching through the windows. Jack's flashbacks take us back over past months. He lives in an unnamed American city and has a well-paid job as a risk assessor in an insurance company, calculating the costs of recalling defective cars against the costs of losing cases in court. In an early scene, we watch him investigate a car filled with flesh of the victims burned into the seats. A central theme is hereby introduced: in capitalism everything is commodified, has a price, even human life. In this context we also get a taste of commodity fetishism; thus the camera shots panning Jack's flat work in exactly the same way as browsing through an IKEA catalogue.

> Like everyone else, I had become a slave to the IKEA nesting instinct. If I saw something like a clever coffee table in the shape of a yin and yang, I had to have it. Like the Johanneshov armchair in the Strinne green stripe pattern. ... Or the Rislampa wire lamps of environmentally-friendly unbleached paper. Even the Vild hall clock of galvanized steel, resting on the Klipsk shelving unit. I would flip through catalogues and wonder, 'What kind of dining set defines me as a person?' We used to read pornography. Now it was the Horchow Collection. ... I loved my life. I loved my condo. I loved every stick of furniture. That was my whole life. Everything – the lamps, the chairs, the rugs – were me. The dishes were me. The plants were me. The television was me.

Jack is mobile: he has a career, travels in the space of flows, and fully, but reflexively, participates in consumerism. He is constantly on the move, yet his attitude towards his environment is blasé. As a spectator of his own life, he paradoxically lives in inertia in a mobile network society. Jack also suffers from insomnia, a typical pathology of the network society. But, finding his pain insignificant, his doctor does not want to prescribe him sleeping pills: 'You want to see pain? Swing by Meyer High on a Tuesday night and see the guys with testicular cancer'. Jack does as the doctor says and joins the testicular cancer therapy group, although under false pretences.

This is Jack's first emotional experience in the film. 'Sharing' their pain, he tries to take part in the bond that exists between the mortally ill. He is aroused by this experience and visits the groups for amnesia, prostate cancer and so on, until he is able to sleep again. But only until another 'tourist', Marla Singer, shows up. Marla's reason for attending therapy groups is that they are less expensive than going to the cinema plus free coffee is available. Her presence confronts Jack with his own lies in joining the groups. In this sense Marla 'spoils everything'. Jack becomes sleepless again.

Then Jack meets the charismatic Tyler Durden, who makes a living by selling exclusive soap to rich people. Their encounter changes Jack's emotional and bodily state. After his flat mysteriously has been blown up (later we learn that Jack has in fact done it himself), Jack is invited to move into Tyler's ramshackle place. But there are conditions for Tyler's hospitality: Jack has to hit Tyler as hard as he can. Thus, they start to fight outside the bar where the deal was made. To his surprise, Jack likes it. Indeed, he becomes addicted to fighting. Jack and Tyler start a secret, fraternity-like, rhizomatic group, open to males only: Fight Club, in which men beat each other to a pulp in cellars to experience something authentic and real.

In Fight Club Jack is cured of his insomnia for a second time. He does not worry any more about his job, about his possessions and status, not even about his knocked-out teeth, wounded eyebrows and hurting limbs. Rather, he sees these injuries as proof of his existence. Then Marla returns. She calls Jack after taking an overdose, but he does not respond. Tyler, however, does respond and goes to her place, saving her by having sex with her the whole night. Marla now becomes Tyler's girlfriend. Jack dislikes Marla, but his admiration for Tyler is stronger so the three stay together.

Jack is fascinated by Tyler's criticism of consumer society. Initially, together with other members of the club, they experiment with various kinds of protests: they feed the pigeons in the neighbourhood with laxatives to make them relieve themselves on rich people's cars, they release the airbags of these cars, they paint slogans on advertisements, replace the safety brochures on planes with brochures showing people struggling against flames and smoke, etc. What they want to undermine is, above all, people's trancelike obsession with comfort, which capitalism allows for and feeds upon. One of the more subtle forms of 'subversions' in this context is Tyler's production of soap out of human fat stolen from a cosmetic clinic, which also allows him to make glycerine, that is an explosive.

This takes on an extra significance when fight clubs mushroom everywhere and its agenda changes by the introduction of a new project: 'Project Mayhem'.

Fight Club now becomes a 'revolutionary' organization that uses vandalism as a strategy. Now the home-made explosives are planned to be used to blow up seven skyscrapers, all financial headquarters, in order to delete their client account information so that everybody can make a new start. The structure of the group also changes: Tyler becomes its absolute leader, personal names are forbidden, all members (now called 'space monkeys') are dressed in anonymous black battle uniforms. After a while, Bob, a member, is killed through a Project Mayhem action and his death forces Jack to realize that the emancipatory potential of Fight Club has been taken over by a blind desire for destruction. Thus Tyler must be stopped. But he is nowhere to be found.

In his search for Tyler, Jack visits fight clubs all around the country. But each time he asks for Tyler, Fight Club members are confused. And at this point we are served the most powerful twist in the film, when it becomes obvious that Jack is in fact schizophrenic, that Tyler is a product of his fantasy, his own unconscious wishes. Becoming aware of his schizophrenia, Jack now attempts to stop the terrorist attack on the seven skyscrapers. In the closing scene, we see six of the seven skyscrapers collapse. Jack and Marla stay on the top floor of the seventh one, which also begins to shake, and the question remains whether this skyscraper is going to collapse too.

The collapsing buildings symbolize Fight Club's failure. That is, although Fight Club emerges as a critique of capitalism through perversion and transgression, it ends up transforming into a fascist organization. Violence is turned outwards and culminates in organized terror. Acts of subversion turn out to be repressive. The emerging question is whether and in what ways its critique of capitalism, based on the idea of subversion, still can hold in the network society. What if microfascism itself constitutes a subversive line of flight, a question which preoccupied Bataille and Deleuze? What happens to the idea/project of subversion when power itself goes nomadic? Is the idea of subversion accommodated by a 'new spirit of capitalism' based on inspiration and creativity (Boltanski and Chiapello 1999)? Is it, still, possible and feasible to say 'More perversion!' (Deleuze and Guattari 1983: 321) when perversion has already become big business? *Fight Club* is a film about the possibility of critique in the contemporary society.

Capital and its subterranean other

'The first rule of Fight Club is: you do not speak about Fight Club. The second rule of Fight Club is: you–do–not–speak–about–Fight–Club!' Yet, of course, prohibition is an invitation to transgress the rule: go and tell about Fight Club, but treat this knowledge as a dirty secret that unites 'us', the community of sworn brothers! Fight Club knows well that it cannot exist without secrecy, that, if transgression becomes all too obvious, its attraction would disappear. As we have already discussed, there is no social order without an obscene supplement, and no social bond without a dark, invisible downside. The heterogeneous supplement does not negate a given order but, rather, as *Fight Club* demonstrates, serves as its positive condition of possibility. In the context of *Fight Club*, no Jack without a Tyler Durden! The normalized and law-abiding subject is haunted by a spectral double, through whom the will to transgress the law in perverted enjoyment is materialized. Thus Tyler, Jack's ghostly double, says to him: 'You were looking for a way to change your life. You could not do it on your own. ... I look like you want to look. I fuck like you want to fuck. I'm smart and capable, and most importantly, I'm free in all the ways you're not'.

If the subject internalizes social norms through a superego as Freud claims, one should add that this superego itself is split into two distinct but interrelated figures of the law, between the two figures of the father. First, there is the father of the law, of the symbolic order, castrating the subject through law and language, and second, there is the obscene father who commands transgression and enjoyment. Whereas the first authority simply prohibits, 'Do not!', the latter says: 'You may!' (Žižek 2000c: 132). Because the transgressor needs a law to transgress and because the law is not destroyed but rather confirmed through the act of transgression, any attempt at balancing these two functions is doomed to be fragile. And an important tendency of the contemporary society, be it the 'network society' (Castells 1996) of deterritorialized flows or the de-traditionalized, reflexive 'risk society' (Beck 1993), is the disturbance of this fragile balance.

We are witnessing the demise of symbolic efficiency, the fall of the father (Žižek 1999: 322–34). Socially produced risks are unpredictable, and since there is no master in charge who can reduce complexity, social spheres are 'increasingly "colonized" by reflexivity' (ibid.: 336). Issues are to be decided upon without a symbolic authority who 'really knows' and can bear the burden of choosing. Thus the subjects complain, as Tyler does: 'we are a generation of men raised by women'. Tyler never 'knew his father' (Palahniuk 1997: 49). In the social space within which Fight Club emerges, there is no father, only an experience of a smooth space without symbolic hierarchies. Instead of following the tradition or relying on the solidity of a habitus, one now has to choose one's place in the social space. Hence, one desperately searches for a true identity, tries to find an objective correlated with one's being.

The source of anxiety in this open, smooth space is not lack of freedom; rather, too much pseudo-freedom, e.g. freedom to consume.

> [T]he anxiety generated by the risk society is that of a superego: what characterizes the superego is precisely the absence of a 'proper measure' – one obeys its commands not enough/or too much; whatever one does, the result is wrong and one is guilty. The problem with the superego is that it can never be translated into a positive rule to be followed.
>
> (Žižek 1999: 394)

This is the paradox of postmodern individuality: the injunction to be oneself, to realize one's creative potential, results in the exact opposite, i.e. the feeling of the inauthenticity of all acts. No act, no commodity, is really it. One's 'inner being' is not expressed that way, either (ibid.: 22–3). Extreme individuality reverts to its opposite which causes the subject's experience to be uncertain and faceless, changing from mask to mask, trying to fill the void behind the mask by shifting between idiosyncratic hobbies (ibid.: 373).

What is overlooked in this smooth 'friction-free' space of contemporary capitalism is that fantasies are violated here, not because they are forbidden but because they are in fact not. Under the reign of capital, fantasies are subsumed, allowing a market for the extreme and the perverted to grow. In our post-Oedipal era, the paradigmatic mode of subjectivity is the 'polymorphous perverse' subject who follows the command to enjoy and no longer the Oedipal subject integrated into the symbolic order through castration (ibid.: 248). Thus, the standard situation of the subject is reversed:

> we no longer have the public Order of hierarchy, repression and severe reg-
> ulation, subverted by the secret acts of liberating transgression ... on the
> contrary, we have public social relations among free and equal individuals,
> where the 'passionate attachment' to some extreme form of strictly regu-
> lated domination and submission becomes the secret transgressive source
> of libidinal satisfaction, the obscene supplement to the public sphere of
> freedom and equality.
>
> (ibid.: 345)

Capitalism is no longer characterized by panoptic, place-bounded disci-pline forcing people to overtake given subject positions, but by a permanent movement in which the subject is always in a state of becoming. Foucault's disciplinary society was about reproduction of power through 'strategies with-out subject'. Today, we are confronted with the exact opposite situation, i.e. subjects caught in the consequences of their actions without a master to regulate their interactions (ibid.: 340). The universe of capitalism is imma-nent, infinite, without an end. As Fight Club says, living in it is like living in 'The IBM Stellar Sphere, The Philip Morris Galaxy, Planet Starbucks'. Societies of discipline are replaced by societies of control. 'Control', Deleuze says, 'is short-term and rapidly shifting, but at the same time continuous and unbounded, whereas discipline was long-term, infinite and discontinu-ous' (Deleuze 1995: 181). If the geography of discipline worked in terms of fixed points or positions, control operates in terms of mobility, speed, flexi-bility, anonymity and contingent identities, in terms of 'the whatever' (Hardt 1998: 32). In a control society, subjectivity is 'produced simultaneously by numerous institutions in different combinations and doses'; hence social space tends to lose its delimitation: a person 'is factory worker outside the factory, student outside the school, inmate outside prison, insane outside the asylum – all at the same time. It belongs to no identity and all of them – outside the institutions but even more intensely ruled by their disciplinary logics' (Hardt and Negri 2000: 331–2).

Insomnia/immobility

Fight Club is a film about mobility and mobilization. However, it depicts mobility as a paradoxical topic. 'You wake up at Air Harbor International. ... You wake up at O'Hare. You wake up at LaGuardia. You wake up at Logan ... you wake up and have to ask where you are. ... You wake up, and you're nowhere' (Palahniuk 1997: 25, 33). Jack's extreme geographical mobility leads to 'inertia' à la Virilio's theory (2000). Yet *Fight Club*'s nomadism is not (only) geographical mobility. It is, rather, nomadism in the Deleuzian sense, which is related to deviation, however slowly, instead of fixation and linear movement (Deleuze and Guattari 1987: 371). It is by staying non-socialized, by deviation, and not necessarily by physical movement, that the nomad creates his own space. That is *Fight Club*'s nomadism is also spiritual: 'keep moving, never stop moving, motionless voyage, desubjectification' (ibid.: 159). It is a sort of metaphysical mobility, a schizophrenic connectionism, in search of new possibilities that are to (be)come. 'Let the chips fall where they may', says Fight Club.

Enter Jack's life into a rigidly segmented modern society: he is a white, male, middle-class member of generation X, 'a slave to the IKEA nesting instinct'. His cry is loud and clear: 'my life just seemed too complete. ... Deliver me from Swedish furniture. Deliver me from clever art. ... May I never be content. May I never be complete. May I never be perfect. Deliver me' (Palahniuk 1997: 46, 52). It seems that a paradoxical consequence of mobility is immobility, and this paradox marks the network society, in which sedentariness/inertia is more a post-mobility than a pre-mobility phenomenon. 'Sedentariness in the instant of absolute speed. It's no longer a sedentariness of non-movement, it's the opposite' (Lotringer and Virilio 1997: 68).

Jack's insomnia is an example of this strange mixture of movement and sedentariness. In insomnia, one is literally allowed no rest, but at the same time nothing really happens, one cannot 'connect' to the world. At first, Jack sees the solution in therapy groups. But, as we want to argue below, this solution is not a genuine one; insomnia is not a problem of how one relates to oneself. It is significant in this context that Jack is a risk assessor in a 'risk society'. Should defective cars be recalled, or should one do nothing and accept the cost of liability when cases come to court? The calculus is easily made: the cost of recalling a defective car minus the cost of paying damages to the victims of traffic accidents or their relatives. If the cost of damages is less than recalling a model, the defects will remain a secret, and nothing will be done.

> Risk – life-threatening risk, concealed like a black marble in the lottery of consumer purchase – is also an incurable, perhaps ultimately fatal, by-product of global capitalism ... it signals the entry of a radical new phase of modernity. While the challenge to society under industrial capitalism concerned the distribution of 'goods', late capitalism is more and more inflected by the problem of the distribution of 'bads' – most

significantly, infiltrative, invisible, non-localizable toxic risks – that threatens the whole system of commodities by threatening the basis for desire itself: the body. Risk eludes the consoling logic of exchange; one purchases risk only unwittingly, as dictated by the probability function of corporate risk assessors like Jack. Risk is invisible imposed by the seller, an unwanted by-product. When the seller makes off not only with your money, but with our life, the spell of shopping is broken.

(Brigham 1999)

What is significant about the 'bads' of risk society is the fact that the costs are individualized and the risks are hidden to keep consumerism alive. Instead of systemic error in a car model, a traffic accident becomes a matter of hazardous driving. Likewise, the therapy groups we encounter in *Fight Club* privatize risks that are really social in their origin. In this, sickness becomes a matter of individual lifestyle and relief of living with one's weaknesses. For instance, even though Jack's insomnia is provoked by the fact that he lives a hyper-mobile life in a capitalist society, he tries to find recovery in therapy groups. No wonder he is unsuccessful and Marla can easily 'destroy everything'. Thus *Fight Club* depicts therapy groups as nothing but a trick; they are not real collectivities but only individuals bound together by a utilitarian contract: if you relieve my pain I will relieve yours (Brigham 1999). Such groups remain a testimony to the culture of complaint; people complain about their suffering and demand that it should be relieved, but they only do this as individuals or as groups that aim at satisfying their specific needs. *Fight Club* is a response to this impossibility of collective action, offering a possibility of 'relief' on the basis of social change and criticism.

Master of pain

In insomnia, Jack feels that nothing is real. Everything is like 'a copy of a copy of a copy'. Jack cannot get in touch with reality. Following a career and striving for unnecessary commodities are signs of a lack of 'real' experience. Much action takes place, but never a genuine act. Life passes by. 'We're virgins. Neither one of us has ever been hit' as Jack says. This is what Fight Club allows for: being hit and getting in touch with reality. Fight Club is not merely about physical pain; physical pain is sublated into affirmative joy. The aim is not to become immune towards pain but to live through it. Being hit and feeling pain is a way to re-conquer life, to feel alive. It is in this sense that Jack does not 'want to die without any scars'. As such, Fight Club's members' actions are not acts of aggression and self-destruction but attempts to get a hold in reality and establish some sort of normality (see Žižek 2002: 19). Fighting is a defensive action against a society that does not allow for real experience.

> For modern man's average day contains virtually nothing that can still be translated into experience. Neither reading the newspaper, with its

abundance of news that is irretrievably remote from his life, nor sitting for minutes on end at the wheel of his car in a traffic jam. Neither the journey through the nether world of the subway, nor the demonstration that suddenly blocks the street. Neither the cloud of tear gas slowly dispersing between the buildings of the city centre, nor the rapid blasts of gunfire from who knows where; nor queuing up at a business counter, nor visiting the Land of Cockayne at the supermarket, nor those eternal moments of dumb promiscuity among strangers in lifts and buses. Modern man makes his way home in the evening wearied by a jumble of events, but however entertaining or tedious, unusual or commonplace, harrowing or pleasurable they are, none of them will have become experiences.

(Agamben 1993: 13–14)

Why this emphasis on bodily experiences, and why scars? The body is the only entity that is unique and not just 'a copy of a copy of copy' (Palahniuk 1997: 20–1). It is my body. Capitalism, however, must also be pointed out as the background for this 'sculptural' approach to the body. If capitalism is given by a logic of accumulation and by the production of still more goods and greater comfort, then its critique must take the form of a potlatch, destruction and senseless pain. 'Self-improvement is masturbation. Self-destruction is the answer' (ibid.: 49). The answer to a one-dimensional society governed by only utilitarian concerns.

It is 'only after you lose everything ... that you're free to do anything. ... We have to break everything to make something better out of ourselves' (ibid.: 70, 52). *Fight Club* seeks to attain a 'Body without Organs', the zero-degree of symbolic difference, an undifferentiated body with no face, no privileged zones and forms: 'a chaos so perfect, so pure, so complete that in it all differences, all articulations are effaced. Pure chaos, the undifferentiated reality' (Callinicos 1982: 95). Complete destratification. With Bataille its principle is 'expenditure', with Deleuze and Guattari 'antiproduction', a universal tendency which coexists with exchange and production.

In his 'Programme' from 1936 and his analysis of fascism, Bataille concludes that there is much the Left can learn from the organizational forms of fascism (Bataille 1997a; 1997b). 'Assume the function of destruction and decomposition. ... Take part in the destruction of the existing world. ... Fight for the decomposition ... of all communities' (Bataille 1997a: 121). *Fight Club*, too, seeks 'a prematurely induced dark age. ... The complete and right-away destruction of civilization' (Palahniuk 1997: 125). Bataille had argued that it is necessary to affirm the 'value of violence' and 'to take upon oneself perversion and crime' (ibid.: 121); and *Fight Club*, again, violently lifts the curse: 'yes, you're going to have to kill someone. ... No excuses and no lies. ... You are the same decaying organic matter as everyone else' (Palahniuk 1997: 125, 134). *Fight Club* wants the whole world to 'hit the bottom' (ibid.: 123).

Fight Club also searches for a non-consumerist domain outside capitalist exchange, heading toward a total anti-production, a potlatch: the destruction of Jack's perfectly appointed condo, his moving into Tyler's ramshackle mansion on the edge of a toxic-waste dump, terrorizing the food industry, blowing up the financial buildings to sabotage the credit-card society and so on. The ultimate aim of these actions is the destruction of capitalism. Capitalism survives by sublimating commodities, transforming them into objects of desire, and Fight Club is obsessed by the desire to escape from the lure of the commodity form.

Yet, is this desire for anti-production not the other side of the very capitalist fantasy? The reverse case of commodity fetishism is waste: the object devoid of its fetish-value; totally de-commodified and de-sublimated object, which is indeed, according to Jacques-Alain Miller, the main production of contemporary capitalism. What makes *Fight Club* postmodern is precisely the realization that all consumption artefacts will become obsolete before being used and ending as waste, thus transforming the earth into a gigantic wasteland, which is a permanent feature of the capitalist drive (see Žižek 2000c: 40–1).

So how genuinely critical are these strategies? Let us answer this question through a short detour to the British performance artist Michael Landy and his 'Project Break Down' exhibited in Tate Modern. The essence of the project was that Landy destroyed everything he owned. Landy rented a shop in Oxford Street in London and transformed it into a small processing plant. Here, he and his team, all dressed in blue coveralls, systematically destroyed Landy's possessions: his porcelains, his passport, his records, his old Saab, etc. On the window of Landy's shop, it was ironically written that 'Everything must go'. Capitalism is not just about the production of objects but also of rubbish. To set up a small factory in the centre of London producing rubbish is an ironic gesture through which Landy attempts at short-circuiting the logic of capital.

But is Landy telling us something that we do not already know? Do we not regularly fill our containers with rubbish? Would a more radical approach not be to insist on the use-value of commodities? Worse yet: is Landy's art not as subjectivist and individualistic as the social order he criticizes? Landy explains his potlatch as an attempt to show that he is ready to give up on everything. But is it not also true that doing this he also produces a work of art, an identity as an avant-garde artist. He loses his possessions but gains cultural and symbolic capital. Destruction brings with it more accumulation. Subsequently, with the money he earned by selling his artwork, he is capable of buying more than he has lost. Thus, Robbie Sibthorpe claims that the only way Landy could show true consequentiality would be to make his helper cut him into pieces and turn him into rubbish as well (quoted in Olsen 2001). Are Jack and Tyler falling prey to the same critique?

Let us return to the scene where Jack and Tyler steel fat from a plastic surgery clinic to produce soap and explosives. Here, the intertextual references are dense. The production of soap from human fat reminds us of the Nazi concentration camps. As Tyler puts it: 'I make and sell soap – a yardstick for civilization'. Fat also refers to greed and useless consumption: 'We were selling rich women their own fat'. But isn't Fight Club also about sculpting of the body, creating oneself as a work of art? Perhaps, therefore, *Fight Club* should be criticized for repeating the logic it mocks. It criticizes the capitalist order for reducing everything to an imaginary order, but it is itself caught within that register. Which brings us to the difference between the traditional and postmodern scar or cut in the body:

> [T]he traditional cut ran in the direction from the Real to the Symbolic, while the postmodern cut runs in the opposite direction, from the symbolic to the Real. The aim of the traditional cut was to inscribe the symbolic form on the raw flesh, to 'gentrify' raw flesh, to mark its inclusion into the big Other, its subjection to it; the aim of postmodern sado-masochistic prac-tices of bodily mutilation is, rather, the opposite one – to guarantee, to give access to the 'pain of existence', the minimum of the bodily Real in the universe of symbolic simulacra. In other words, the function of today's 'postmodern' cut in the body is to serve not as the mark of symbolic cas-tration but, rather, as its exact opposite: to designate the body's resistance against submission to the socio-symbolic Law.
>
> (Žižek 1999: 372)

The (postmodern) cut in *Fight Club* is closely related to its masochism. As Salecl (1998: 141–68) writes, the masochist is the executioner of his own law. A masochist is a person who longs for the cut of castration. He wishes to feel the pressure of the law, and hence tries to install it himself. To the masochist, castration is not completed, i.e. the symbolic is not fully oper-ative; hence, in his rituals of torture, the masochist stages castration, trying to operationalize the law, which does not work at a symbolic level, at an imaginary level.

Not all scars in the film are related to such practices, though. One day, producing soap at home, Tyler kisses Jack's hand and puts some lye on it. Lye and water make a chemical reaction whereupon the substance heats to over 200 degrees. Such a burn is of course a source of terrible pain and does leave a scar. Yet, this act does not necessarily reveal any trace of pleasure in Jack's face, nor can it necessarily be linked to masochism or sadism. It is another kind of cut. Hence, later in the film, in Project Mayhem, we understand that all mem-bers have a burn like Jack's on their right hand. This wound, remembered by any and every member, marks the membership of a community. It signals that one has passed through a rite of passage. The passage from a cut inscribed in the imaginary register to one forming a social bond, i.e. one that is inscribed in the symbolic, reflects a change in the structure of Fight Club too: from being a rhi-zomatic structure, it is now transformed into a stratified, segmented structure. Fight Club is the undifferentiated mass resembling Canetti's 'crowd' (1962), while Project Mayhem is internally stratified in line with Freud's 'mass' (1985). In Freud's theory, the mass is organized like a family, it has a father, a leader or a master, and the members' being is constituted through identification with this father. Such an internal differentiation also emerges within Fight Club when its rules shift from commanding secrecy to obedience, when Jack/Tyler, as a fascist leader, becomes an object of desire and of identification.

Microfascism

'We are segmented from all around and in every direction. ... Dwelling, getting around, working, playing: life is spatially and socially segmented' (Deleuze and Guattari 1987: 209). The 'social' is segmented in two ways simultaneously: one molar/rigid, the other molecular/supple. Masses or flows, with their molecular segmentarity (based on mutations, deterritorialization, connections and accelerations) are different from classes or solids, with their rigid segmentarity (binary organization, resonance, overcoding). Rhizomatic flow versus rigid structure, lines versus points/positions, micropolitics versus macropolitics: a qualitative distinction, not between 'society' (macro) and the individual or mass phenomena (micro), but between the molar and the molecular segments, both traversing the 'social' and the 'individual' at the same time.

The two different segmentarities 'are inseparable, they overlap, they are entangled. ... Every society, and every individual, are thus plied by both segmentarities simultaneously ... every politics is simultaneously a macropolitics and micropolitics' (ibid.: 213). There is always something that flows, that escapes from social segmentation. Every creative potential and every profound movement in society originates from 'escape', not from antagonisms or contradictions between rigid segments (ibid.: 220). 'What matters is to break through the wall' (ibid.: 277).

'Realize ... the irony of the animal world', continues Bataille's *Programme* (1997a: 121). In one of the therapy groups, the members are asked to think of themselves as an animal. In his imagination, Jack walks up to the entrance of a cave, and out comes a penguin. 'Slide', it says, smiling. 'Without any effort, we slid through tunnels and galleries' (Palahniuk 1997: 20). It is no coincidence that the social space in which Jack/the penguin 'slides' is a smooth social space. Losing the social bond is freedom, and in this sense Fight Club is a Deleuzian 'war machine', a free assemblage oriented along a line of flight out of the repressive social machinery. It is that which cannot be contained in the striated, rigidly segmented social space; it consists of flows (speed), operates in a smooth space, and unties the social bond (codes) in multiplicity (mass phenomena). In this respect 'war', or 'fight', is the surest mechanism against social organization: 'just as Hobbes saw clearly that the State was against war, so war is against the State, and makes it impossible' (Deleuze and Guattari 1987: 357).

It is crucial in this context that Deleuze and Guattari recognize a war machine as an assemblage that has as its object not war – war is only 'the supplement' of the war machine – but the constitution of a creative line of flight, a smooth space. War is simply 'a social state that wards off the State' (ibid.: 417). In this sense, violence is Fight Club's supplement, not necessarily its object; Fight Club is above all a social state that wards off 'society'. Fight Club proliferates in, or, even better, constructs a nomadic social space without zones, centres, segments: a flattened space, in which one can 'slide' through connections: 'and ... and ... and'. Lines rather than points; connection rather than conjugation. Fight Club does not have a fixed spatiality, a permanent address; it grows like a rhizome. And temporally, it 'exists only in the hours between when fight club starts and when fight club ends' (Palahniuk 1997: 48).

Lines of flight, according to Deleuze and Guattari, are neither good nor bad in themselves; they are open-ended processes. There is not a dichotomy between schizophrenia and paranoia, between the rhizome and the tree, between the strata and lines of flight. And then it is not enough to be against the strata, to oppose the strata (organization) and the lines of flight (becoming body without organs). Lines of flight have their own dangers, which are interesting in relation to Fight Club.

The first danger is that a line of flight can become re-stratified: in the fear of complete de-stratification, rigid segmentation and segregation may seem attractive. Whenever a line of flight is stopped by an organization, institution, interpretation, a black hole, etc., a 're-territorialization' takes place. In spite of the fact that Fight Club makes a mockery of an 'illusion of safety' in the beginning, its line of flight is followed by re-territorialization. It evolves into a project, Project Mayhem. Becoming a 'bureaucracy of anarchy' (ibid.: 119), Project Mayhem is the point at which Fight Club re-territorializes as 'the paranoid position of the mass subject, with all the identifications of the individual with the group, the group with the leader, and the leader with the group' (Deleuze and Guattari 1987: 34). In comparison with Fight Club, Project Mayhem is centralized on Jack/Tyler, who gives the multiplicity of lines of escape a resonance. Methods change too: 'We have to show these men and women freedom by enslaving them, and show them courage by frightening them' (ibid.: 149). The new rules are: 'you don't ask questions'; 'you have to trust Tyler', and so on (ibid.: 125). Fight Club was a gang, Project Mayhem is more like an army. Fight Club produces a microcosm of the affections of the rigid: it deterritorializes, massifies, but only in order to stop deterritorialization to invent new territorializations.

The second danger of the line of flight, which is less obvious but more interesting, is 'clarity'. Clarity arises when one attains a perception of the molecular texture of the 'social', when the holes in it are revealed. What used to be compact and whole seems now to be leaking, a texture that enables de-differentiations, overlappings, migrations, hybridizations. Clarity emerges with the transformation of Fight Club into Project Mayhem. 'Everything is nothing, and it's cool to be enlightened' (Palahniuk 1997: 64). Clarity is also the reason why Fight Club fascinates its members. In this sense, Fight Club not only reproduces the dangers of the rigid on a miniature scale, it is microfascism.

Instead of the great paranoid fear, we are trapped in a thousand little monomanias, self-evident truths, and clarities that gush from every black hole and no longer form a system, but are only rumble and buzz, blinding lights giving any and everybody the mission of self-appointed judge, dispenser of the justice, policeman, neighbourhood SS man.

(Deleuze and Guattari 1987: 228)

The third danger: a line of flight can lose its creative potentials and become a line of death. This is precisely what happens in *Fight Club*: 'the line of flight crossing the wall, getting out of the black holes, but instead of connecting with other lines and each time augmenting its valence, turning to destruction, abolition pure and simple, the passion for abolition' (ibid.: 229). In fact, fascism is the result of an intense line of flight that becomes a line of death, wanting self-destruction and 'death through the death of others' (ibid.: 230), a line of flight that desires its own repression. The point at which escape becomes a line of death is the point at which war (destruction) becomes the main object of the war machine rather than its supplement.

Fight Club, transforming into Project Mayhem, becomes an instrument of pure destruction and violence, of complete de-stratification, a war machine that has war as its object. In other words, the regression to the undifferentiated or complete disorganization is as dangerous as transcendence and organization. Tyler, the alluring and charismatic, the free-wheeling pervert of *Fight Club*, is as dangerous as society. If there are two dangers, the strata and complete de-stratification, suicide, *Fight Club* fights only the first. Therefore a relevant question, never asked by microfascists, is whether it is 'necessary to retain a minimum of strata, a minimum of forms and functions, a minimal subject from which to extract materials, affects, and assemblages?' (ibid.: 270). The test of desire is not denouncing false desires but distinguishing between that which pertains to the strata, complete de-stratification, and that which pertains to line of flight, a test which *Fight Club* does not pass (ibid.: 165).

It is this lack of discrimination among diverse forms of violence and the conditions for their emergence, use, and consequences coupled with a moral indifference to how violence produces human suffering that positions Fight Club as a morally bankrupt and politically reactionary film. Representations of violence, masculinity, and gender in Fight Club seem all too willing to mirror the pathology of individual and institutional violence that informs the American landscape, extending from all manners of hate crimes to the far right's celebration of paramilitary and proto-fascist subcultures.

(Giroux 2000: 37)

We have so far interrogated the three modes of critique offered by the film but have only focused on its narrative rather than its status as commodity. Thus, we now want to move from interrogating the film's narrative to the context for its production.

Fight Club as critique

As a whole, *Fight Club* constantly makes use of a schizophrenic logic. For instance, the motif of 'decomposition' throughout the film is a double reference to poststructuralist French philosophy and to post-apocalyptic primitivism à la *Planet of the Apes* and *12 Monkeys*. The film is both a commercial block-buster and a critique of consumer society. It demonstrates both modernist techniques (e.g. flashbacks-in-flashbacks, Brechtian epic cuts in which the narrator directly addresses the audience by breaking dramatic illusions) and pop-art. It is simultaneously loaded with motifs of Christ (e.g. fights take place in parking lots and basements as the early Christian meetings in caves) and Nietzschean motifs of the anti-Christ. It refers both to the Frankfurt style of pessimism/elitism (may I never be content, deliver me from) and to mass movements (fascism), and so on. *Fight Club* is both violence and comedy, both popular culture and avant-garde art, both philosophy and pop-philosophy at the same time, in the same schizophrenic package. As a commentator put it, 'for all its revolutionary, fuck-it-up fervor Fight Club's dirty little secret is it's one of the best comedies of the decade. Forget the blood, the explosions, the Nietzschean verbal jousting, the weird gender mutation ... this is some funny, subversive stuff' (Savlov 1999).

Palahniuk is celebrated as an 'anti-institutional writer' (see Spear 2001: 37). At first sight *Fight Club* does not really fit into the universe of Hollywood. Indeed, publishers initially refused the first version of the book, claiming it to be too dark, too offensive and too risky. Yet, as a response, Palahniuk only took its violence to the extreme rather than toning it down: 'I made it even darker and riskier and more offensive, all the things they didn't want. ... And it turns out, boom – they loved it' (quoted in Tomlinson 1999). Why? Why does 'more' excess sell better? Is the aesthetic critique of capitalism, which *Fight Club* enjoins, really 'anti-institutional', or subversive, in today's world? It is the poststructuralist French philosophers who most visibly opposed capitalism and power with an aesthetic critique: inspiration, perversion and transgression versus the power of inertia, paranoia and the law. Nomadism versus sedentariness; situationism versus the society of spectacle. Yet, what *Fight Club* ironically highlights once more is that lines of flight emanating from critique are open-ended and that they can be accommodated today by a power which itself goes nomadic.

Aesthetic creativity, which is related to the idea of transgressing one-self, industrialist productivity, and the market's grandeur, willingness to take risks, are no longer exclusive worlds. Boltanski and Chiapello call this new compromise 'project regime', a new regime of justification and cri-tique adjusted to network mobility whose grandeur is connectionism, by always being on the move towards a new project, new ideas, living a life of simultaneous and successive projects. In this connectionist, reticular world, in which a pre-established habitus is not desirable, one 'should be physically and intellectually mobile' and be able to respond to the call of 'a moving world': the 'grand person is mobile. Nothing must disturb his displacements' (Boltanski and Chiapello 1999: 168, 183).

The development of contemporary society confirms that critique is not a peripheral activity; rather, it contributes to capitalist innovations that assimilate critique, which is why it is constantly confronted with the danger of becoming dysfunctional. Capitalism had received mainly two forms of critique until the 1970s: the social critique from the Marxist camp (exploitation) and the aesthetic critique from the new French philosophy (nomadism). Since the 1970s, capitalism has found new forms of legitimation in the artist critique, which resulted in a 'transfer of competencies from leftist radicalism toward management' (Boltanski and Chiapello, quoted in Guilhot 2000: 360). Consequently, the aesthetic critique has dissolved into a post-Fordist normative regime of justification, the notion of creativity is re-coded in terms of flexibility, and difference is commercialized. This is perhaps nowhere more visible than in the production process of *Fight Club* itself as an aesthetic commodity: 'David [Fincher] said to me, "You know, Chuck, we're not just selling the movie *Fight Club*. We're selling the idea of fight clubs"' (Palahniuk, quoted in Sult 1999).

Thus, *Fight Club* is hardly an 'anti-institutional' response to contemporary capitalism, just as creativity, perversion or transgression are not necessarily emancipatory today. Power has already evacuated the bastion *Fight Club* is attacking, and it can effortlessly support *Fight Club*'s assault on sedentariness. Palahniuk says: 'We really have no freedom about creating our identities, because we are trained to want what we want. What is it going to take to break out and establish some modicum of freedom, despite all the cultural training that's been our entire existence? It's about doing the things that are completely forbidden, that we are trained not to want to do' (quoted in Jenkins 1999). What Palahniuk enjoys the luxury of overseeing here is precisely that such strategies are emancipatory only in so far as power provides hierarchy exclusively through essentialism and stable binary divisions. But many of the concepts romanticized by Palahniuk's *Fight Club* find a correspondence in the network capitalism and its aesthetic Mecca, Hollywood, today.

As Deleuze and Guattari repeatedly emphasized, smooth space and nomadism do not have an irresistible revolutionary calling but change meaning drastically depending on the context (see 1987: 387). Neither mobility nor immobility are liberating in themselves. Subversion or liberation can only be related to taking control of the production of mobility and statis (Hardt and Negri 2000: 156). In this respect, *Fight Club*'s aesthetic critique sounds, if not cynical, naïve. Asked by CNN if he is amused by the irony that Hollywood decided to make a violent film about anti-consumerism by spending millions of dollars, Palahniuk answers that 'it seems like the ultimate absurd joke.

In a way it's funnier than the movie itself' (CNN 1999). Yes, indeed, but as we tried to show, there are reasons why it is so.

Palahniuk himself emphasizes *Fight Club*'s social critique. 'The system is more frightened of our anti-consumerist message than they are of our violence. The violence is just an excuse to trash us' (ibid.). This is correct. *Fight Club* overtly takes issue with strategies of social critique too and launches an articulated critique of the contemporary society. While Marx is disregarded by much mainstream academia, his philosophy seems to reappear as a Hollywood brand. Indeed, although *Fight Club* has been called 'nihilism for dummies' by some reviewers, it is perhaps more adequate to label it 'Marxism for dummies'.

Fight Club's critique takes two moves: first, it experiments with (aesthetic) sublimation of violence as an alternative to commodity fetishism and, second, it calls for a (social) potlatch that aims at destructing the exchange system, at escaping the lure of the commodity form. What both have in common is of course a search for an outside, for what is exterior to capitalism. But how is an ethical and political act possible when there is no outside? It is relevant in this context that the narrator of *Fight Club*, Jack/Tyler, speaks from an impossible position, namely the position of the dead. Speaking from this phantasmatic outside, he places himself outside the symbolic order. In this sense, *Fight Club* exempts itself from the concrete historical context and from an actual involvement with politics. Rather than being a political act, *Fight Club* seems to advocate a trancelike subjective experience, a kind of pseudo-Bakhtinian carnivalesque activity in which the rhythm of everyday life is only temporarily suspended. 'You know the rage is coming out some way. And if this stuff can be sort of vented in a consensual controlled situation like a fight club, I just see that as an improvement' (Palahniuk, quoted in Tomlinson 1999).

Significantly in this context, *Fight Club* contains no concrete economic analysis and completely overlooks social and class inequalities. The middle classes and the underclass are portrayed as people who merely want to find a relief for their masculine energies (Giroux 2000: 34). Economic problems are sexualized and re-framed as a question of how to relate to one's desire. It is telling that in a scene where Tyler draws his gun and forces Raymond, an employee at a shop, down on his knees, telling him that he is going to die, he asks him as a 'final gesture' what has been his greatest wish. Raymond answers that he always wanted to be a vet but that he had had to give it up because he could not finance his studies. Tyler responds that he will kill Raymond if he does not restart his studies within six weeks. He explains to Jack that this would be the happiest day in Raymond's life and he would remember it as the day he learned to take responsibility for his own destiny. But then again, *Fight Club* repeats what it mocks:

> This privatised version of agency and politics is central to understanding Tyler's character as emblematic of the very market forces he denounces. For Tyler, success is simply a matter of getting off one's back and forging ahead; individual initiative and the sheer force of will magically cancels out

institutional constraints, and critiques of the gravity of dominant relations of oppression are dismissed as either an act of bad faith or the unacceptable whine of victimisation. Tyler hates consumerism but he values a 'Just Do IT' ideology appropriated from the marketing strategists for the Nike Corporation and the ideology of the Regan era.

(Giroux 2000: 34)

Just joking?

The phantomlike platform of enunciation we mentioned previously can also be given a more positive interpretation. Such reading is possible if we move from the question of economic analysis to the question of social change, e.g. the plan to blow up the financial centres. The question here is whether this act is paralleled by Jack/Tyler's suicide. Here, we could return to the distinction between act and action. The act differs from action in that it radically transforms the agent. That is why suicide is the act par excellence. In the act,

> the subject is annihilated and subsequently reborn (or not), i.e. the act involves a kind of temporary eclipse, aphanisis, of the subject. Which is why every act worthy of this name is 'mad' in the sense of radical unaccountability: by means of it, I put at stake everything, including myself, my symbolic identity; the act is therefore always a 'crime', a 'trangression', namely of the limit of the symbolic community to which I belong.
>
> (Žižek 1992: 44)

And likewise, to Palahniuk, it is destruction that allows for the character to develop into something stronger that is not burdened by his past (Palahniuk 1999: 3).

Jack acknowledges that a revolutionary act cannot focus solely on public rules and identities but must strike at this order's downside, its obscene fantasies. One could here return to the scene where Jack tries to force his boss to finance his activities. His ways are untraditional. He throws himself at the glass table, against the bookshelves and so on, and then screams for help. When the guards enter the office, he is down on his knees, begging the boss not to hurt him anymore. The boss is afraid of being taken to court to pay Jack compensation. Thus Jack achieves his goal on the condition that he never again visits the office. Here, two aspects should be noted: first that Jack literally becomes a 'Body without Organs'. His left hand takes over and operates independently of Jack's will in an act of total de-subjectivation. Second, the act is efficient because it realizes the disavowed fantasy of his boss: his desire to beat him to a pulp (Žižek 2003a: 112–17).

This scene might also be seen as a prologue to the final scene where Jack kills Tyler. Tyler was the person Jack wished to be, his object of desire. Again, it is an act directed against the realm of fantasy; this time Jack's fantasies. Marla's role in the film is crucial in this respect. She is the one who prevents Jack from finding rest, that is she keeps his desire in motion; she reveals his lying in the therapy groups; she stands between Jack and Tyler and prevents their homoerotic relationship fully to develop; and at the end of the film, Jack's love for Marla forces him to halt Project Mayhem. Jack finally acknowledges that external hindrances (Marla) are nothing but an attempt to avoid confronting his own desire, that the objects of desire are nothing but a materialization of a void.

In a way, in the beginning of the film Jack is already dead and excluded (as reduced to an office worker, a consumer) even though biologically speaking he is still alive. 'Dying people are so alive', he says. And it is true: it is only in the final scene that he confronts his desire and truly lives. But still, we should be suspicious of this nihilism. An act is not only beyond the 'reality principle', that is a given socio-symbolic order, it also needs to redefine the coordinates of the social order (Žižek 2001c: 167). *Fight Club* is critical of the dominant economy of desire, but it does not attempt to define or install another one. An act is only revolutionary if it contains a constructive aspect. Such a project is exactly what Jack/Tyler lacks.

> Tyler represents the magnetism of the isolated, dauntless anti-hero whose public appeal is based on the attractions of the cult-personality rather than on the strengths of an articulated, democratic notion of political reform. Politics for Tyler is about doing, not thinking. As the embodiment of authoritarian masculinity and hyper individualism, Tyler cannot imagine a politics that connects to democratic movements, and is less a symbol of vision and leadership for the next millennium than a holdover of early-twentieth-century fascism.
>
> (Giroux 2000: 33)

There is much action but not much act in *Fight Club*. In this respect, it is thought-provoking that, when asked about 'consumerism is bad … but what is good?', Palahniuk can only reply with irony: 'Ha ha. I want to sidestep that one! Seriously, buy my book … or better yet … just send me gobs of money. Please don't make me wrestle that intellectual greased pig any more' (CNN 1999). The problem with *Fight Club* is that it falls into the trap of presenting its problematique, violence, from a cynical distance. *Fight Club* is of course extremely reflexive and ironic. It can even be said that it is an irony on fascism. Thus of course it should not be taken literally. Further, does not Fight Club even deny its own existence?

Let us, at this point, return to the destruction of the six skyscrapers. Is the seventh going to collapse? Has Jack been successful in defusing the bomb, or is it a classic Hollywood ending in which love finally conquers all (Jack and Marla standing hand in hand)? Or will the seventh tower also go down, allowing everybody to start afresh? This undecidability is multiplied by the phallus image that reappears for a split second in this final scene. At this point in the film we already know that Tyler used to work in a cinema where he included pornographic images in, for instance, children's films, which is of course just another attack on the indifference of the consumer society. It could be argued that this forced inclusion of an uncanny fetish object, the phallus, in an irrelevant context testifies to the fact that the cinematic apparatus itself might function as a substitute for the phallus or its absence (see Metz 1979: 11). Yet the appearance of the phallus in *Fight Club* provokes another series of questions regarding the nature of critique in Fight Club, too. Is the phallus just a joke, an ironic comment on the impossibility of critique in the contemporary society? Does Fincher wish something more than just to entertain? Or, is he 'ironically' accepting that *Fight Club* turns anti-consumerism itself into a commodity, that it sells the consumers their own fat in the form of soap, their own critique as institutionalized norm?

> Then a magazine editor, another magazine editor, calls me, angry and ranting because he wants to send a writer to the underground fight club in his area. 'It's cool, man', he says from New York. 'You can tell me where. We won't screw it up'. I tell him there's no such place. There's no secret society of clubs where guys bash each other and gripe about their empty lives, their hollow careers, their absent fathers. Fight clubs are make-believe. You can't go there. I made them up.
>
> (Palahniuk 1999)

It is perhaps the case that 'today's neo-Fascism is more and more "postmodern", civilized, playful, involving ironic self-distance ... yet no less Fascist for all that' (Žižek 1997: 64).

6 *Brazil*

From error to terror

The Cold War apologist Georg Kennan once claimed that the concept of totalitarianism, that is the image of a state that exercises total control over its subjects through a massive bureaucratic apparatus and planned economy, a society disciplined through a huge police corps and a vast number of secret informers, is merely a phantasm. Like Lévi-Strauss's concept of totemism, it signifies a social institution with no actual or even historical existence and marks off 'certain human phenomena ... which scholars preferred to regard as alien to their own moral universe, thus protecting the attachment they felt toward the latter' (Pietz 1988: 56).

Interestingly, this concept allowed both the Left and the Right to fantasize, each in its own way. While the Right used this concept/phantasm to dream away from the malfunctions of their society, bringing to mind Lévi-Strauss's totemism, to the Left, to social theorists such as Marcuse for instance, it served as a mirror reflecting everything that was wrong with consumerism and with the 'one dimensional man' it produced. As Kennan puts it, stressing the dream-work involved in right-wing discourse:

> When I try to picture totalitarianism to myself as a general phenomenon, what comes to my mind most prominently is neither the Soviet picture nor the Nazi picture as I have known them in the flesh, but rather the fictional and symbolic images created by such people as Orwell, or Kafka or Koestler or early Soviet satirists. The purest expression of the phenomenon, in other words, seems to me to have been rendered not in its physical reality but in its power as a dream, or a nightmare.
>
> (quoted in Pietz 1988: 57)

To Kennan, Orwell's *1984* turned a generation's nightmare into words and images (Gleason 1984: 145). And as such it quickly became a battleground for a struggle between the Left and the Right. What did this dystopia resemble the most: the USA or the USSR? Capitalism at its highest stage aided by thought control, television surveillance, manipulated masses and techno-science or Stalinism characterized by the 'drabbest of greys, with police helmets atop the dour heads of half the population stomping across the supine bodies of the other half' (Glass 1986: 22). Although Orwell undoubtedly had Stalin(ism) in mind, the grandeur of his work is its timelessness. The dystopia he depicted can be perceived as a capitalist or a socialist society gone awry.

Orwell wrote his masterpiece in 1948, and to give it its hyperbolic form, he framed it as a science fiction taking place in 1984. In 1949, with a one-year delay, the book was published, which also happened to Terry Gilliam's film *Brazil*, a work indebted to Orwell's classic novel. Missing 1984 by a year, the film appeared in 1985. And, like Orwell, Gilliam does his best to de-contextualize the narrative; hence *Brazil* opens with the following information: '8:49 p.m., somewhere in the 20th century'. Gilliam's use of a variety of filmic references, narrative reversals and particularly dramatic use of music supports this timelessness allowing us to distance ourselves from an overwhelming reality and thus to be able to reflect upon it.

No doubt that our nightmares are not exactly those of Orwell, Arendt, Koestler and Aron; the East and the West are no longer fighting a cold war, Stalinism is an issue of the past, etc. And yet a film like Gilliam's seems as fresh as ever. Why? Perhaps because *Brazil* portrays a contemporary nightmare: the horrors of the twenty-first century's totalitarian state. At first sight, *Brazil* is a rather bizarre comedy; thus it is, like *Monty Python's Flying Circus* for instance, excessive in its exaggerations. However, on closer inspection, *Brazil* stands as a pertinent commentary on the contemporary war against terror. *Brazil* is, in Gilliam's words, a kind of swindle: 'we give no answers. We only highlight things that are obvious, but they are obvious things that people almost never take into account' (Gilliam, quoted in Noblejas 2004). The more we are immersed in everyday reality, the less we see what is in fact obvious. For the obvious to be seen, it must be 'hidden' in the guise of a fiction. Orwell did this to the nightmare of the Cold War, and Gilliam repeats the same gesture by putting *our* nightmare into fiction.

In contrast to the above-mentioned definition (inspired by thinkers such as Brzezinski, Orwell, Arendt and Aron), to Gilliam totalitarianism simply designates a society that cannot question itself. This understanding uncannily links the former totalitarian society of the East with that of the contemporary West: the market is always right, in its optimum condition, and so is the party constellation in power in being forced to obey the iron laws of the economy – international competition, etc. Is this so different from the way the iron laws of history were conceived of by the Stalinists? Gilliam's *Brazil* can show that it is not.

It is no surprise that the whole narrative of *Brazil* is set off by a simple mistake. In a system that cannot question itself, an error easily becomes terror. Everything that happens in the film might be traced back to a beetle that has entered the Ministry of Information and caused an electronic typewriter to misspell the name of the supposed enemy terrorist Mr Tuttle, by typing Buttle instead of Tuttle. By this mistake, Mr Tuttle becomes Mr Buttle, an ordinary man who repairs shoes for a living and spends the rest of his time together with his family. Based on the piles of intelligence reports, the unfortunate

Mr Buttle is violently arrested and brought to the Ministry of Information for 'information retrieval', that is for torture. He knows nothing and has nothing to tell which, however, makes him seem even more dangerous. Unsurprisingly, therefore, he is tortured to death. The society we meet in *Brazil* is one in which surveillance and intelligence pervade all spheres of life and where the omnipresent threat of terrorism has turned the population into privatized individuals who hardly notice the attacks and the victims anymore. This is Buttle's bad luck.

Sam Lowly, an employee at the Ministry of Information, is one of these privatized and indifferent individuals. Unluckily, he is stuck with the mistake that cannot be made. At first, he simply follows the ministerial procedures for dealing with error, but as time goes by, he becomes morally involved, not at least due to the inspiration of his 'dream girl', Jill, who teaches him 'the moral way'. As Sam tries to eradicate the error, he faces still more difficulties. Irregularities pile up and, in the end, Sam himself becomes seen as an enemy of the state. A systemic error, the Buttle/Tuttle affair, is rephrased as part of a greater terrorist plot involving Sam. Sam is thus captured and sent for information retrieval. To a certain extent he escapes, but only by paying a high price: he retreats into his dream world and becomes mad. The film's title tune, a Latin escapist song called 'Brazil', here serves as an ironic comment on the prospect of utopia. Dreaming away from the present realities is no solution. Choosing between the Left and the Right fantasies, Gilliam thus sides with the Left. He wishes to link the work of dream (and utopia) with that of collective action.

Gilliam himself understands *Brazil* as a parallax of scepticism and optimism. It is a work of scepticism in so far as the system always wins: anybody who attempts to challenge the system is crushed mercilessly. But it is also optimistic in the way that it experiments with different ways of resistance. There is Sam, who tries to escape the grip of the police; there is Jill's sceptical attitude: 'Sam, have you ever seen a terrorist?' and her concern for the victims of the numerous terrorist bombings; and, finally, there is Tuttle, the man who should have been arrested instead of Buttle. Tuttle works as a freelance repair man, who fixes what the Central Services (the department in charge of infrastructure, gas, water, heating, etc.) has broken. He surpasses governmental forms and bureaucratic procedures and simply makes things work.

All three characters, the heroes, are situated in two spaces simultaneously: they are characters in both a realm of (empirical) reality and one of fiction/dream. Sam dreams about striking a deadly blow against the system in a gigantic war of good against evil. Jill is a real person living next to the Buttles (she witnesses Mr Buttle's arrest and tries to get him released), but she is also Sam's 'dream girl', and Tuttle is the 'empirical' person who helps Sam by repairing his flat – the hero in Sam's visions, rescuing him from the grip of the Ministry.

The crucial question emerging here is this: is fantasy a way of escaping an absolutist state, or is it through fantasies that people are subdued? Is fantasy a precondition for action – why resist if we cannot imagine something better – or, is it a form of escapism, making us able to endure our sufferings? This question is subtly posed in the opening scene and in some dream sequences in which Sam flies away like a big bird. The sky, of course, marks a route of escape. But remarkably such scenes in the film also bring to mind those shot by Leni Riefenstahl in the *Triumph of the Will*, a masterpiece of Nazi cinema.

In *Brazil* reality and fiction intertwine in two ways: there is the allegorical relationship between the film (fiction) and reality (the war on terror, our predicament that is), and there is the relationship between the realms of reality and dream portrayed in the film's narrative. We discuss both aspects in this chapter, especially how one slips from one world into the other, in three steps. First, we outline the vision of the totalitarian security state in *Brazil* and then we compare it to our own war against terrorism. Second, we examine various ways fiction/ideology might cover a burdensome reality. How do people position themselves *vis-à-vis* the security apparatus? And, third, we consider how resistance is portrayed. Finally, in the conclusion, we take a broader perspective and contextualize the disagreement between Gilliam and the film studio concerning *Brazil*'s form and release. Does the studio's unwillingness to release the film testify to a greater potential of fiction that Gilliam imagined?

(Anti)-terror

Brazil portrays a society in which terror is a part of everyday reality: the opening sequence shows a TV retail shop being bombed, later the same happens in a restaurant and later on a shopping centre is blasted; Mr Helpmann, the deputy minister of the Ministry of Information, has lost his legs due to a terrorist attack; in Sam's final dream Tuttle blows up the Ministry; the children in the street arrest suspected terrorists as a part of their play and so on. However, this reality is most clearly manifested in the restaurant scene. Sam, his mother Ida and her friend Mrs Terrain and Mrs Terrain's daughter, Shirley, are dining together when a bomb suddenly goes off. Wounded customers and waiters are lying on the floor, moaning, but the incident hardly affects any of our four guests. To avoid the horrific sight, a group of waiters, those not arrested by the security corps, arrange for a folding screen to be set up around the table. This cuts off the sight but not the noise of the suffering victims. What appears as an exceptional act is experienced as a normal state of affairs and handled with indifference. One cannot avoid the suspicion that it is the government itself that organizes all these small explosions in order to keep the population at bay, because the anti-terror corps is present in the restaurant only a few seconds after the explosion. As Gilliam puts it:

> The other question that always came up in these discussions was: are the terrorists real? To which I would always say that I don't know if they are,

because this huge organization has to survive at all costs, so if there is no real terrorism it has to invent terrorists to maintain itself – that's what organizations do. This always came as a bit of a surprise to them, and they wanted answers: was the explosion in the restaurant a terrorist one? Again, I said I didn't know, it might just be part of the system that went bang, which happens all the time. But if you assume that that technology works, then, if it blows up, it must be because someone blew it up: this is what I was trying to get across in *Brazil*.

(Gilliam 1999: 131–2)

The ongoing attacks are, if we develop this sceptical attitude further, a way of teaching people to live in the shadow of terror and thus a way of legitimizing the government and its harsh policies. One of the things which proved to be most difficult in the making of *Brazil* was, Gilliam relates, to make the actors act as if nothing happened while a lot of special effects were going on (1986). Only skilled actors can behave so 'professionally'. Likewise, the behaviour of the four (Sam, Ida, Mrs Terrain and Shirley) is also only possible after a lot of 'practice' – they react in this way because they have become used to terror attacks which are now experienced merely as annoying inconveniences.

Might the Department of Homeland Security's morbid mixture of excitation and tranquillization be interpreted along the same lines? As a way of interpellating people through their readiness for the next attack. Even though the ultimate catastrophe looms, you should go on with your everyday activities and just leave the rest to the government (Žižek 2003b: 98–9). Those interpellated by the threat barometer are situated somewhere in between a situation of no threat (which is in fact a category missing on the barometer) and total destruction. What we get in the interval is instead a row of possible minor attacks and a corresponding generalized state of exception. On the one hand, these small eruptions of violence remind us that the ultimate catastrophe is a real threat and that harsh initiatives should be undertaken to avoid it (thus whatever a government might have in mind is legitimized); on the other hand, there is a need to communicate that peace is possible when the threat is no longer imminent (this explains why government initiatives are presented as limited ones, restrictions are made with sunset clauses, etc.).

Sam and Jill pass by a poster at a processing plant which reads 'Power today. Pleasure tomorrow': the hardship ('power') is a temporary and necessary precaution on the way to the best of all worlds ('pleasure'). Another phrase found on a statue in the Department of Records reads 'The Truth Shall Make You Free': 'freedom' is waiting for us on the horizon, but first we must do whatever it takes to deliver 'truth', that is accept the ways of the Ministry. The restrictions on liberties as temporary measures are necessary to fight an alarming problem; they are, to paraphrase Michael Ignatieff's (2005) words, a lesser evil on the way to a greater good.

But how can one speak of a free society when many are interrogated and tortured to death? It might be that all these lesser evils become a greater one.

Perhaps the way of the Ministry is a greater threat to society than the terrorists are. The 'remedy' itself, in other words, might turn out to be poisonous:

> The state in which we live now, in the 'war on terror', is one of endlessly suspended terrorist threat: the Catastrophe (the new terrorist attack) is taken for granted, yet endlessly postponed. Whatever actually happens, even if it is a much more horrific attack than that of 9/11, will not yet be 'that'. And it is crucial here that we accomplish the 'transcendental' turn: the true catastrophe *already* is this life under the shadow of the permanent threat of catastrophe.
>
> (Žižek 2003b: 165)

The first time we visit the Ministry, we see a printer processing arrest warrants: Tonsted, Simon; Topper, Martin F.; Trollope, Benjamin G; Turb, William K; Turner, John D ... and then Tuttle, Archibald – a well-known and dangerous terrorist, who, as we know, has become Archibald Buttle by the interference of a beetle. The machine continues: Tutwood, Thomas T; Tuzczlow, Peter. ... And this is only the names beginning with 'T' and the arrest warrants processed on this particular day. When Sam is promoted and gets a job at the Ministry, we get a closer picture of what is going on. Mr Warren, Sam's new boss, is on his way through the endless corridors, bombarded with questions from his employees, including one about what to do with 15 suspects who are still 'outstanding'. 'Put half as terrorists and the rest as victims', Warren suggests. The actual arrests seen in the film are randomized in a similar way: in the blasted restaurant approximately half the waiters are arrested; and the customers and employees who work in the lingerie department that has been attacked are dealt with in the same way.

The arrestees are all taken to the Ministry for torture. The official purpose is to get information, but the 'need' to scare the population into privacy and show effectiveness is just as important. 'In a free society, information is the name of the game', Mr Helpmann says in a televised interview, and his words are echoed on numerous signs and posters at the Ministry of Information. One of which reads: 'Information – the Key to Prosperity'. In the fight against terrorism it has become a commonplace that information is the key. Terror differs from regular warfare in numerous ways: the most important is that terrorists and guerrilla fighters avoid an open battle against a standing army. Hence, they cannot be beaten in a regular way. What can be done is preventing future attacks. Intercepting telephone calls, suspicious emails, money transfers and the like is of vital importance for uncovering the secret structures and plans of terrorist organizations.

Is this not the rationale behind the Patriot Act? We think so. Access to registers, bank information, travel information, etc., is perceived to be the way of fighting terrorism. Another and perhaps more interesting parallel to what goes on in *Brazil* is to be found in the way information is retrieved in the 'war' against Afghanistan and Iraq. It has been claimed that 70 to

90 per cent of those imprisoned in the 'American Gulag' – on the Guantanamo naval base, in Abu Ghraib and other prisons in Iraq, in various places in Afghanistan and in secret prisons elsewhere – are innocent (Danner 2004: 3). Many of these 'unlawful combatants' have simply been in the wrong place at the wrong time – like the waiters in the restaurant or those shopping or working in the lingerie department. These arrests might simply be understood as desperate and unfocused attempts to gain information on the terrorist cells: if a sufficient number of persons are arrested, hopefully somebody will know and tell something.

In Abu Ghraib, prisoners were routinely subjected to 'information retrieval'. The tools used were dissimilar to those seen in *Brazil*: 'classic' torture causing physical suffering in *Brazil* versus psychological torture through sexual humiliation and profanation of Islam in Abu Ghraib. The aim, however, seems to be the same: to soften people up and make them talk. The use of torture is prohibited by the 1949 Geneva Conventions, and those who have defended the use of torture have done so by claiming torture to be a lesser evil necessary to protect a greater good. 'It's going to be vital for us to use any means at our disposal, basically to achieve our objective', Vice President Dick Cheney said in his first interview after 11 September. President Bush stressed that the attacks on 11 September required 'a new paradigm as a response', 'a new way of thinking the laws of war' (Strauss 2004: 6). 'All I want to say is that there was a before 9/11 and an after 9/11' – this was how Cofer Black, the US Central Intelligence Agency's (CIA) director for counter terror measures, put it, but the view is widely shared (Brown 2005: 978).

The torture in Abu Ghraib was perceived as 'torture light', as torture without torture. People would not be harmed permanently, psychological torture was thought to be less harmful than physical torture, and there were guidelines on how far one could go: no further than what would be comparable to an organ failure, as James Bybee proposed in his infamous memorandum. Then Secretary of Defense Donald Rumsfeld could easily have been offered a role in *Brazil*, claiming that what went on in Abu Ghraib was something 'technically different from torture' (Sontag 2004). The torture we see in *Brazil* is also 'torture light'. As Jack, the doctor who tortures the victims, claims, there are rigid parameters laid down to prevent the arrestees from dying. Buttle's death is therefore not premeditated but caused by a confusion of journals making Jack use the wrong parameters in Buttle's electro-memory therapy.

How is torture legitimized in a free society, in a democracy? Robert Jackson, a columnist, has claimed that torture might be accepted in cases where national security is under threat. To him and to other neoconservatives, the constitution is not to be understood as a suicide pact: we must 'keep an open mind about certain measures to fight terrorism, like court sanctioned psychological interrogation. And we'll have to think about transferring some suspects to our less squeamish allies, even if that's hypocritical. Nobody said this was going to be pretty' (Jackson, quoted in Macmaster 2004: 3). Within the academic field, Michael Ignatieff (2005) and Alan Dershowitz (2002) offer similar arguments.

The laws of war, the Geneva Conventions, have to be adjusted to the new realities of postmodern warfare. Torture might be necessary in ticking-bomb scenarios. Besides its limited use and its 'light' character, torture has to be authorized by a judge. Special permissions could, Dershowitz suggests, be given on a case-by-case basis: 'I'm not in favour of torture, but if you're going to have it, it should damn well have court approval; there is no "good" realistic third alternative. This is a classic "choice of evils"' (quoted in Cohen 2005: 27). Dershowitz would allow for needles to be inserted under the fingernails or for a tooth to be drilled without a tranquillizer being given (Macmaster 2004: 4).

Let us return to *Brazil*. Here the arrestees can either confess to being terrorists or plea not guilty in which case they will just face more torture. There are only two options: to confess immediately or to do it after torture. Arrestees are thus perceived to be guilty no matter what. Rumsfeld's way of seeing the prisoners in Guantanamo as ticking bombs repeats this argument. The prisoners had to stay in Guantanamo as long as the war against terror was on (which could take decades) because they would otherwise go off like a bomb. They were potential suicide bombers just waiting for the right movement. Thus, they were not accused of something they had done but of something that they might do in the future. Their religious commitment and anti-American values were enough proof of their 'explosiveness'. To Rumsfeld, there were only terrorists and potential terrorists, and both groups, of course, had to be imprisoned.

This argument brings to mind the water test used to deal with witches in the Middle Ages. With her hands and feet tied together, thus incapable of moving/swimming, the supposed witch was thrown into a lake. If she kept floating, it proved that she was a witch (had supernatural powers, etc.), if not, she was innocent, which was, however, worth nothing since she would then have drowned. Gilliam got his idea of payment for torture from some medieval documents on witch processes. Those who were sentenced to death had to pay for the wood that was used for the fire (Gilliam 1999: 132). Sam is likewise advised to plea guilty to save his own and the taxpayers' money or at least plea guilty to some of the charges to keep the cost of his information retrieval within reach.

What he is going to pay for is, of course, not torture but 'therapy', 'service' or 'assistance'. The arrestees are thus treated as both prisoners and customers (Cowen 1998). On the one hand, the guards refer to the prisoners as 'government property'. Prisoners are taken to the 'depot', and are, as Agamben (1998) has put it, *homini sacri*: people who are subjected to state power but simultaneously placed outside the realm of law. After their arrest, the detainees literally look like a bag of flesh: they are placed in baglike canvas covering them from head to waist, they have a metal clamp around their neck, and a metal bar slides up the back of the bag to which they are handcuffed. These 'bags' are transported like slaughtered pigs: the baglike arrangement is fastened to a hook in the roof of the transporters from which the 'bags' dangle as the car moves on. Again, a parallel with the real world intrudes: are the prisoners leaving Afghanistan for Guantanamo Bay not experiencing something similar, all dressed in overalls or jumpsuits, wearing nappies and strapped onto the floor of military transporters? Or what about the way the prisoners are dressed when moving about in 'public' areas in Guantanamo? They are forced to wear orange jumpsuits, their ability to see is blocked by blackened goggles and a surgical mask and a hearing protector prevent them from speaking and hearing.

People like Buttle, on the other hand, are *invited* to *assist* the Ministry of Information with its *enquiries*. Jack tells Sam that he is busy because he has a queue of *customers* to deal with. When Sam is imprisoned, he is asked to contribute to a survey aimed at providing a better service: 'Official: do you think the present system is A. efficient, B. inefficient? Official: as a taxpayer are you A. impressed, B. unimpressed?' And so it goes on and on. A crucial question is then: can what goes on with Buttle and the other detainees be compared to what happens to people when they act in a market economy?

The reign of the commodity

Gilliam's film offers a double diagnosis. Obviously, one flank of attack is a totalitarian security state. The other, however, is the consumer society. These two simultaneous lines of criticism force us, the viewers, to reflect upon the similarities between the ways in which the state and the market produce subjectivities. At first sight, the two realms seem to be very different. In a totalitarian state, bureaucracy reduces freedoms: it restricts the freedom of expression, narrows down the realm of free choice, cripples consciousness (doublespeak, newspeak) and so on. The panoptic state uses discipline as a tool to restrict movement and behaviour. In a market economy, in contrast, individual differences are stimulated, differentiated goods are produced as long as there is a demand for them, everybody has a right to start an enterprise etc.

These ideas are of course, as generations of Marxists have shown, ideological in essence: there is only a freedom of choice for those who can afford it, people are not autonomous agents but are subjected to the whim of the capitalists, demands do not emerge spontaneously but are produced through advertising. Indeed, as Orwell put it:

> Capitalism, as such, has no room in it for any human relationship; it has no law except that profits must always be made. Not much more than a century ago, children as young as six were brought up and worked to death in the mines and cotton mills, more ruthlessly than we should now work a donkey. This was not more cruel than the Spanish Inquisition, but it was more inhuman, in that the men who worked those children to death thought of them as mere units of labour, things, whereas the Spanish Inquisitor would have thought of them as souls.
>
> (quoted in Kellner 2006: 10)

Capitalism reduces man to labour, to a commodity. To Agamben, *homo sacer* is a person who can be killed without the executioner facing punishment. Likewise, a labourer in a capitalist economy is someone you can dismiss without moral scruples. In each case morality is perceived to be something alien to the system. In other words, in each case, morality ceases to be a register for critical reflection.

The labourers we meet in *Brazil* are treated exactly in this spirit, as objects. They live in ramshackle houses crammed with rubbish, junk and old worn-out furniture. Ordinary workers are poor and can afford no more than subsistence. As a whole, the capitalist economy is depicted as a gigantic machine which leaves nothing but rubbish in its trail. As Sam and Jill drive towards the processing plant, we get a bird's-eye view of the industrial area: rubbish piles up, there are no trees, no grass, nothing. Yet, people passing by in their cars see only the advertisements that are placed on both sides of the road.

Marxist thought has always been divided into two branches. One has mainly focused on production and the other on consumption: Marxism as political economy and as cultural theory. The kind of criticism we have just outlined above belongs to the first branch: the role of labour in the production process and the irrationalities of the capitalist machinery. The second branch focuses not on what is produced but on how demands are stimulated. Consumers desire what the market makes them desire. In this respect, the distinction between need and desire is crucial. People need clothes, food, shelter, etc., and make demands for these goods no matter how the economy is organized. Yet desire, the attraction of goods, only has little to do with the satisfaction of such demands. We buy something not when we actually need it, but when we *discover* a need for it.

There are even rites of shopping, Christmas being perhaps the most important of them. Unsurprisingly, in *Brazil*, it is Christmas time, and everybody is busy inventing demands. What to give a friend or a family member who already has everything? Do they have a need that they are not aware of? Christmas in *Brazil* seems to be nothing more than an excuse for shopping. We get no closer to a religious statement than a band that marches through a shopping centre while carrying a banner: 'Consumers for Christ'. Christmas is the time for exchanging presents, which is also the case in *Brazil*. But nobody seems to take pleasure in giving or receiving these presents. Giving gifts has become a habitual act deprived of meaning (Wheeler 2005: 101). All the presents exchanged are the same commodity: a toy for executives, allowing the recipient to randomize 'yes' and 'no' answers. As a commodity, the present massifies and individualizes at the same time. People get a present, an item which is meant only for them. At the same time, however, they are reduced to a type, to a member of an indistinct group as just one of many consumers who get the same toy.

This allegorical commodity is a commentary on the social structure in more than one way. First, the toy illustrates how the totalitarian state apparatus works (e.g. how people are randomly placed in the victim and terrorist categories). Thus it hints at a possible symbiosis of a totalitarian state apparatus and a capitalist economy. Second, the toy alludes to the amoral character of the capitalist economy. It is as pleased with a 'yes' as it is with a 'no'. Its axiomatic nature wants nothing in particular and thus produces whatever is demanded from its owner. Third, the toy makes it clear that commodities are desired and not demanded.

However, the capitalist economy does not work in a conformist fashion, making everybody desire the same objects. It has no problem with producing different commodities; in fact, it thrives on difference (e.g. the difference between this year's and last year's fashion; the difference among consumer segments: young, middle-aged, elderly; and the difference among cultural groups: the adventures, the traditionalists, the snobs and so on). As such, Gilliam's portrait of the capitalist economy is wrong and old-fashioned. Perhaps he had to exaggerate in order to illustrate the point that goods are not demanded but desired. If the characters in the film had bought different goods, his point would have been weakened. We do not all have the need for the same object. However, even the porter, who has no executive functions, has one of these toys. The capitalist economy is totalitarian in this sense: 'through the manipulation of needs by vested interests' (Marcuse 1964: 3). The products do:

> indoctrinate and manipulate; they promote a false consciousness which is immune against its falsehood. And as these beneficial products become available to more individuals in more social classes, the indoctrination they carry ceases to be publicity; it becomes a way of life. It is a good way of life – much better than before – and as a good way of life, it militates against qualitative change.
>
> (ibid.: 12)

We should also note that the toy for executives is an object with no real functions. This hints at the fourth aspect stressed in Gilliam's allegory. The toy is made of exclusive materials, and it is promoted as the perfect present for those at the top – for the very important decision-makers. As such the commodity becomes part of the identity-building process. It has a magical aura which can be transferred to the owner; it is, to use Marx's concept, a fetish. Fifth, as an illustration of the power of advertising, those who give the toy as a present simply pass on the slogan for the toy to the recipients by saying that it is a toy for executives. The customers are, in other words, buying statements. The sign-value of the commodity becomes more important than its use-value.

The importance of sign-value is further stressed by two other commodities encountered in the film: the dinner served in the restaurant, and Ida and Mrs Terrain's cosmetic operations. In the restaurant scene, our four guests study the menu card, which has colourful photographs of the dishes, while the waiter, with a fake French accent, makes exclusive recommendations to each guest on what to order: 'Between you and me, Madam, today the number two'. It seems to be a very exclusive and upper-class place. However, all the dishes turn out to be identical: each guest gets three scoops of a brown lumpy substance to which four different photographs of the dishes from the menu card are attached. What is encountered here is a capitalist economy in its simulated phase.

The capitalist economy turns everything into commodities and all commodities into signs. Cosmetic surgery testifies to this final conquest. Both Ida and Mrs Terrain undergo several cosmetic operations each altering their looks and appearance. They are both reduced to a surface and a semblance. They always talk about how they look, and they are thrilled by the prospects of being able to buy and give the so-called 'medical gift tokens' for Christmas. Ida and Mrs Terrain each get a treatment at a celebrity doctor's clinic. Ida gets a classical 'cut and paste' treatment making her look even younger. Mrs Terrain undergoes an acid treatment to give her a 'wonderfully subtle shading' and 'delicate nuances like a Rembrandt etching'. Unfortunately, however, there are some 'teensy-weensy complications', and while Ida becomes still younger, Mrs Terrain looks even older and finally dies from her complication. When Sam tips her coffin over by accident, it is revealed that she has been reduced to a slimy substance and some bones.

It is the movement towards a simulated economy that gives the film its 'totalitarian' twist and links it with the way the war on terror is conceived of and fought. As the reference to use-values disappears (Baudrillard 1994: 22), so does the reference to actual and real terror attacks – they can be simulated by the state (hence the alert code system mentioned previously). Several additional parallels could be mentioned: are the consumers not 'terrorized' by the market imperative and by advertisements allowing them no rest? May cosmetic surgery be seen as a form of torture? We will not comment on these possibilities but instead investigate how subjects position themselves vis-à-vis the capitalist economy and the security state.

The cynic

Who is Sam? He is, above all, a bureaucrat, and Mr Kurtzmann's most cherished employee at that. He is also a good and decent guy. Perhaps too good indeed; in his eagerness to assist Mr Kurtzmann, he ends up as the one responsible for all the irregularities. He forges Mr Kurtzmann's signature when Mr Kurtzmann suddenly claims to have a broken arm. Kurtzmann is a master of passing the buck. Sam, on the contrary, works according to the rules and obviously has no idea of the perverted practices that keep the system running (such as the colleagues watching *Casablanca* on their screens when Mr Kurtzmann is in his office and looking busy when he is nearby). Sam does not care about promotions, prestige and wants to distance himself from the system. He minds his own business, dislikes responsibilities and adjusts to the circumstances he cannot control. He tries to escape the grip of the system.

On a second look, however, Sam might be caught in an ideological trap. His reflective distancing from reality works as a form of ideology. We can develop this idea with Arendt and Havel.

Adolf Eichmann, in charge of logistics, did send millions of Jews to the concentration camps, and Arendt claims that he did not realize the true impact of his actions. Eichmann was banal: he did not reflect on his actions within a moral register (Arendt 1992: 287–8). Sam, too, is banal in this sense. Both believe that evil resides elsewhere, thus unable to contaminate them. Both treat people (Jews, suspected terrorists) as goods to be delivered, and any departure from this line of thinking is conditioned by personal sympathies or love. Eichmann tries to help Storfer, a Jew who has been brought to Auschwitz, because he sees him as a personal friend and as one who has worked hard to solve the Jewish question (ibid.: 50–1). When Sam tries to help Jill, it is because she is his dream girl. Storfer and Jill serve as constitutive exceptions confirming the rule, that the rest have got what they deserve.

Eichmann and Sam are professionals who invest all their morality in doing their duty, in carrying out the orders with outmost precision. Thus, in reply to Mrs Buttle's enquiry into her husband's death, Sam can only answer in officialese: 'I assure you Mrs Buttle, the Ministry is always very scrupulous about following up and eradicating errors. If you have any complaints which you'd like to make, I'd be more than happy to send you the appropriate forms.' And he can say this all to a Mrs Buttle who is paralysed, crying, and certainly does not look as if she were capable of filling out governmental forms. How is such denial, such ignorance of the other possible? Eichmann knew of course that it was not cargo but Jews he sent to the concentration camps, and Sam knows that Mr Buttle is dead. However, they both also know how to avoid moral involvement by rephrasing and passing on information by means of Orwellian newspeak.

Arendt mentions how extermination, liquidation and killing became 'the final solution', 'evacuation' and 'special treatment'. Deportation became 'change of residence' and so on (ibid.: 85). When Kurtzmann tries to make a compensation to the Buttle family, who have been overcharged for Archibald's memory therapy, he discovers that Population Census has registered Mr Buttle as 'dormated', the Central Collective Storehouse computer as 'deleted', the Information Retrieval as 'inoperative', and Security as 'completed'. Newspeak also plays an important role in the war on terror, allowing us to distance ourselves from the realities of the war. Thus casualties on the enemies' side become 'collateral damage', prisoners of war can be treated outside the rules of the Geneva Conventions when their activities are labelled 'illegal combats', war becomes 'humanitarian intervention', enemies form an 'axis of evil', attacks become 'surgical strikes'.

In *The Power of the Powerless* (1985), Havel mentions a shopkeeper who decorates his windows with the party's slogans and flags to show that he is a good communist. When he retreats to his private room, however, he mocks the system for its stupidity (Žižek 2001c: 90). Sam's identity is split in a similar way. After the attack in the restaurant, Mrs Terrain encourages Sam to do something about these terrorists, but Sam just responds that it is his lunch hour. Mrs Terrain (who links up the restaurant incident and Sam's job) and Sam's mother (who sees promotion as a way of gaining social prestige) perceive the private and public self as inseparable. Sam, however, does not make such a link. This explains why a common ground for a discussion cannot be established. Again, there is a linguistic strategy attached to this split personality. Doublethink is:

> the power of holding two contradictory beliefs in one's mind simultane-ously, and accepting both of them … to tell deliberate lies while genuinely believing them, to forget any fact that has become inconvenient, and then, when it becomes necessary again, to draw it back from oblivion for just so long as it is needed, to deny the existence of objective reality and all the while to take account of the reality which one denies.
>
> (Orwell, quoted in Pietz 1988: 62)

Sam knows that one who is 'inoperative' is in fact dead, but the euphemistic language still helps him to cope with his job. In front of Kurtzmann, he speaks bluntly about Buttle's death but not in front of Mrs Buttle. He has two different vocabularies, one to use in the private and one in the public sphere. The two vocabularies only collide when the two spheres overlap, as in the case of Jill.

Sam, in short, suffers from enlightened false consciousness. He knows that the ideological notions are false, that they hide something, but he insists on acting as if they were true. And precisely this reflective distancing allows the system to work unhindered. Ideology works exactly because it can depict itself as its own opposite. 'Ideology is not a dreamlike illusion that we build to escape insupportable reality; in its basic dimension it is a fantasy-construction which serves as a support for our "reality" itself: an "illusion" which structures our effective, real social relations' (Žižek 1989: 45). The question here is a pragmatic one: reality demands of us that we play our roles even though we prefer another and more just society. We know that we participate in objective mechanisms which structure the political settings, but we are not *really* involved because our goal is not consciously to support the real effect caused by the given social and political order. We work hard in an unjust and environmentally disastrous and repressive system, but we are really not the ones who work, our masks do. And when we come home, we can put our masks aside and enjoy our private life together with our family. However, this idea of a mask concealing a truer self is false:

> There is more truth in a mask than in what is hidden beneath it: a mask is never simply 'just a mask' since it determines the actual place we occupy in the intersubjective symbolic network; what is effectively false and null is our 'inner distance' from the mask we wear (the 'social role' we play), our 'true self' hidden beneath it. … The performative dimension at work here

consists of the symbolic efficiency of the 'mask': wearing a mask actually *makes us* what we feign to be.

(Žižek 1992: 34)

In *Brazil*, the idea of a split personality is even more evident in the case of Jack. He literally carries a mask while doing his dirty job retrieving information. When Sam meets Jack in his office for the first time, Jack is wearing a suit, his child is playing on the floor with some toys, the room looks cosy and the tone is informal and friendly. The next and last time they meet is in the room next to Jack's office: in a gigantic silo, the torture chamber. Jack now wears a doctor's uniform and a mask with a baby doll face. Jack has two selves, two faces. Everything is neatly organized until the day Sam becomes his 'client':

Sam: Jack?
Sam: Jack? ... Jack?
Jack: Shut up!
Sam: Jack, I'm innocent! Help me.
Jack: Bastard!!!
Sam: This is all a mistake. Jack, please take that mask off.
Jack: You stupid bastard!
Sam: What?
Jack: How could you do this to me?
Sam: Help me, Jack! I'm frightened!
Jack: How do you think I feel? You're shit!
Sam: Jack...
Jack: Shut up! This is a professional relationship!
Sam: Jack!! ... You can't ... No, don't!

The neat distinction between the private and the public self is short-circuited. But Jack resists the ethical injunction by putting on his mask. Jack is skilled at taking his mask on and off.

And precisely at this point there emerges an obvious question: for whom is this carnival staged? The Lacanian answer is the Big Other. The Big Other is the idea of a divine authority, a master mind, the list of reason, a conspirator or the like. It is the one we blame for all our miseries and the one we believe to be responsible for those orders we do not wish to follow. This Big Other does not exist but is a product of the mind. Still, it works, it organizes our world. Who plays the role of the Big Other in *Brazil*? In Ida's case, it is Sam's biological father, Jeremiah, and she urges Sam to make his father proud. Jeremiah is also the father figure to and an old friend of Mr Helpmann. It is as if Jeremiah is always around, speaking to him; he even describes him as 'the ghost in the machine'.

Who is Sam's Big Other? No one, or rather Sam's frustration stems from the lack of a father figure. He searches for the man on the top but never finds him.

His real father, Jeremiah, is dead, and throughout the film he searches for an ersatz father: Kurtzmann, Helpmann or perhaps even the samurai. When he enters Mr Helpmann's office, it is empty apart from a machine processing arrest warrants. Later, when Mr Helpmann visits Sam in his cell just before his information retrieval, Helpmann explains that the rules of the game are laid down and that not even he can do anything! The Big Other is exactly this: an anonymous machine that works independently of human will. Indeed it brings to mind Orwell's Big BrOther or the authority that K in Kafka's stories searches for but never finds.

The Big Other is an imaginary father figure. This is why Helpmann appropriately visits Sam dressed as Father Christmas. Father Christmas is a father whom we know does not exist but who is still capable of influencing our daily lives. That is our stance is cynical. Or, as Jack puts it: 'there are not coincidences, Sam. Everything's connected, all along the line. Cause and effect. That's the beauty of it. Our job is to trace the connections and reveal them.' This pre-established gigantic pattern of causes and effects is the system; it is the Big Other. The ducts that appear all over the city could also be taken as a metaphor for the Big Other. The system is knit together by an anonymous power that nobody seems to control or know the extent of (Gilliam 1999: 130). Here is Gilliam's own version of the non-existence of the Big Other:

> I didn't want it to be a totalitarian system like in *1984* or *Brave New World*. Even Mr Helpmann isn't the top guy, he's the deputy. There probably is no top guy, since everybody abdicates responsibility; the buck doesn't stop here, it always stops at the next person up. Although it's often described as a totalitarian world, I don't think it is, since the sum of the parts isn't quite the total that we're looking at in a totalitarian system.
>
> (ibid.: 144)

When Sam fights the forces of evil that prevent him from entering his paradise, the system, the Big Other, takes the form of a gigantic samurai warrior. After having beaten the monster, he removes its helmet, and his own face is revealed. Sam is the system! It is made up of ordinary people like him. There is no Big Other – the system is us! The word samurai is a pun. When the word is divided into two syllables, it can mean 'Sam and I' or 'Sam, you are I'. In a talk show, Gilliam further explained:

> The fears of *Brazil* are not so much that the world is spinning out of control because of the system, because the system is us. What *Brazil* is really about is that the system isn't great leaders, great machinating people controlling it all. It's each person performing their job as one little cog in this thing.
>
> (Gilliam 1991)

Resistance

Sam resists the system by retreating into his fantasy world. All his dreams, however, seem to reflect the reality in which he is immersed, and as such their emancipatory potential is limited. The dreams condense experiences from his everyday life: people he knows, the psychological relationship between Sam and the oppressive social structures he refuses to face directly (Glass 1986: 22–3). They offer an 'ersatz substitute for the imagination that could solve or at least analyse the problem' (ibid.: 26). Here, Glass proposes a useful distinction between imagination and fantasy, a distinction that allows us to separate the repressive and utopian functions of dreams, at least in theory.

> Imagination might be defined as the ability to project something other than what is, in such a way as to be able to realize the image in reality. It is a hopeful response and alternative to the external pressure of social oppression. Fantasy, as poor second choice, is the ghost of imagination strangled, where one's own felt oppression is turned inward and relief sought helplessly in images shaped by that oppression.
>
> (ibid.: 25)

Glass convincingly shows that the true context of Sam's dreams is his unresolved relationship to his mother and late father. His dreams are confined to his personal context, and, as such, they do not allow for a wider political involvement. When Sam escapes the forces of darkness by entering the chapel in which the unfortunate Mrs Terrain is going to be buried, he encounters his mother, now looking 20 years younger, being the same age as Jill. The two characters are in fact played by the same actor. The organizing principle behind his visions is, in other words, an Icarus dream.

Yet, a more optimistic way of reading Sam's fantasies is also possible. First, there is the idea of blowing up the Ministry of Information. The scene in the hall mirrors the famous scene in *Battleship Potemkim* and may as such be read as an ode to the Russian revolution. The guards march and lower their rifles in exactly the same way as in *Battleship Potemkim*. *Brazil*'s counterpart of the mother loosing her grip on the pram as she gets shot is a cleaning lady letting go of her floor polisher as she, too, gets shot (Cowen 1998). It might be that there is no utopian vision here, that the act is just an act *against* the system and not *for* something. On the other hand, the demand for an articulated vision of a coming society easily turns into blackmail: if you cannot imagine a realistic alternative, then shut up! It is also not entirely true that Sam's rebellion is just a work of his dreams. When Sam short-circuits the tube in his office, pressure builds up and finally the tube system explodes like a volcano erupting; lots of papers are dispersed throughout the corridors and in the streets, a scene that reminds us of the collapse of the Third Reich.

We might even unpack a utopian vision in Sam's dreams. His vision of a life together with Jill looks very much like a communist society as it is envisioned without oppression, pollution and exploitation. In Sam's dream, he and Jill have parked their truck in a beautiful valley. In front of the house there is a garden with plants, a cow and some chickens. It is morning, and Jill asks Sam if he has slept well. Sam answers that he has and that he does not dream anymore. This is the realization of utopia – there is no longer a need to dream (for escapism). Earlier in the movie, Jill had told Sam how tired she was of his 'fucking dreams'. Jill prefers action (she is the one who helps the victims of the explosion in the shopping centre). The two characters melt together in the final scene: Sam's vision of something better and Jill's realism and preference for action. A change/revolution might in fact be conditioned by this synthesis.

As for the blackmail described above, do we find an uncanny parallel to this in our ongoing war on terror? If you criticize the government, you side with the terrorists! It is either them or us! But it ought to be possible to criticize *both* terrorism and the way we fight it. The war on terror might delegitimize all attempts at political reform. Who are the terrorists really? One man's terrorist is another man's freedom fighter as the saying goes. Tuttle in *Brazil* testifies to this. He is a middle-aged heating engineer, a short, tough character with dark clothes, balaclava and a gun, resembling 'a cross between a cat burglar and a night raid commando'. The Ministry sees him as a 'freelance subversive' who has a grudge against society. Tuttle's explanation is that he is in the game for the adventure and because he is tired of state bureaucracy.

The Central Services do not respond when the central heating in Sam's apartment breaks down, but luckily Tuttle arrives and fixes the problem. This is Tuttle's only crime. This might not sound as a big deal, but in a totalitarian system it is the capital crime: initiative. So when the Central Services finally arrive, they do not take this 'sabotage' lightly. As punishment they tear Sam's apartment apart. Thus, we have two kinds of terror: partisan activities and state terror – good and bad terror. Evidently, Gilliam sides with Tuttle. Anti-terror, he claims, might become terror in itself.

As an American adviser in Iraq put it, echoing General Lefevre's 'you will have to fight like a partisan wherever there are partisans' (quoted in Schmitt 2004: 18): 'The only way we can win is to go unconventional. We're going to have to play their game. Guerrilla versus guerrilla. Terrorism versus terrorism. We've got to scare the Iraqis into submission' (Moreias 2005: 10). Gilliam warns us about seeing terrorists everywhere and urges us to be cautious about whom we define as terrorists. The definition is often fuzzy and deeply subjective; more a political than a legal one. Terrorists are often just defined as all those who aim at destabilizing the present economic and social order. The result is, among others, the criminalization of protest movements (Paye 2004: 172–4).

Terrorists are those defined as such by the state. They are people of weapons who do not belong to a regular army. Four conditions define members of regular troops: the presence of responsible officers, firm and visible symbols, open display of weapons, observance of rules and application of laws of war (Schmitt 2004: 26). The partisan, such as Tuttle, does not meet any of these criteria.

Tuttle works alone without the guidance of a superior, he does not show his weapons, is dressed as a black cat in the dark, and finally he does not follow the rules laid down by the state. As a guerrilla fighter, he moves only at night and stays in the woods during the day (ibid.: 27). Or, as Helpmann puts it in the televised interview shown in the beginning of the film:

Interviewer:	Deputy Minister, what do you believe is behind this recent increase in terrorist bombings?
Helpmann:	Bad sportsmanship. A ruthless minority of people seems to have forgotten certain good old fashioned virtues. They just can't stand seeing the other fellow win. If these people would just play the game, instead of standing on the touch line heckling –
Interviewer:	In fact, killing people –
Helpmann:	– In fact, killing people – they'd get a lot more out of life.

Bad sportsmanship, irregular fighting, terror! The partisan defies the neat distinctions between inside and outside, war and peace, combatants and non-combatants, enemies and common criminals, that is all the distinctions that uphold the state (ibid.: 16). The partisan is as such the political figure per se. He expects neither law nor mercy from the enemy (ibid.: 17). He puts his life at risk, but not for his own sake. The word 'partisan' is derived from the word 'party' – the partisan fights for a party, he sides 100 per cent with one of the parties (Schmitt and Schickel 1995: 631). This applies to Tuttle as well: he does not seek enrichment; he is not an ordinary criminal. He fights for ordinary people suppressed by a repressive system. And unlike Sam, he resists the cynical split between being both against (in words and fantasies) and for (in practice) the party. Thus, Gilliam's positive conclusion is that *this* kind of action and *this* way of being are still possible alternatives, and, we might add, more needed than ever.

A parallax of scepticism and optimism

Is *Brazil*, then, an optimistic or a pessimistic film? In the end, Sam loses his mind and retreats into his private dream world. He escapes the system but at the cost of becoming a vegetable. So, yes and no: yes, because resistance is a possibility, we can imagine something better, there are acts of resistance, etc.; and no, in so far as all these ways of resistance are crushed. Better yet: it might be the very antithesis between 'optimism' and 'pessimism' that is wrong. Pessimistic ideas can mobilize people against oppression (Kellner 2006: 23). The best example is perhaps the story of the suffering of Christ. Here, the ultimate defeat is turned into the ultimate victory. Are the marks on Sam's hands, of which we get a glimpse in the torture scene, stigmata? And is Jack a Judas who performs a lobotomy on Sam to save him from his suffering and deliver him to another world, to Brazil/heaven (the instrument seen in Jack's hand is a device used to perform a frontal lobotomy, Cowen 1998)? Defeat or victory? What matters is not the story itself but how it is continued. What Gilliam does is to analyse our present predicament. The rest is up to us. As he puts it, answering a question on the cynical tone of his films:

> It's amazing that you say cynical because that's come up before. I don't think I'm cynical. I'm sceptical; I don't think I'm cynical about things. The terrible fact is that I'm terribly optimistic about things. I have a theory about *Brazil* in that it was a very difficult film for a pessimist to watch but it was okay for an optimist to watch it. For a pessimist it just confirms his worst fears; an optimist could somehow find a grain of hope in the ending. Cynicism bothers me because cynicism is in a way an admission of defeat, whereas scepticism is fairly healthy, and also it implies that there is the possibility of change.
>
> (Gilliam 1986)

There is a possibility of change. Criticism might even be effective. The fact that *Brazil* was released confirms this. Gilliam's struggle with the studio might be seen as yet another instance of the fight between a totalitarian system and the power of the imagination, an important aspect being of course that Gilliam won. When Sidney Sheinberg received the film from Gilliam, he refused to release it. He thought it lacked commercial potential. Hence, he re-edited the film, cutting out the film's dark ending, the scenes showing the dehumanizing power of bureaucracy as well as most of the witty and dark orchestral score. He suggested to replace those scenes with rock music in order to attract teens. What was left was the story of Sam's pursuit of his dream girl and most of the humoristic scenes. The result was a shorter film, well, a totally different film produced according to the standard Hollywood ideology, a happy ending in which the emotional tensions are finally resolved, social criticism is internalized as problems of the actor's psyche, etc. Gilliam, however, would not accept these alterations, and the result was a fairly long saga. The case was resolved when friends started to set up the original version of the film in private homes. At the yearly vote on the best film, *Brazil* won three prizes, and Universal's big film, *Out of Africa*, none. Hence, the studio was finally forced to run the film (ibid.). Thus, it would not be a cliché to say that *Brazil* was a dream that finally came true.

7 *Life is Beautiful*
The ghost of Auschwitz

Who can bear testimony to Auschwitz, given that its 'true' witnesses died in the gas chambers (Lyotard 1988: 3)? Herein lays the revisionists' most serious trump: nobody can *prove* that he or she died there. But do we not have survivors, testimonies, museums and miles of literature on the Holocaust? Why, then, take the problems of testimony and revisionism seriously? Because it is a symptom of a more fundamental problem: how are we to preserve the status of the Holocaust as a unique and living memory? Is it to be inscribed in the history books as one chapter among others, or is to be understood as a singular and traumatic event beyond comprehension?

The will to preserve the living memory of the Holocaust principally relies on testimonies. Despite being 'only' second-hand witnesses to the gas chambers, the survivors may through their unsuccessful attempts to depict the horror of camps testify to this very incomprehensibility. However, this 'puritan' strategy suffers from the fact that the Holocaust generation will not be with us much longer, that is in the absence of living memory we will soon have to make do with history. In this situation the problem of Holocaust denial revival might be the reason for the ever-increasing quantity of Holocaust-related cultural production. Indeed, if it is denied historically and pushed aside, the Holocaust is today, if anything, an overexposed topic.

We are here confronted with two equally unsatisfactory alternatives. The first consists of accepting the Holocaust as the ultimate mystery that cannot be represented for it is rooted in the survivors' experience. Thus, many attempts at demystification are perceived as negations of the unique in the catastrophe, and this, of course, makes a critical reflection on the Holocaust difficult (Žižek 2001c: 66–7). Further, there is a problematical conformity between the imperative to let the events (or the survivors) speak for themselves and the depersonalizing silencing produced by the Third Reich (Trezise 2001: 51). The other alternative is to abandon the Holocaust to history; to see it as just one of many incidents of genocide. However, to explain the Holocaust in this way is to normalize it, that is to ignore that the Holocaust enabled the West to develop a critical self-consciousness and a moral and political will to resist evil.

Rejecting these two strategies, Agamben investigates the possibility of a third in which the Holocaust is neither elevated to a mystery that escapes representation, nor reduced to an object that can be exhausted by understanding (1999: 13). Auschwitz materializes the aporia of historical knowledge: that facts and truth, verification and understanding can never coincide (ibid.: 12). Inasmuch as 'aporia' refers to a tension without which ethics, memory and the political cannot exist, the aporia of the Holocaust consists of bearing testimony to something to which it is impossible to bear testimony. Remembrance is impossible but imperative (ibid.: 13).

Agamben's work on Auschwitz, *Remnants of Auschwitz*, is an interesting intervention into the philosophical debate on the Holocaust. Equally interesting is the more popular discussion of the Holocaust in Benigni and Cerami's film *Life is Beautiful* (La vita è bella 1997). Here we attempt to establish a dialogue between these two discussions, hopefully allowing for mutual fertilization. This raises the stakes in relation to both discourses. Thus, the ethical problematic of *Remnants of Auschwitz* opens up an interesting line of interpretation regarding *Life is Beautiful*, while this interpretation in turn becomes a test for its own ethical strength. Indeed, *Life is Beautiful* sets up the problem of remembrance more radically, focusing not 'only' on the survivors' testimony, but also on post-remembrance as practised by the postwar generation. We begin with a short summary of the film and then move on to a more abstract reflection on the character of the Holocaust as memory. In this, we deal with the question of how we, the postwar generations, might relate to the memory of the camps in an ethical way. Or, in a nutshell, how is post-remembrance possible?

The accident

The film plunges in headlong with Guido's (played by Benigni himself) entrance. Together with his friend Ferruccio, he is in his car on the way to a Tuscan town. Going down a hill, they discover that the brakes do not work. At full speed, they approach the cheerfully decorated town expecting the King's visit. Without brakes, Guido and Ferruccio overtake the King. When they approach the festive gathering, Guido feverishly moves his arms to warn the gathering who, misunderstanding the gesture, ecstatically address Guido with a 'Heil Hitler', which was originally prepared for the King. The leitmotif of the movie is thus disclosed: the Jew Guido drifts towards an unavoidable catastrophe. To be sure, Guido can avoid the barriers on his way, but the course (towards the final solution) cannot be changed. The Nazis will become his fate.

The opening scene ends rather pleasantly at a farm outside the town, where the charming Dora literally falls into Guido's arms as if she were sent from heaven. From this moment, Guido is obsessed with the desire to win her heart. He employs comic tricks. The logic of his tricks is Schopenhauer's will. Schopenhauer is mentioned for the first time just before Guido and Ferruccio, who have arrived in the town and been given a double bed by their uncle, start calming down. Asked how it is possible to fall asleep quickly, Guido says that Schopenhauer is the answer: 'I am what I want to be'. Like a hypnotizer, he attempts to make Ferruccio fall asleep: 'sleep, sleep, sleep ...' he whispers, while he waves his fingers over Ferruccio's head. Ferruccio says good night and falls asleep. Guido tries his technique a last time: 'wake up, wake up, wake up ...', and Ferruccio wakes up. Guido is surprised by the effect of his trick.

Guido needs his sense of humour and his Schopenhauerian tricks because Dora's object of choice is the local Party boss, no less. Luckily, Guido gets to be a servant at Dora's engagement party. The 'cheerful' conversation around the table is about children's calculating abilities (Dora is a teacher in the local primary school). The head teacher refers to a task, which she has come across in the teaching material: a mentally disabled person costs four marks a day, a crippled person four and a half, and an epileptic three and a half. Given that the average daily expense is four marks and that there are 300,000 patients, how much money would the state then save by eliminating these people? One cannot demand such a difficult task from seven-year-olds, the head teacher declares! They are, after all, not German children. Dora's future husband does not think the calculation is difficult and quickly multiplies 300,000 by four. Dora herself is shocked by the dry indifference demonstrated by her future husband, as are some of the other guests. So, when she sees her chance, she seeks contact with Guido and asks him to take her away. Guido comes to fetch her, riding his uncle's white horse, which is now painted green and covered with skulls, invectives and other indicators that it belongs to a Jew. But, as he often does, Guido turns the fascist harassment to his own advantage, and the two lovers ride off on his uncle's horse. Guido and Dora are happy and their son, Giosuè, is born.

Giosuè's growth is characterized by the protection provided by his parents on the one hand, and fascism on the other. Guido does much to protect him from the latter. For instance, Giosuè sees a shop sign that reads 'no entrance for dogs and Jews' and then asks his father: 'Dad, why are dogs and Jews not allowed to enter the shop?' And Guido answers: 'it is because, they don't like Jews and dogs, exactly in the same way as the ironmonger wouldn't like Spaniards and horses inside his shop and the pharmacist, Chinese and kangaroos'. 'But dad, with us, everybody is allowed to enter?' 'Yes', answers the father, and asks Giosuè what he does not like. 'Spiders', Giosuè says. Guido adds that he is himself not crazy about Visigoths. So they decide that when they open the shop next morning, they will hang a sign that forbids Visigoths and spiders to enter.

When, in the film, we arrive at the year 1945 the story takes an abrupt turn. On Giosuè's sixth birthday, Dora finds their house devastated. Her husband, son and Guido's uncle have disappeared. After a short while, she finds them at the local train station, from whence they are to be deported to a concentration camp in cattle wagons. She desperately tries to convince the authorities that there has been a mistake, but is then told that according to race laws, her husband and son are both Jewish. There is no mistake. When she cannot free them, she asks the authorities whether she could get on the train with them and, after a short hesitation, she is permitted to do so. The rest of the film is set in an unspecified concentration camp. Upon arrival the Jews are sorted. Guido's uncle is sent directly to the gas chamber because he is old; Dora is sent to the women's barracks, Guido and Giosuè to the men's barracks.

Again Guido tries to protect his son from the Nazi reality. To this end he has invented a story, in which he presents camp life for Giosuè as a competition with other children to win 1,000 points and thereby a tank. Guido has arranged everything, exactly as his father had done for him when he turned six. Giosuè, though, becomes increasingly sceptical, while Guido does his best to keep up the illusion, taking considerable risks. For instance, he volunteers to translate the camp regulations, which a soldier reads to the residents of the barrack. The three most important rules of the camp are that one must not attempt to escape, that all orders must be obeyed without question, and that riots are punished by hanging. In Guido's translation these three rules become that one loses all one's points if one cries, if one asks about one's mother, or asks for a snack.

Guido is aware of the seriousness of the situation and desires, like all other inmates, to escape. He sees his chance when he is asked to work as a servant at the camp commandant's dinner parties. Here he meets an old acquaintance, Dr Lessing. We met Dr Lessing for the first time in the film six years before, in the uncle's hotel, where Guido serves and where Lessing regularly eats, while he ponders riddles together with a friend of his. He often asks Guido for help. The intelligent and humoristic Guido charms Dr Lessing to the extent that the film hints at a friendship between the two. When we meet Dr Lessing for the second time in the camp he is working as a doctor, that is he inspects the new inmates and sorts them, often very quickly, through a 'glance selection'. Guido tries, in the brief moment when Dr Lessing checks him, to make him aware that he is Guido from the restaurant. The doctor at first does not remember him, but when Guido recites a riddle, he is immediately remembered. Guido can now avoid the showers. We then suspect that he becomes Lessing's 'favourite Jew', that a human being is hidden behind the SS officer, empathy behind racism, at least for one's former friends and acquaintances.

This is the necessary condition for the third and final meeting of Lessing and Guido. Guido now serves at the official dinners. He immediately understands his 'participation' in the dinner as Lessing's attempt to help him to escape. Guido therefore hides Giosuè among the German officers' children, who are busy eating sweets in the adjacent room. Lessing finally manages to talk to Guido without being seen. His only aim, however, turns out to be asking Guido for his help to solve a tortuous riddle. *He* needs Guido's help! Guido is paralysed. The contrast between the two life-worlds is further emphasized when Guido gets lost in the fog on the way back to his barracks and runs into a pile of dead bodies. Here we see the limits to his humour and his Schopenhauerian will. Now reality is revealed in all its horror and nakedness.

The final scene of the film shows the moment of liberation. The camp is slowly being emptied. Trucks take the inmates away and return empty. We understand from the conversation among the inmates that the Germans are liquidating all the inmates. Guido therefore hides Giosuè and, dressed as a woman, he goes to the women's barracks to look for Dora. She is however not there. On the way back, he is caught by a Nazi guard and killed. Shortly after, we see that the whole camp is deserted. Together with a few others, Giosuè comes out of his hiding place. We hear a rumbling, which becomes stronger and stronger, and finally an American tank rolls into the camp. Giosuè has won his tank. Together, they leave the camp. On the way out Giosuè catches a glimpse of his mother on a truck, and the film ends with their reunion. In the epilogue we learn that the narrator of the film is Giosuè; the film is a testimony to his father, who sacrificed himself to save him.

Holocaust as comedy

Life is Beautiful breaks many of the implicit rules regarding the representation of the Holocaust. Indeed, a special Holocaust etiquette seems to have evolved that prescribes a rigorous realism, under-toned artistic affects and a deep seriousness. 'A Holocaust conformism has arisen, along with a Holocaust sentimentalism, a Holocaust canon, and a system of Holocaust taboos together with the ceremonial discourse that goes with it; Holocaust products for Holocaust consumers have been developed' (Kertész 2001: 269). To use the Holocaust as a frame for a love story, which *Life is Beautiful* does, and go on to tell this story in the form of comedy was thus, for many, an unforgivable mistake. And, of course, every time an etiquette is transgressed, it causes public outcry. The criticism against *Life is Beautiful* can be grouped under three main points. First, it is criticized as misrepresenting camp life; second, its genre, comedy, is found improper; and lastly, its plot is described as unrealistic and unconvincing, even impossible, implying that it should have represented camp life as realistically and precisely as possible (Siporin 2002: 346). Let us now dwell on these three points.

According to some commentators, Benigni's film presents an idyllic camp. Art Spiegelman, for example, thinks the film banalizes the Holocaust (Celli 2000: 1). To be sure, the film does not include much violence and mass death is only hinted at (Tatara 1998). Many critiques emphasize that children were gassed immediately upon arrival at Auschwitz, and that those who escaped this fate in the first place were constantly humiliated. The camps were characterized by systematic degrading, torture and starvation (Flanzbaum 2001: 282). Thus, according to Teachout, who reviewed *Life is Beautiful*, 'it is no exaggeration to say that nothing that happens in *Life is Beautiful* could possibly have occurred in real life, and that the film consists of one historical distortion after another' (ibid.: 281). Likewise, Schickel complains that Benigni's lack of understanding of the terror that characterized the camps is the first step towards Holocaust denial (ibid.: 282). The coming generations will think that Benigni's fictive camp depicts camp life as it was (Celli 2000). Indeed, Schickel goes as far as accusing Benigni of fascism:

> The witnesses to the Holocaust – its living victims – inevitably grew fewer each year. The voices that would deny it ever took place remain strident. In this climate, turning even a small corner of this century's horror into feel-good entertainment is abhorrent. Sentimentality is a kind of fascism too.
>
> (quoted in Flanzbaum 2001: 281)

To counter this predictable form of critique in advance Benigni employed Marcello Pezzetti from the Jewish centre for documentation in Milan as a historical consultant and, before its premier, the film was shown to a group of Italian Jews who had survived the Holocaust (Ben-Ghiat 2001: 254). Further, Pezzetti claimed that in reality some children were indeed found in the camps after the inmates were emancipated; some were waiting to be gassed, and others were to be used in medical experiments (Celli 2000). One could also claim, as Haskins (2001) does, that the film is in fact a realistic depiction of camp life. Benigni's film cannot depict this horror; no doubt about that. After all, who could? However, Benigni is able to depict another aspect of camp life, namely the survival instinct, which consisted of building a protective shield against camp reality. Surviving the camp necessitates 'a benign form of Holocaust denial' (ibid.: 380).

> But does not this device of the 'game' correspond in an essential way to the lived reality of Auschwitz? One could smell the stench of burning human flesh, but still did not want to believe that all of this could be true. One would rather find some notion that might tempt one to survive, and a 'real tank' is, for a child, precisely this kind of seductive promise.
>
> (Kertész 2001: 271)

Benigni does not defend himself by stating that his film is realistic. Instead, he claims that the terror of the camp was so incomprehensible that nobody can depict it as it was. The most responsible solution was therefore to depict it indirectly through allegory or comedy (Viano 1999: 53). Lanzmann, whose own 'film' consisted of eight and a half hours of documentary material and interviews, is perhaps the most radical exponent of the realist approach. If this strategy is defended with reference to the danger of otherwise delivering material for Holocaust denial, then one should also ask whether the best weapon against this is not precisely to broaden the knowledge of the Holocaust. After all, is not a film like Benigni's better than no film or films nobody wants to see (Flanzbaum 2001: 282–3; Kertész 2001: 267)? Certainly, films like Lanzmann's *Shoah* do not have mass appeal. Furthermore, art that depicts the Holocaust is precisely art, not the thing itself (Flanzbaum 2001: 275; Trezise 2001: 47). We have enough testimonies and 'relics'; what we lack is pedagogical and experimental strategies that can frame the Holocaust as an active remembrance (Hartman 1996: 152).

The other main criticism against *Life is Beautiful* targets its form. The Holocaust was a tragedy; therefore, the form of comedy with its redeeming laughter is both improper and false. Genocide cannot be redeemed (Celli 2000: 3). It should be recalled here that Pezzetti was against the idea of letting Giosuè live, while Benigni felt that his death would give the film a tragic tone (ibid.). The most serious criticism that can be directed against Benigni's choice of genre is perhaps not the choice of comedy as a form but the use of the Holocaust as a frame for a love story. Benigni's primary interest was not to make a film on the Holocaust but to create a radical and challenging framework for his plot (Viano 1999: 51).

Pezzetti has defended *Life is Beautiful* by stating that the comical elements are limited to the first half of the film, after which Benigni respectfully lets the tragic form take over (Celli 2000). Laughter is then replaced by tears, optimism by fear. The use of humour in the first half aims to 'purify' the final part, thereby strengthening the tragic effect (Viano 1999: 55). Comedy may convey a tragic message (Žižek 2001c: 72). *Life is Beautiful*, claims Pezzetti, laughs not at the Holocaust, but directs the power of laughter against the destructive effect of the catastrophe (Viano 1999: 63). Comedy and laughter are enemies of the camp. The question is therefore which aspect of camp life one would like to depict: the Nazi attempt at dehumanization of the victims, or the victims' attempt to preserve their humanity or simply survive. Following this, one could claim that humour was the weapon of the inmates against their executioners. It helped them to preserve their humanity (Frankl 1984: 63; Appelfeld 1988: 85). In addition, comedy can also be seen as an attempt to re-establish a human universe after the Holocaust (Ezrahi 2001: 287). In this respect, Benigni expressed the idea that only laughter can save us (Viano 1999: 51).

Third, it is claimed that *Life is Beautiful* urges identification with Giosuè's point of view. Just as Guido tries to protect Giosuè against the camp, so does the film do the same with the audience (see Celli 2000: 3). When in the final scene Giosuè is saved by a tank, his imaginary world remains intact.

> *Life is Beautiful* is soothing and anodyne – a hopeful fable of redemption. It is also one of the most unconvincing and self-congratulatory movies ever made. … In the end, Benigni protects his audience as much as Guido protects his son; we are treated like children. … *Life is Beautiful* is a benign form of Holocaust denial. The audience comes away feeling relieved and happy and rewards Benigni for allowing it, a last, to escape.
>
> (Denby, in Haskins 2001: 375)

Bruno Bettelheim's reaction against Des Pres's (1980) contested work *The Survivor* is worth recalling here. 'It will be startling news to most survivors that they are "strong enough, mature enough, awake enough … to embrace life without reserve", since only a pitifully small number of those who entered the German camps survived. What about the millions who perished? Were they "awake enough ... to embrace life without reserve" as they were driven into the gas chambers?' (quoted in Agamben 1999: 93). Accordingly, the weakness of *Life is Beautiful* is its 'survivalism', or its assumption that survival depends on talents and skills.

In fact, it is not true that Guido's imaginary world is not shattered. On the way to his barracks from the officers' dinner, he mumbles in the fog: 'what if it is just a dream?' Shortly after, he runs into the dead bodies. What appears to be fog turns out to be the smoke from the crematorium (Viano 1999: 57). Even daydreaming does not allow him to escape the reality of the camp. Indeed, in this context it is relevant to discuss the character of Guido's fictive universe. His motto is, as mentioned before, 'I am what I want to be'. The same could be said about the Nazis, however. Benigni's merit is to show that the power of imagination can work in the service of both good and evil (Ben-Ghiat 2001: 254). Guido's reversal of Schopenhauer is interesting in this context. Schopenhauer counted, together with Nietzsche, as one of the favourite philosophers of the Nazis. Guido's Schopenhauer is of course simplified and naïve, but in no way seems further from the truth than the strongly revised and vulgarized Nazi version; one distortion versus another!

Guido's use of Schopenhauer is not a denial of the terrors of the camp. He is clearly aware that one cannot just become whoever one wants to be. Further, Guido is not in himself a comic person, but one who strategically makes use of humour and imagination. The condition for this is seriousness and a sense of reality. The fourth time Guido uses his Schopenhauerian trick is thus in a deadly serious situation, in which the Nazis' dogs sniff out Giosuè. We are here confronted not with a man who thinks he can form his world according to his wishes, but with a desperate father who hopes for a miracle. Perhaps the film is not so much about the ability to fictionalize but about the ability to have faith. Leslie Epstein wrote in the programme for the Jewish film festival in Boston, where Benigni's film was shown, that:

> [t]he war against the Jews was in many ways a war against the imagination (and at bottom the Jewish conception of God): to suppress the workings of that imagination to deny the sufferings of the Jews any sort of symbolic representation – would make that a war that Hitler had won.
>
> (Epstein, quoted in Viano 1999: 53)

The unspeakable

The debate over *Life is Beautiful* did not, of course, take place in a vacuum; it was strongly influenced by philosophical discussions of ethics and representation. Trezise counts three meanings of the 'unspeakable', which can sum up the debate on the uniqueness of the Holocaust. First, the unspeakable is what cannot be uttered, what cannot be understood and therefore cannot be represented. The Holocaust transgresses our categories and therefore no description can do it justice. The second meaning of the unspeakable emerges in terms of the dimensions and character of an evil act, e.g. the 'unspeakable evil' of Nazism. Finally, there is a third meaning, which takes the form of a prohibition against utterance or narration. In this sense, the unspeakable refers to something sacred or a taboo (Trezise 2001: 39).

Adorno's famous dictum 'To write poetry after Auschwitz is barbaric' and 'after Auschwitz one cannot write poetry', and even that 'all post-Auschwitz culture, including its urgent critique, is garbage' (1973: 367), is often utilized as an axis around which the discussion of the representation of the Holocaust revolves (Trezise 2001: 43). In an essay entitled 'Commitment', Adorno emphasizes that he wants to stick to his original wording and explains that it has two central meanings: first, every artistic representation of naked violence contains in itself the possibility of being in receipt of a desire to confront it. Following this, and second, any representation will invest meaning in what has no meaning. There is thus established an emancipating distance through which horror is relieved (ibid.: 44). 'The pleasure principle to upstage the pain principle' (Ezrahi 2001: 297). Hence, Lanzmann argues that strong affective reactions (e.g. laughter and crying) have a cathartic effect. One must avoid these and instead confront the Holocaust with 'dry eyes' (Flanzbaum 2001: 227). What is central here from our point of view is the question of distance. The ideal is presence. The catastrophe must be remembered as an ever present and haunting trauma. An undesired distance emerges when one adds something (Trezise 2001: 48–9).

However, when Agamben claims that the Holocaust is unspeakable, he does not do so with reference to aesthetics but to Arendt's and Primo Lévi's understandings of the Holocaust as an event that explodes the frame of any past evil (1999: 31–2). What horrified Arendt was the mass production of dead bodies. The Nazis did not kill, but eliminated the Jews. The camps were a radical manifestation of biopolitics. Whereas ordinary biopolitics targets the health of the population – as a kind of 'life politics' – the Nazi biopolitics aimed at the opposite. The Nazis not only wished to open up a *Lebensraum* for the Aryans, but also a *Todesraum* for the Jews and others.

The camps verified the Nazi politics, the essence of which was, in Goebbels's words, the art of making the impossible possible (ibid.: 77). As God created the world out of nothing, the Nazis created a world in the image of their power. The essence of Aryans was, as repeatedly emphasized by Rosenberg and Hitler, their creative power. They did not owe their existence to anybody else. The camps confirmed this imagery of self-referential sovereignty. A distorted understanding of self-interest could perhaps explain the will to kill the Jews, but not the systematic humiliation and torture. It was this lack of self-interest, regardless of how distorted it was, that distinguished the Nazis from other extremes like those in Cambodia or Hiroshima (ibid.: 31–2). The radical evil is radical precisely because it cannot be explained as being a consequence of a default or lack; it materializes as an evil will. Herein lies the reason why every rational explanation of the camps is necessarily mistaken. To see them as rational would be to understand them as a means for something else. On the contrary, the camps were an end in themselves and as such they materialized an unspeakable evil (Seeskin 1988: 110).

For Agamben, too, the Holocaust is unique in its dimensions and character (the second meaning of the unspeakable). Similarly, the Holocaust is the limit of the language and the speakable (the first meaning of the unspeakable). Agamben claims, for instance, that the unfortunate term Holocaust is an attempt to give meaning to something that has no meaning (1999: 31). He does not, however, accept that the Holocaust is a mystical event that contains a sacred aura (the third meaning of the unspeakable) (ibid.: 31–3). To say this would be to play the Nazis' own game. How can one avoid the apparently logical step from the first two understandings of the unspeakable to the third? The solution is to emphasize the aporetic character of testimony. We are urged to communicate that which is incommunicable.

> This is why those who assert the unsayability of Auschwitz today should be more cautious in their statements. If they mean to say that Auschwitz was a unique event in the face of which the witness must in some way submit his every word to the test of an impossibility of speaking, they are right. But if, joining uniqueness to unsayability, they transform Auschwitz into a reality absolutely separated from language, if they break the tie between an impossibility and a possibility of speaking that, in the Muselmann constitutes testimony, then they unconsciously repeat the Nazi's gesture; they are in secret solidarity with the *arcanum imperii*.
>
> (ibid.: 157)

Before focusing on the *Muselmann*'s testimony, let us here draw a parallel to Adorno's thought. What is central in Adorno's dictum and more generally in his negative dialectics is a dialectic tension between aesthetics and ethics. This tension does not allow for redemption. Literature is, on the one hand, a waste, rubbish, something that brings with it enjoyment and moral well-being, which is why it is impossible to unite it with a universe after the Holocaust. But on the other hand, it is exactly the survivors' suffering that demands the sustained existence of the very art it forbids (Trezise 2001: 50). To demand the art that it prohibits is the aporia of the Holocaust, which is a problematic that could be displaced onto the relation between naked life and testimonial memory. A similar aporia is taking form here.

The *Muselmann*

The *Muselmann* is often described as a worthless being who lacks the ability to distinguish good and evil, noble and base. This condition was primarily defined physically as a consequence of the malnutrition, stress and cold that reduced the *Muselmann* to a mere bodily existence (Agamben 1999: 42–3). Hence, the *Muselmann* had only one aim: survival. Even worse, he did not even register the guardians' physical violence and only occasionally protected himself. The *Muselmann* had no sense of a self; like an autistic child, he pulled himself into his own delirium and fantasy world (ibid.: 46). The *Muselmann* reminds us above all of a walking corpse (ibid.: 41). The term *Muselmann* originates in Auschwitz and alludes to the Muslims bending forward in prayer (ibid.). In Majdanek the term in use was 'donkeys', in Dachau 'cretins', in Stutthof 'cripples', in Mauthausen 'swimmers', in Neuengamme 'camels' and in Buchenwald 'tired sheikhs' (ibid.: 44). In addition, it is worth recalling Primo Lévi's telling term here: 'the drowned'.

The *Muselmann* was the product of an absolute power. As is well known from Hegel's master–slave dialectic, death is the limit of power. When the slave dies, the master's power over him disappears too. By reducing the inmates to *Muselmänner*, however, the Nazis delimited a space between life and death and thereby continued their exercise of power over the Jews even in death. They robbed the *Muselmann* of his death (ibid.: 48). The camps were thus in a sense the epitome of dehumanization. The Nazis did not call the inmates by their names but tattooed a number on their skins (Appelfeld 1988: 83). This extreme dehumanization culminated in the killing of the Jews. Nobody died in his or her own name in the camps (Agamben 1999: 104). Nobody died as individuals but as parts of an industrial production of corpses. They died, in other words, as numbers.

It is this aspect that gives Auschwitz a special status and defines the character of its horror (ibid.: 72). Death has always been thought of as a limit, as a figure of nothingness against the background of which the finite, life itself, finds meaning. The Nazis appropriated this limit, reducing the infinite to the finite, or, in other words, turned the exception into the rule. Death was no longer something distant, an external limit, but the condition in which the *Muselmann* lived. Against this background, we can also understand the reason why the inmates of the concentration camps distanced themselves from *Muselmänner*. One avoided them, because in their eyes one saw one's own coming death (ibid.: 45, 52).

Almost regardless of how the *Muselmann* is described, it is not possible for him to attain a distance from himself. To kill one*self* requires precisely a self, which is what the *Muselmänner* lacked. Autonomy, self-determination and freedom necessitate a reflexive distance to oneself. Likewise, conscience entails that one can relate to one's self as if it were somebody else. Agamben uses the concept of shame to describe this relationship. What is central here is not the subject of shame, but its object. What is it that which we are ashamed of? The answer is: our nakedness. We are ashamed of those acts from which we can establish no distance.

What one is ashamed of is something that cannot be appropriated and this something is the nakedness of the subject. Shame does not originate from a consciousness of a lack from which one attempts to distance oneself. One is ashamed of not being able to escape oneself. More technically, shame is produced when the subject acts as a subject for his own de-subjectivation. Here one might recall Sophie in *Sophie's Choice*. She is forced by the guards of the camp to choose between her two children – one will survive, the other will be sent to the gas chambers. She is forced to choose. And even though it is a forced choice, it is one that, because she is actively acting, produces shame. Shame is thus not a feeling but a condition of being (ibid.: 104–6). One can live in shame – and certainly all in the camp did. Those who did not hit bottom avoided this fate by stealing from other inmates or by working in the *Sonderkommando* or by taking on policing functions in the camps (ibid.: 24). It was impossible to preserve one's dignity (ibid.: 60). We mentioned earlier that nobody died in their own name. It must be added that nor was there anybody who survived in their own name. They survived because others died instead of them (ibid.: 104).

Shame, however, has both an active and a purely receptive pole. The *Muselmann* incarnates the first and the person who bears testimony the other (ibid.: 111). What is significant is the relationship between these two poles. Testimony as the appropriation of something that cannot be appropriated is exactly such a relation. Agamben seeks to identify this relationship through a series of concepts such as auto-affection, immanence and the existence of the grammatical 'I'. This 'I' has no substance in itself. It is merely the link between a series of utterances. As such, the grammatical 'I' refers to the same nakedness that the *Muselmann* incarnates (ibid.: 116). The 'grammatical I' marks a non-being, which is the condition of all being. We started with the nakedness of the *Muselmann* and now end up with this nakedness as the fundament of every speaking subject. Testimony emerges at the point at which the mute gives the speaking subject a voice, and the speaking subject bears testimony to the impossibility of speaking with one's own voice (bears testimony to that which cannot be communicated and represented) (ibid.: 120). It is only because we all share in common the fundamental nakedness of the *Muselmann*, because human life is precarious and vulnerable, that we can bear testimony to the *Muselmann*. 'The witness' survival of the inhuman is a function of the *Muselmann* survival of the human. What can be infinitely destroyed is what can infinitely survive' (ibid.: 151).

Lévi repeatedly emphasized that those who survived were not the real witnesses. The *Muselmann* would have been a real witness. But those who have seen the *Gorgon* either did not come back or came back without the ability to witness. The survivor is the exception, the drowned the rule (ibid.: 33). Therefore, meaningful remembrance must relate itself to the fundamental nakedness of the subject, and thus always take place per delegatation.

At first it appears that it is the human, the survivor, who bears witness to the inhuman, the Muselmann. But if the survivor bears witness for the Muselmann – in the technical sense of 'on behalf of' or 'by proxy' ('we speak in their stead, by proxy') – then according to the legal principle by which the acts of the delegated are imputed to the delegant, it is in some way the Muselmann who bears witness.

(ibid.: 120)

Testimony does not guarantee the factual truthfulness of a given utterance and thus does not enable a definitive historical archivation. The Holocaust is that which resists being archived for it escapes both the appropriating memory and the willed forgetting (ibid.: 158). But how can we then keep alive the aporia, the tension between speech and naked life, between the traumatized testimony and the appropriating forgetfulness, and thus 'mediate' between the past and the present? How can one represent the impossibility of depicting horror?

The riddle of the Holocaust

As we have seen before, many critics think that Benigni misused the Holocaust for his own comical ambitions. What they overlook, however, is that the film refers to a series of riddles that strengthens the descriptions in the film and thus marks the existence of a horrific reality that can only be depicted indirectly. Let us discuss the four allegorical riddles that appear in the film.

The first one is: 'the bigger it is, the less one sees', and the answer is 'darkness'. Darkness is here a metaphor for fascism and Nazism as well as cynicism and hate (Siporin 2002: 349). The more one hates, the less one will experience the other, who no longer appears as a singular and vulnerable being. Fascism and Nazism darkened the souls of its supporters and blinded them. It is Lessing who gives Guido the riddle, and the riddle is more than anything else a key to understanding his personality. When Lessing meets Guido in the camp, he is morally blind to Guido's situation. For Benigni, Lessing incarnates the evil of Nazism.

Indeed, apropos Arendt's (1992) discussion of Adolf Eichmann, one could claim that Lessing stands for the banality of the evil. Both Eichmann and Lessing perceive their activities as part of a normal job. And in both cases, the relationship between the executioner and the victim is reversed. As Lessing is tortured by his riddles, Eichmann was pained by his lack of promotion and loss of pleasure in his work. Just like Eichmann, Lessing has isolated himself from the world and thus dehumanized himself. For both, there exists a sharp distinction between the private and the public realm, and their empathy does not reach outside the private sphere. The one who is a friend in the private sphere is reduced to an ideological stereotype when encountered in the public sphere: to a Jew, an inmate or a subhuman being. Dr Lessing is banal exactly in the same way as is Eichmann. Neither of them thinks, that is reflects on their acts morally. One does not need to be a psychopath to function in the service of evil. A lack of thinking and callousness will do. The first riddle condenses this terrifying message.

The second riddle is the only one told by Guido and is therefore not surrounded by the same darkness as Lessing's riddles. 'Snow White among the dwarfs. Solve this riddle, genius, in the time that the solution gives you (in seven seconds; among seven small ones)'. The answer is already given in the formulation of the riddle. The Italian word 'second' is ambivalent and means both second (time unit) and small (a reference to the dwarfs' height). Central here is not the latent content of the riddle; it does not have any. It must be understood precisely as that which it is, as part of an innocent children's game. It expresses joy over life and optimism (Siporin 2002: 350). It is significant for Benigni that there is room for hope, humour and redemption amidst the terror of the camp. Even more significantly, it is *after* the Holocaust that room is made for these abilities that are symbolized by children's games.

The third riddle is posed by Lessing to Guido while he serves him in the restaurant: 'If you say my name. I'm no longer there, who am I?' The answer is 'silence'. To call somebody a Jew was during the Holocaust to eliminate them (ibid.: 351). Siporin suggests a further plausible interpretation. Silence also refers to the lack of protest or resistance against the deportation of the Jews, which was characteristic of the Italian population. The riddle is repeated by Guido when he tries to contact Dr Lessing during the selection process. He examines their bodily structures, their hands, feet and eyes. It all takes place very quickly, and Guido's examination is almost over before he notices its beginning. Lessing whispers after every examination his judgement to a nurse, who notes down whether the person in question is to be gassed or not. Lessing does not recognize Guido, which is why Guido reiterates Lessing's riddle. The nurse shouts resolutely: 'silence!' and thus answers the riddle without knowing it herself. Here the riddle is explicitly linked to disappearance or elimination. Lessing's verdict when it does not favour the inmates is a death sentence. What is left after the final solution is a massive silence.

The fourth riddle is perhaps the most interesting one: 'Fat, fat, ugly, ugly. All yellow in truth. If you ask me where I am. I tell you "quack, quack, quack!" While walking I defecate. Who I am, tell me a little.' In contrast to the previous three riddles, there is given no answer to this one. Or rather, Lessing explains that the answer is not a duck. The riddle is without a solution. It is asked of Guido by Lessing during the officers' dinner in the camp, and it is implied that Lessing will help Guido if Guido helps him with the riddle. Benigni himself has explained the riddle as pure nonsense, which emerges when Guido expects a rational and emphatic act from Lessing (Celli 2000). The riddle blocks Guido's escape. It 'prevents' Lessing from experiencing Guido for what he is, a human being in need. The riddle is a 'neck-riddle', one whose solution is a question of life and death. The best examples are perhaps Samson in the Bible and the riddle fight in Tolkien's *The Hobbit*. Guido cannot solve Lessing's riddle and is shot dead (Siporin 2002: 357). The riddle is, to use Falassi and Ben-Amos's concept, an 'anti-riddle', a riddle that does not contain the possibility of an objectively correct answer. Either the rule that riddles ought to have only one correct answer is violated or, alternatively, the correct answer is not verified (for instance the 'duck' above). Siporin understands this as a metaphorical expression of a situation in which civilization disappears. The Nazis transgressed all norms. They did not play according to the rules. The Holocaust is a riddle beyond comprehension and understanding (ibid.: 357). As Lévi said apropos the Holocaust: 'I find no solution to the riddle. I seek, but I do not find it' (quoted in ibid.: 345).

Post-remembrance

We have mentioned several types of critique that could be levelled against Benigni's film, all of which are essentially variations on the same theme, namely that the film misrepresents the Holocaust. However, we can move beyond this critique, which is mistaken already in its assumptions. The Holocaust cannot be represented in all its horror and all its essence for this essence consists precisely in rendering testimony impossible. Following this, the smoke in the beginning and the end of the film (and the corresponding 'fog' scene in between) does not express a defensive distance towards the Holocaust, but rather the recognition that the horror of the camp can be depicted only indirectly. *Life is Beautiful* seeks to represent the impossibility of representing the Holocaust.

This structure is mirrored in the narrative of the film. Just like the fog represents the impossibility of representation, the final scene reveals that the narrator of the film is Giosuè, and that his narration is an attempt to remember his father, who sacrificed himself for him (Ben-Ghiat 2001: 255). Benigni himself says that the film is to a certain extent autobiographical. Benigni's father, Luigi Benigni, spent two years in a German labour camp after the end of the alliance between Germany and Italy. When he told his children about the camp after the war, he always tried to protect them from knowledge of the real horror of the camp. His stories were not painful accounts of the camp but marked by humour and anecdotes (ibid.: 255). *Life is Beautiful* repeats his gesture.

Further, the film is Benigni's attempt to fill the holes he sensed in his father's account of the camps. In the same way as Benigni reflects over his father's fate, Giosuè reflects over his own father's life. Such remembrance, which does not claim the authenticity of the testimony, is vulnerable to criticism. But Kertész is fully justified when he writes: 'I notice that Benigni, the creator of the film, was born in 1952. He is the representative of a new generation that is wrestling with the *ghost of Auschwitz*, and has the courage (and also the strength) to lay claim to this sad inheritance' (Kertész 2001: 272, our italics). It is as if there exists a mystical and invisible bond between Benigni and Auschwitz. Agamben aspires to precisely such a bond when he speaks of 'remnants' of Auschwitz. 'Remnant' is a messianic concept that expresses that which cannot be destroyed, a residue of the past that refuses to disappear. Or, in Kertész's words: 'the ghost of Auschwitz'. The word remnant appears in the biblical narrative of Isaiah as *shear yisrael* (bearer of Israel's spirit) and Amos as *sherit Yousef* (bearer of Joseph's spirit) (Agamben 1999: 162). The parallel to the relation between *Muselmann* and the survivor, between the drowned and the saved, is thus obvious.

> In the concept of remnant, the aporia of testimony coincides with the aporia of messianism. Just as the remnant of Israel signifies neither the whole people nor a part of the people but, rather, the non-coincidence of the whole and the part, and just as messianic time is neither historical time nor eternity but, rather, the disjunction that divides them, so the remnants of Auschwitz – the witnesses – are neither the dead nor the survivors, neither the drowned nor the saved. They are what remains between them.
>
> (ibid.: 163–4)

'The ghost of Auschwitz' is thus neither incarnated in those who died in the gas chambers, nor in those who survived, but in the bond that exists between them. It is in this context central that Guido's name stems from the Italian 'guidare', to guide. Guido guides Giosuè out of the camp; leads him towards redemption. Giosuè thus becomes the bearer of 'the ghost of Auschwitz'. He bears testimony to the father's, to Guido's, acts. Giosuè is in the biblical context the one who guides the Jews to the Promised Land. Moreover, Giosuè's nickname Joshua refers to the biblical leader who saved the Jews from extinction by leading them through the desert (Viano 1999: 60). But neither Benigni nor Agamben stops here. For them we are all descendants of Auschwitz. And we are all obliged to bear testimony.

Afterword
Aesthetics against postpolitics

In an interesting article, Davis shows that the term 'ground zero' was put into use, long before 9/11, to single out the epicentre of the first atomic bomb to be able to measure its power and effects (2003: 127). In a sense, therefore, it is perfectly possible to make an ethical link between Hiroshima and 9/11 – does the latter not, after all, signify the uncanny return of the repressed in the American psyche? In other words, ground zero could have paved the way for a fundamentally ethical recognition, for, to paraphrase Derrida, our unconditional compassion for the victims does not and should not prevent us from acknowledging that regarding 9/11 nobody is politically guiltless (Derrida 2001). Has the 9/11 attack become the Holocaust of our age – a traumatic act that is elevated to the position of a sacred and sublime event beyond reflection and critique? And can cinema play a role in reopening the space of reflection?

When speaking about Hiroshima and the American psyche we are hinting at a kind of religiousness, which takes the acknowledgement of guilt and sin as its point of departure, not as certainty and absolutes but rather fear and trembling, if we are to use Kierkegaard's terms. Why has such an attitude not developed; why this closure and lack of ethical reflection? Apropos Hiroshima, the answer could be that

> we have learned to recite, by route, what has now become a national article of faith: that the bombings of Hiroshima and Nagasaki were justified, almost idealistic acts, undertaken with reluctance, as 'the least abhorrent choice' but finally the only way to end the war, thereby saving perhaps a million lives. This explanation was first articulated in an article ghost-written for Secretary of State Henry Stimson by his aide McGeorge Bundy. It is a pretty story, the only problem being Bundy's admission in a book published shortly before his death that the entire thing was a fabrication, a deliberate myth, carefully constructed after the fact to disguise the actual reason why we dropped the bomb: (1) to avenge Pearl Harbor, (2) to justify the amount of money spent developing the bomb, (3) to create laboratories so that our scientific, medical, and military personnel could

study the affects of the bomb, and (4) to impress the Russians and the rest
of the world with this opening salvo in the Cold War.

(Davis 2003: 128)

This story was the perfect cover-up. Because it verges on a securitized and
quasi-religious logic according to which purity, innocence and good intensions
are safely on our side. We have it all here including the idea of vanguardism
and the willingness to accept a huge cost to save a cherished good – what
are the innocent victims of two Japanese towns compared to the lives of
millions? Moreover, we have the idea of the radical act as a desperate last
resort. The willingness to carry out a monstrous act is even a proof of the
strength of our faith. True idealists are those for whom their dignity and
moral worth is second to the cause for which they are fighting. But the
whole plot could also be seen as a cynical strategy using these ideas to create
support for acts which might otherwise be subject to moral condemnation.
Might this also be the script for American foreign policy after 9/11? Do
the wars against Afghanistan and Iraq hide motives which are just as suspect as those informing the bombs that fell on Hiroshima and Nagasaki?
Suffice it to emphasize here that such hermeneutics of suspicion seem increasingly difficult to exercise in today's political climate characterized by a clash
of fundamentalisms: on the one hand religious fundamentalism and on the
other Bush's self-assured rhetoric. What both fundamentalisms silence is
the voice of those who advocate for a culture of self-doubt and critique (see
Bernstein 2005). But why has ours become a society that cannot question
itself?

Boltanski's *Distant Suffering* (1999) emphasizes that the relationship
between morality and suffering is a political problem, a problem of action.
Watching the suffering in Afghanistan and Iraq, the Westerners can be shocked
but this does not need to have a consequence; the spectator may still refuse
commitment. Considering that people can only consume a certain amount
of horror at a time and that indifference to distant others is an easy option
in a 'war', commitment at a distance has a weak chance (see ibid.: 10). If it
takes place, however, there are two common forms of commitment: denunciation (e.g. finding indignation by denouncing the perpetrators of the horror)
or sentimentalism (ibid.: 132). But there is a third kind of commitment, by
which one dares to cast eyes on the unfortunate and look at the evil without
the imaginary benefits of denunciation and sentimentalism. This form of commitment, related to trust in the power of speech, is the only realistic basis for
political action informed by morality. Pity can be a political issue only through
engagement (ibid.: 186). Hence the contemporary crisis of pity in the shadow
of fundamentalisms:

> That is the true meaning of Hiroshima. Ground-zero haunts us not because
> we feel guilt about it but because we don't. Which is why, whenever we
> are traumatized, we repeat the psychological operation we perfected in

Hiroshima in a progressive self-reification that we remain powerless to reverse as long as we refuse to internalize what actually happened on 8-6-45.

(Davis 2003: 130)

Against this background there are several reasons for turning to an analysis of film. Thinking about this kind of terror is, as Weber claims, 'almost impossible without thinking about film' (2006: 3). The strategic alliance formed between Hollywood and the Pentagon shortly after 9/11 is also telling in this respect. In this, Hollywood filmmakers were encouraged both to brainstorm about future terror scenarios and to make patriotic films (Žižek 2002:16). However, we did not want to produce yet another book on 9/11 or films about it. In fact, it is by using films released before 9/11 that our analyses gain their resonance; it is their 'non-contemporariness' that allows for an allegorical reading. Allegory is, in today's political climate, one of the most effective tools to do critical sociology. It allows one to distance oneself from one's present predicament and reflect upon it.

Further, art and the political can be activated against the present postpolitical constellation, in which everything is subjected to critique but critique ceases to have consequence. Hence the major focus on the concept of critique in this book. In Bauman's formulation, politics is 'the ongoing critique of reality' (Bauman 2002: 56). Politics is politicization. Yet ours is a postpolitical age, in which politics is becoming increasingly difficult. As an ambiguous concept, postpolitics designates a political way of emptying out the political and interestingly in this respect it resembles Althusser's notion of ideology. Postpolitics is a depolitized politics that hides the fundamental antagonisms in society. It takes two major forms. It is either ideological blackmail imposing a forced choice, e.g. a choice between fundamentalism and the politics of security (see also Žižek 2002: 3). The other major form is closely related to a 'hospitality to critique'. Critique is accepted but reduced to something without consequence, to something that can only lead to pragmatic negotiations and strategic compromises. In both cases, politics in the sense of a radical questioning of the social disappears.

In the postpolitical condition the aesthetic and the political share in common an interest in influencing the way people perceive the world, a transformative capacity enabled through critique. In this respect, the cinematic apparatus is an important site of ideological struggle. Today, while avant-garde art has to a large extent lost its critical edge and its shock value, mainstream films consumed by many are increasingly becoming an arena for critique.

Political statements and literary locutions produce effects in reality. They define models of speech or action but also regimes of sensible intensity. They draft maps of the visible, trajectories between the visible and the sayable, relationships between modes of being, modes of saying, and modes of doing and making. They define variations of sensible intensity, perceptions, and the abilities of bodies. They thereby take hold of unspecified groups of people, they widen gaps, open up space for deviations, modify the speeds, the trajectories, and the ways in which groups of people adhere to a condition, react to situations, recognize their image.

(Rancière 2004: 39)

Cinema is much more than reflections of a reality. Rather, it offers alternative ways of being in the world, opening up the social to change, modifying its conditions of transformations, the speed of transformations. Cinema is an Event. Or better, it might become so through a critical reading that releases its critical potential.

Let us now, to end with, turn to a mainstream film, Roland Emmerich's *Independence Day* (1996), which might condense the kind of ethical and critical attitude we are advocating. If anything *Independence Day* is *the* film on 9/11. The earth is attacked by hostile powers from outer space. The gigantic spaceship approaching the earth is an evil empire inhabited by aliens/nomads, who move from planet to planet and exploit their resources. They are prepared to annihilate human beings to realize their aim. The attack is initiated in a series of big cities, and the American Army quickly and resolutely counter-attacks the spaceship. However, protected by an electro-magnetic shield, the alien ship turns out to be indestructible. The rescuer is a scientist (David), who discovers a strange signal emanating from the spaceship. It turns out to be a counting-down mechanism. Time to attack comes, and Washington is the target. The residents of the White House are evacuated to an underground military bunker. It turns out that the bunker contains a research centre for outer space. It includes a UFO that had crashed in an American desert. All of which had naturally been top secret before the aliens' arrival. Meanwhile, David's father happens to warn him against catching a cold when he sees him sitting on the floor. This of course triggers the redeeming idea: the virus. David develops a virus that can penetrate the protective shield of the spaceships. If this works, that is if their protective shield can be destroyed, the aliens can also be attacked with conventional weapons. The plan is to contaminate the alien's network with the virus. Having no choice, the president accepts the plan and contacts the other nations which without hesitation 'unite' against the enemy.

The film seems to have anticipated the American reaction to September 11. Evil alien powers attack the house of God and their actions are totally unexplainable. The film never attributes to the aliens a depth in the form of an insight, ability, motives or emotions. Further, they are invincible; their networked weaponry is infinitely superior to what is available on earth. The only choice: us or them, the Good or the Evil. As the sublime incarnation of humanity the USA gathers a world-encompassing alliance for the war against the enemy. Such a reading, however, is slightly boring and, what is worse, reifying. It is much more interesting to play with the basic assumption of the film, that it is narrated from an American perspective. What if we saw the hostile spaceship as a metaphorical description of a global American empire, which suffocates the local life forms in consumerism and indifference? Is it so clean-cut a matter to decide what the Good and the Evil consist of?

We deliberately excluded a point in our narration of the plot. After the protective shield of the alien ship is penetrated, there emerges an intense battle between American fighter-planes and the aliens. Towards the end of the film every American fighter has been shot down or has no missiles left, except one. When the last fighter is to fire its missiles, it turns out that the missiles cannot be detonated. Then its pilot chooses to lead the fighter against the target, transforming his plane into a missile and himself into a suicide attacker. What if the 9/11 pilots conceived of their acts as such a heroic gesture whose aim was to destroy the empire of the evil? The movie condenses the self-conception of the terrorists.

Needless to say, the point of such a dialectic reversal is not to make excuses for terrorism. Terrorism is not only violence; it is the enemy of democracy. It is therefore central also to insist that the Western tradition is a tradition for democracy and criticism. Rather than undermining democracy in the war against terrorism we must support it; and rather than keeping away from criticizing Bush's international policies in the name of patriotism and unity of the nation, we must criticize it mercilessly (see Kellner 2002: 154–5). Indeed, 'independence' could refer to independence in classical Kantian sense, namely as *selbstdenken*: independent thinking.

References

Adorno, Theodor W. (1973) *Negative Dialectics*. New York: Continuum.

Agamben, Giorgio (1993) *Infancy and History. Essays on the Destruction of Experience*. London: Verso.

Agamben, Giorgio (1998) *Homo Sacer. Sovereign Power and Bare Life*. Stanford, CA: Stanford University Press.

Agamben, Giorgio (1999) *Remnants of Auschwitz. The Witness and the Archive*. New York: Zone Books.

Agamben, Giorgio (2000) *Means Without End. Notes on Politics*. Minneapolis: University of Minnesota Press.

Althusser, Louis (1984) *Essays on Ideology*. London: Verso.

Appelfeld, Aharon (1988) 'After the Holocaust', in Berel Lang (ed.) *Writing and the Holocaust*. New York: Holmes & Meier, pp. 83–92.

Arendt, Hannah (1973) *The Origins of Totalitarianism*. New York: Harcourt Brace.

Arendt, Hannah (1978) *The Life of Mind*. San Diego, CA: Harcourt Brace.

Arendt, Hannah (1992) *Eichmann in Jerusalem – A Report on the Banality of Evil*. London: Penguin.

Aries, Philippe (1962) *Centuries of Childhood: A Social History of Family Life*. New York: Vintage.

Badiou, Alain (2005) *Infinite Thought*. London: Continuum.

Bataille, Georges (1993) *The Accursed Share*, vols II and III. New York: Zone Books.

Bataille, Georges (1997a) 'Programme (Relative to Acéphale)', in Fred Botting and Scott Wilson (eds) *The Bataille Reader*. London: Blackwell, pp. 121–2.

Bataille, Georges (1997b) 'The Psychological Structure of Fascism', in Fred Botting and Scott Wilson (eds) *The Bataille Reader*. London: Blackwell, pp. 122–46.

Bataille, Georges (2001) *Eroticism*. London: Penguin.

Baudrillard, Jean (1990) *Fatal Strategies*. Paris: Semiotext(e)/Pluto.

Baudrillard, Jean (1994) *Simulacra and Simulation*. Ann Arbor: University of Michigan Press.

Baudrillard, Jean (2005) *The Intelligence of Evil or the Lucidity Pact*. Oxford: Berg.

Baudry, Jean-Louis (1974) 'Ideological Effects of the Basic Cinematic Apparatus', *Film Quarterly* 28(2): 39–47.

Bauman, Zygmunt (1993) *Postmodern Ethics*. Oxford: Blackwell.

Bauman, Zygmunt (2000) *Liquid Modernity*. Cambridge: Polity Press.

Bauman, Zygmunt (2002) *Society Under Siege*. Cambridge: Polity Press.

Bauman, Zygmunt (2003) *Liquid Love*. Cambridge: Polity Press.

Beck, Ulrich (1993) *Risk Society*. London: Sage.

Ben-Ghiat, Ruth (2001) 'The Secret Histories of Roberto Benigni's *Life is Beautiful*', *The Yale Journal of Criticism* 14(1): 253–66.

Benigni, Roberto (dir.) (1997) *Life is Beautiful*. Buena Vista Home Entertainment.

Benigni, Roberto and Vincenzo Cerami (1999) *Life is Beautiful*. London: Faber & Faber.

Benjamin, Walter (1992) *Illuminations*. Fulham: Fontana Press.

Bennington, Geoffrey (1994) *Legislations. The Politics of Deconstruction*. London: Verso.

Bernstein, Richard J. (2005) *The Abuse of Evil. The Corruption of Politics and Religion since 9/11*. London: Polity Press.

Betts, Christopher J. (1973) 'Introduction', in Charles de Secondat Montesquieu, *Persian Letters*. London: Penguin, pp. 17–33.

Bhabha, Homi (1972) 'The Other Question', *Screen* 24(6): 18–36.

Boer, Inge E. (1996) 'Despotism from Under the Veil: Masculine and Feminine Readings of the Despot and the Harem', *Cultural Critique* 32(1): 43–73.

Boltanski, Luc (1999) *Distant Suffering. Morality, Media and Politics*. Cambridge: Cambridge University Press.

Boltanski, Luc and Chiapello, Ève (1999) *Le nouvel esprit du capitalisme*. Paris: Gallimard.

Boltanski, Luc and Thévenot, Laurent (1999) 'The Sociology of Critical Capacity', *European Journal of Social Theory* 2(3): 359–77.

Bourdieu, Pierre (1982) *Leçon sur la leçon*. Paris: Éditions de Minuit.

Bourdieu, Pierre (1990) *In Other Words. Essays Towards a Reflexive Sociology*. Stanford, CA: Stanford University Press.

Bourdieu, Pierre (1992) *Les règles de l'art. Genèse et structure du champ littéraire*. Paris: Seuil.

Bourdieu, Pierre (1994) *Raisons pratiques. Sur la théorie de l'action*. Paris: Seuil.

Bourdieu, Pierre and Wacquant, Loïc J.D. (1992) 'The Purpose of Reflexive Sociology', in Pierre Bourdieu and Loïc J.D. Wacquant, *An Invitation to Reflexive Sociology*. Cambridge: Polity Press, pp. 61–216.

Brians, Paul (1998) 'Plato: The Allegory of the Cave, from *The Republic*', http://www.wsu.edu:8080/~wldciv/world_civ_reader/world_civ_reader_1/plato.html

Brigham, Linda (1999) 'Taking it IS Dishing it Out: The Late Modern Logic of Fight Club', in *ebr*, http://www.altx.com/ebr/reviews/rev10/r10bri.htm

Brown, Michelle (2005) '"Setting the Conditions" for Abu Ghraib: The Prison Nation Abroad', *American Quarterly* 53(3): 973–97.

Burton, C. Emory (1988) 'Sociology and the Feature Film', *Teaching Sociology* 16: 263–71.

Çaglar, Ayse (1995) 'German Turks in Berlin: Social Exclusion and Strategies for Social Mobility', *New Community* 21(3): 309–23.

Caldeira, Teresa P.R. (2000) *City of Walls. Crime, Segregation, and Citizenship in Sao Paulo*. London: Routledge.

Callinicos, Alex (1982) *Is There a Future for Marxism?* London: Macmillan.

Canetti, Elias (1962) *Crowds and Power*. London: Phoenix.

Castells, Manuel (1996) *The Information Age. Vol. I: The Rise of Network Society*. Oxford: Blackwell.

Celli, Carlo (2000) 'The Representation of Evil in Roberto Benigni's *Life is Beautiful*', *Journal of Popular Film and Television* 28(2): 74–9.

CNN (1999) 'CNN Chat Transcript "Fight Club" Author Chuck Palahniuk', http://www.joblo.com/fightclubchat.htm

Cohen, Stanley (2005) 'Post-Moral Torture: From Guantanamo to Abu Ghraib', *Index on Censorship* 1: 24–30.

Comolli, Jean-Louis and Narboni, Jean (1980) 'Cinema/Ideology/Criticism', in Ellis, John (ed.) *Screen Reader 1. Cinema/Ideology/Politics*. London: Society for Education in Film and Television, pp. 477–88.

Connolly, William E. (2005) *Pluralism*. Durham, NC: Duke University Press.

Cowen, David S. (1998) 'Frequently Asked Questions', http://www.trond.com/brazil/b_faq00.html

Danner, Mark (2004) *Torture and Truth. America, Abu Ghraib, and the War on Terror*. London: Granta.

Davis, Walter A. (2003) 'Death's Dream Kingdom: The American Psyche After 9-11', *JPCS: Journal for the Psychoanalysis of Culture & Society* 8(1): 128–32.

Davis, Walter A. (2005) 'Passion of the Christ in Abu Ghraib: Toward a New Theory of Ideology', *Socialism and Democracy* 19(1): 67–93.

Day, Gail (1999) 'Allegory: Between Deconstruction and Dialectics', *Oxford Art Journal* 22(1): 103–18.

Dayan, Daniel (1976) 'The Tutor-Code of Classical Cinema', in Bill Nichols (ed.) *Movies and Methods*, vol. 1. Berkeley: University of California Press, pp. 438–51.

Deleuze, Gilles (1989) *Cinema 2. The Time-Image*. London: Athlone Press.

Deleuze, Gilles (1993) *The Fold. Leibniz and the Baroque*. Minneapolis: University of Minnesota Press.

Deleuze, Gilles (1994) *Difference and Repetition*. London: Athlone Press.

Deleuze, Gilles (1995) *Negotiations*. New York: Columbia University Press.

Deleuze, Gilles (2004) 'Desert Islands', in Gilles Deleuze, *Desert Islands and Other Texts 1953–1974*. Los Angeles, CA: Semiotext(e), pp. 9–14.

Deleuze, Gilles and Guattari, Felix (1983) *Anti-Oedipus. Capitalism and Schizophrenia I*. Minneapolis: University of Minnesota Press.

Deleuze, Gilles and Guattari, Felix (1987) *A Thousand Plateaus. Capitalism and Schizophrenia II*. Minneapolis: University of Minnesota Press.

Demerath III, N.J. (1981) 'Through a Double-Crossed Eye. Sociology and the Movies', *Teaching Sociology* 9(1): 69–82.

Denzin, Norman K. (1995) *The Cinematic Society. The Voyeur's Gaze*. London: Sage.

Derrida, Jacques (1986a) *Glas*. Lincoln: University of Nebraska Press.

Derrida, Jacques (1986b) *Margins of Philosophy*. Chicago, IL: University of Chicago Press and Harvester Press.

Derrida, Jacques (1987) *The Post Card: From Socrates to Freud and Beyond*. Chicago, IL: University of Chicago Press.

Derrida, Jacques (2001) 'Niemand ist unschuldig', http://www.hydra.umn.edu/derrida/unschuldig.html

Dershowitz, Alan M. (2002) *Why Terrorism Works: Understanding the Threat, Responding to the Challenge*. New Haven, CT: Yale University Press.

Des Pres, Terrence (1980) *The Survivor: An Anatomy of Life in the Death Camps*. Oxford: Oxford University Press.

Dolar, Mladen (1993) 'Beyond Interpellation', *Qui Parle* 6(2): 75–96.

Dowd, James J. (1999) 'Waiting for Louis Prima. On the Possibility of a Sociology of Film', *Teaching Sociology* 26: 324–42.

Emmerich, Roland (dir.) (1996) *Independence Day*. Twentieth Century Fox Film Corporation.

Ezrahi, Sidra DeKoven (2001) 'After Such Knowledge, What Laughter?', *The Yale Journal of Criticism* 14(1): 287–313.

Fincher, David (dir.) (1999) *Fight Club*. 21st Century Fox Home Entertainment.

Flanzbaum, Hilene (2001) 'But Wasn't it Terrific?: A Defense of Liking *Life is Beautiful*', *The Yale Journal of Criticism* 14(1): 273–86.

Foucault, Michel (1983) 'Preface', in Gilles Deleuze and Felix Guattari, *Anti–Oedipus. Capitalism and Schizophrenia*. Minneapolis: University of Minnesota Press, pp. xi–xiv.

Frankl, Victor E. (1984) *Man's Search for Meaning*. New York: Washington Square.

Freud, Sigmund (1960) *Totem and Taboo*. London: Routledge & Kegan Paul.

Freud, Sigmund (1985) 'Group Psychology and the Analysis of the Ego', in *Civilization, Society and Religion, Group Psychology, Civilization and its Discontents and Other* (The Pelican Freud Library, vol. 12). London: Penguin, pp. 91–178.

Frichot, Helene (2005) 'Stealing into Deleuze's Baroque House', in Ian Buchanan and Gregg Lambert, *Deleuze and Space*. Edinburgh: Edinburgh University Press, pp. 61–79.

Gilliam, Terry (dir.) (1985) *Brazil*. 20th Century Fox Home Entertainment.

Gilliam, Terry (1986) 'The Saga of Brazil. Terry Gilliam Discusses the Making and Near Unmaking of His Dystopian Fantasy', http://members.aol.com/morgands1/closeup/text/brazil.htm

Gilliam, Terry (1991) Interview on the *South Bank Show* (filmed 29 June).

Gilliam, Terry (1999) '1984½ Becomes Brazil, With the Aid of Ducts and De Niro; and What Happened Next', in Ian Christie (ed.) *Gilliam on Gilliam*. London: Faber, pp. 111–51.

Girard, René (1977) *Violence and the Sacred*. London: Continuum.

Giroux, Henry A. (2000) 'Brutalised Bodies and Emasculated Politics. *Fight Club*, Consumerism, and Masculine Violence', *Third Text* 4: 31–41.

Glass, Fred (1986) 'Brazil', *Film Quarterly* 34: 22–8.

Gleason, Abbott (1984) '"Totalitarianism" in 1984', *The Russian Review* 43(2): 145–59.

Goffman, Erving (1959) *The Presentation of Self in Everyday Life*. New York: Anchor Books.

Golding, William (1954) *Lord of the Flies*. London: Faber & Faber.

Grosrichard, Alain (1998) *The Sultan's Court*. London: Verso.

Guilhot, Nicolas (2000) 'Review of Luc Boltanski and Eve Chiapello's *Le nouvel esprit du capitalisme*', *European Journal of Social Theory* 3(3): 355–64.

Halsband, Robert (ed.) (1965) *The Complete Letters of Lady Mary Wortley Montagu*, vol. 1. London: Oxford University Press.

Hardt, Michael (1998) 'The Withering Civil Society', in Eleanor Kaufman and Kevin Jon Heller (eds) *Deleuze and Guattari. New Mappings in Politics, Philosophy, and Culture*. Minneapolis: University of Minnesota Press, pp. 23–39.

Hardt, Michael and Negri, Antonio (2000) *Empire*. Cambridge, MA: Harvard University Press.

Hartman, Geoffrey H. (1996) *The Longest Shadow. In the Aftermath of Holocaust*. Bloomington: Indiana University Press.

Haskins, Casey (2001) 'Art, Morality, and the Holocaust: The Aesthetic Riddle of Benigni's *Life is Beautiful*', *Journal of Aesthetics and Art Criticism* 59(4): 373–84.

Havel, Vaclav (1985) *Power of the Powerless: The Citizens Against the State in Central Eastern Europe*. New York: M.E. Sharpe.

Hook, Harry (dir.) (1990) *Lord of the Flies*. MGM Home Entertainment Ltd.

Ignatieff, Michael (2005) *The Lesser Evil. Political Ethics in an Age of Terror*. Edinburgh: Edinburgh University Press.

Jaguaribe, Beatriz (2003) 'Favelas and the aesthetics of realism: representations in film and literature', unpublished paper.

Jameson, Frederic (1981) *The Political Unconscious. Narrative as a Socially Symbolic Act*. London: Routledge.

Jameson, Fredric (1988) *The Ideologies of Theory: Essays 1971–1986. Vol. 2: Syntax of History*. Minneapolis: University of Minnesota Press.

Jay, Martin (1993) *Downcast Eyes. The Denigration of Vision in Twentieth-Century French Thought*. Berkeley: University of California Press.

Jenkins, Emily (1999) 'Extreme Sport. An Interview With Thrill-Seeking Novelist Chuck Palahniuk', http://www.villagevoice.com/issues/9941/jenkins.php

Johnson, Barbara (1988) 'The Frame of Reference: Poe, Lacan, and Derrida', in John P. Muller and William J. Richardson (eds) *The Purloined Poe: Lacan, Derrida and Psychoanalytic Reading*. Baltimore, MD: Johns Hopkins University Press, pp. 213–51.

Jonas, David and Klein, Doris (1970) *Man–Child. A Study of the Infantilization of Man*. New York: McGraw-Hill.

Joubin, Rebecca (2000) 'Islam and Arabs through the Eyes of the Encyclopédie: The Other as a Case of French Cultural Self-Criticism', *International Journal of Middle East Studies* 32(2): 197–217.

Kaiser, Thomas (2000) 'The Evil Empire? The Debate on Turkish Despotism in Eighteenth-Century French Political Culture', *Journal of Modern History* 72: 6–34.

Karten, Harvey (2003) 'City of God', http://www.all-reviews.com/videos-5/city-of-god.htm

Kellner, Douglas (2002) 'September 11, Social Theory and Democratic Politics', *Theory, Culture & Society* 19(4): 147–59.

Kellner, Douglas (2006) 'From 1984 to One-Dimensional Man: Critical Reflections on Orwell and Marcuse', http://www.uta.edu/huma/illuminations/kell13.htm

Kertész, Imre (2001) 'Who Owns Auschwitz?' *The Yale Journal of Criticism* 14(1): 267–72.

Lacan, Jacques (1966) *Écrits*. Paris: Seuil.

Lacan, Jacques (1973) *Télévision*. Paris: Seuil.

Lacan, Jacques (1975) Le Séminaire: livre XX, Encore, 1972–73. Paris: Seuil.

Lacan, Jacques (1977) *Écrits: A Selection*. London: Routledge.

Lacan, Jacques (1988) 'Seminar on "The Purloined Letter"', in John Muller and William J. Richardson (eds) *The Purloined Poe*. Baltimore, MD: Johns Hopkins University Press, pp. 28–54.

Lacan, Jacques (1993) *The Seminar. Book III. The Ego in Freud's Theory and in the Technique of Psychoanalysis, 1954–55*. New York: Norton.

Lapsley, Robert and Westlake, Michael (2006) *Film Theory. An Introduction*, second edition. Manchester: Manchester University Press.

Lash, Scott and Urry, John (1994) *Economies of Signs and Space*. London: Sage.

Latour, Bruno (1990) 'Drawing Things Together', in Michael Lynch and Steve Woolgar (eds) *Representation in Scientific Practice*. Cambridge, MA: MIT Press, pp. 19–68.

Le Bon, Gustave (2002) *The Crowd. A Study of the Popular Mind*. New York: Dover.

Levinas, Emmanuel (1985) *Ethics and Infinity*. Pittsburgh, PA: Duquesne University Press.

Lotringer, Sylvia and Virilio, Paul (1997) *Pure War*. Semiotext(e). New York: Columbia University Press.

Lowe, Lisa (1991) *Critical Terrains: French and British Orientalisms*. Ithaca, NY: Cornell University Press.

Luhmann, Niklas (1994) 'The Idea of Unity in a Differentiated Society', paper presented at the Thirteenth Sociological World Congress 'Contested Boundaries and Shifting Solidarities', Bielefeld, Germany.

Luhmann, Niklas (2002) 'Inklusion og eksklusion', *Distinktion* 4: 121–39.

Lund, Kátia and Meirelles, Fernando (dir.) (2002) *City of God*. Buena Vista Home Entertainment.

Lyotard, Jean-François (1988) *The Differend: Phrases in Dispute*. Manchester: Manchester University Press.

McAlpin, Mary (2000) 'Between Men for All Eternity: Feminocentrism in Montesquieu's *Lettres Persanes*', *Eighteenth-Century Life* 4(1): 45–61.

McGowan, Todd and Kunkle, Sheila (2004) 'Introduction: Lacanian Psychoanalysis in Film Theory', in *Lacan and Contemporary Film*. New York: Other Press, pp. xi–xxix.

Macmaster, Niel (2004) 'Torture: From Algiers to Abu Ghraib', *Race and Class* 46(2): 1–21.

Maffesoli, Michel (1996) *The Time of the Tribes. The Decline of Individualism in Mass Society*. London: Sage.

Marcuse, Herbert (1964) *One Dimensional Man*. Boston, MA: Beacon.

Metz, Christian (1979) 'The Cinematic Apparatus as Social Institution – An Interview with Christian Metz', *Discourse* 1(3): 7–37.

Miles, M. (2000) 'Signing in the Seraglio: Mutes, Dwarfs and Gestures at the Ottoman Court 1500–1700', *Disability and Society* 15(1): 115–34.

Montesquieu, Charles de Secondat (1973[1721]) *Persian Letters*. London: Penguin.

Montesquieu, Charles de Secondat (1989[1748]) *The Spirit of the Laws*. Cambridge: Cambridge University Press.

Moreias, Alberto (2005) 'Preemptive Manhunt: A New Partisanship', *Positions* 13(1): 9–30.

Morin, Edgar (2005) *The Cinema or the Imaginary Man*. Minneapolis: University of Minnesota Press.

Mourao, Koki (2003) 'City of God', movie review, http://www.hollywood.com/movies/review/id/1704573

Neumann, Iver B. (1999) *Uses of the Other: 'The East' in European Identity Formation*. Minneapolis: University of Minnesota Press.

Neumann, Iver B. and Welsh, Jennifer M. (1991) 'The Other in European Self-Definition: An Addendum to the Literature on International Society', *Review of International Studies* 17(4): 327–48.

Noblejas, Juan J.G. (2004) 'Personal Identity and Dystopian Film Worlds', paper presented at the conference 'Virtual Materialities', Syracuse, May.

Olsen, Nils (2001) 'Alt skal væk', *Politiken*, 15/2, 2. section, p. 1.

Oudart, Jean-Pierre (1977) 'Cinema and Suture', *Screen* 18(4): 33–47.

Özpetek, Ferzan (dir.) (1997) *Hamam* (aka *The Turkish Bath*). Parasol Peccadillo Releasing Ltd.

Palahniuk, Chuck (1997) *Fight Club*. London: Vintage.

Palahniuk, Chuck (1999) 'I Made Most of It Up, Honest', *LA Times Memoir*, http://www.chuckpalahniuk.net/essays/latimes.htm

Palaver, Wolfgang (1992) 'A Girardian Reading of Schmitt's Political Theology', *Telos* 94(3): 43–68.

Paye, Jean-Claude (2004) 'Antiterrorist Measures, a Constituent Act', *Telos* 127(2): 171–82.

Pietz, William (1988) 'The "Post-Colonialism"of Cold War Discourse', *Social Text* (19/20): 55–75.

Poe, Edgar Allan (1988) 'The Purloined Letter' in John P. Muller and William J. Richardson (eds) *The Purloined Poe: Lacan, Derrida and Psychoanalytic Reading.* Baltimore, MD: Johns Hopkins University Press, pp. 3–27.

Rancière, Jacques (2004) *The Politics of Aesthetics.* London: Continuum.

Said, Edward (1978) *Orientalism: Western Conceptions of the Orient.* London: Penguin.

Salecl, Renata (1998) *(Per)versions of Love and Hate.* London: Verso.

Savlov, M. (1999) 'Fight Club', a review, http://www.auschron.com/film/pages/movies/9207.html

Schlegel, Friedrich (1967) *Kritische Ausgabe seiner Werke, Zweiter Band.* Paderborn: Verlag Ferdinand Schöningh.

Schmitt, Carl (2004) 'Theory of the Partisan: Intermediate Commentary on the Concept of the Political (1963)', *Telos* 127: 11–78.

Schmitt, Carl and Schickel, Joachim (1995) 'Gespräch über den Partisanen', in Günther Maschke (ed.) *Staat, Grossraum, Nomos.* Berlin: Duncker & Humbolt, pp. 619–42.

Schwarz, Roberto (2001) 'City of God', *New Left Review* 12: 103–12.

Seeskin, Kenneth (1988) 'Coming to Terms with Failure: A Philosophical Dilemma', in Berel Lang (ed.) *Writing and the Holocaust.* New York: Holmes & Meier, pp. 110–21.

Sennett, Richard (1994) *Flesh and Stone.* London: Faber & Faber.

Sheila (2003) 'Review of City of God', http://www.girlposse.com/reviews/movies/city_of_god.html

Shohat, Ella (1997) 'Gender and Culture of Empire: Toward a Feminist Ethnography of Cinema', in Matthew Bernstein and Gaylyn Studlaw (eds) *Visions of the East: Orientalism in Film.* New Brunswick, NJ: Rutgers University Press, pp. 19–68.

Siporin, Steve (2002) *'Life is Beautiful*: Four Riddles, Three Answers', *Journal of Modern Italian Studies* 7(3): 345–63.

Sontag, Susan (1977) *On Photography.* London: Penguin.

Sontag, Susan (2004) 'Regarding the Torture of Others', *New York Times*, 23/5, http://mailer.fsu.edu/~jgm8530/Terror/Regarding%20the%20Torture%20of%20Others.pdf

Spear, Ryan (2001) 'Chuck Palahniuk: Ben Aslinda Tatil Kitabi Yazmak Istiyordum', *Varlik* 69(1127): 36–9.

Strauss, Marcy (2004) 'The Lesson of Abu Ghraib', *Legal Studies Paper* No. 2004–18, September, http://ssrn.com/abstract=597061

Sult, E. (1999) 'To Get Famous, Punch Somebody. Fight Club Rains Down on Chuck Palahniuk', http://192.245.12.37/1999–10–21.bookguide5.html

Tatara, Paul (1998) 'Unbelievable Optimism in *Life is Beautiful*', CNN.com/showbiz/movies/9811/10/review.lifeisbeautiful

Theweleit, Klaus (1989) *Male Fantasies. Vol. 2: Male Bodies: Psychoanalyzing the White Terror.* Minneapolis: University of Minnesota Press.

Tomlinson, Hugh and Galeta, Robert (1989) 'Translators' Introduction' in Deleuze, Gilles, *Cinema 2. The Time-Image*. London: Athlone Press, pp. xv–xviii.

Tomlinson, Sarah (1999) 'Is It Fistfighting, or Just Multi-Tasking?', http://www.salon.com/ent/movies/int/1999/10/13/palahniuk/index.html

Trezise, Thomas (2001) 'Unspeakable', *The Yale Journal of Criticism* 14(1): 39–66.

Trumpener, Katie (1987) 'Rewriting Roxane: Orientalism and Intertextuality in Montesquieu's *Lettres Persanes* and Defoe's *The Fortunate Mistress*', *Stanford French Review* 11(2): 177–91.

Viano, Maurizio (1999) '*Life is Beautiful*: Reception, Allegory, and Holocaust Laughter', *Jewish Social Studies* 5(3): 47–66.

Virilio, Paul (1997) 'The Overexposed City', in Neil Leach (ed.) *Rethinking Architecture. A Reader in Cultural Theory*. London: Routledge, pp. 381–9.

Virilio, Paul (2000) *The Information Bomb*. London: Verso.

Wacquant, Loïc J.D. (1992) 'Towards a Social Praxeology: The Structure and Logic of Bourdieu's Socilogy', in Pierre Bourdieu and Loïc J.D. Wacquant, *An Invitation to Reflexive Sociology*. Cambridge: Polity Press, pp. 1–60.

Weber, Cynthia (2006) *Imagining America at War. Morality, Politics, Film*. London: Routledge.

Wheeler, Ben (2005) 'Reality is What You Can Get Away With: Fantastic Imaginings, Rebellion and Control in Terry Gilliam's *Brazil*', *Critical Survey* 17(1): 95–108.

Woman's Own, 31 October 1987.

Žižek, Slavoj (1989) *The Sublime Object of Ideology*. London: Verso.

Žižek, Slavoj (1990) 'Beyond Discourse-Analysis', in Ernesto Laclau (ed.) *New Reflections on the Revolution of Our Time*. London: Verso, pp. 249–60.

Žižek, Slavoj (1992) *Enjoy Your Symptom: Jacques Lacan in Hollywood and Out*. London: Routledge.

Žižek, Slavoj (1993) *Tarrying With the Negative. Kant, Hegel, and the Critique of Ideology*. Durham, NC: Duke University Press.

Žižek, Slavoj (1994) 'Introduction. The Spectre of Ideology', in Slavoj Žižek (ed.) *Mapping Ideology*. London: Verso, pp. 1–33.

Žižek, Slavoj (1997) *The Plague of Fantasies*. London: Verso.

Žižek, Slavoj (1999) *The Ticklish Subject: The Empty Center of Political Ontology*. London: Verso.

Žižek, Slavoj (2000a) 'Class Struggle or Postmodernism? Yes Please!' in Judith Butler, Ernesto Laclau and Slavoj Žižek, *Contingency, Hegemony, Universality. Contemporary Dialogues on the Left*. London: Verso, pp. 90–135.

Žižek, Slavoj (2000b) 'The Thing from Inner Space', in Renata Salecl (ed.) *Sexuation, SIC 3*. Durham, NC: Duke University Press, pp. 216–261.

Žižek, Slavoj (2000c) *The Fragile Absolute*. London: Verso.

Žižek, Slavoj (2001a) *The Fright of Real Tears. Krzýsztof Kieslowski Between Theory and Post-Theory*. London: British Film Institute.

Žižek, Slavoj (2001b) 'The Feminine Excess: Can Women Who Hear Divine Voices Find a New Social Link?', *Millennium* 30(1): 93–109.

Žižek, Slavoj (2001c) *Did Somebody Say Totalitarianism? Five Interventions in the (Mis)use of a Notion*. London: Verso.

Žižek, Slavoj (2001d) *On Belief*. London: Routledge.

Žižek, Slavoj (2001e) 'Hallucination as Ideology in Cinema', *Politologiske Studier* 4(3): 17–25.

Žižek, Slavoj (2002) *Welcome to the Desert of the Real*. London: Verso.

Žižek, Slavoj (2003a) 'The Ambiguity of the Masochist Social Link', in Molly A. Rothenberg, Dennis A. Foster and Slavoj Žižek (eds) *Perversion and the Social Elation. SIC 4*. Durham, NC: Duke University Press, pp. 112–25.

Žižek, Slavoj (2003b) *The Puppet and the Dwarf. The Perverse Core of Christianity*. Cambridge, MA: MIT Press.

Žižek, Slavoj (2005) 'Some Politically Incorrect Reflections on Violence in France and Related Matters', http://www.lacan.com/zizfrance.htm

Žižek, Slavoj (2006) *How to Read Lacan*. London: Granta.

Index